Collective Insecurity

Collective Insecurity

U.S. Defense Policy and the New World Disorder

Stephen J. Cimbala

Contributions in Military Studies, Number 162

GREENWOOD PRESS
Westport, Connecticut • London

Library of Congress Cataloging-in-Publication Data

Cimbala, Stephen J.
    Collective insecurity : U.S. defense policy and the new world
disorder / Stephen J. Cimbala.
        p.   cm. — (Contributions in military studies, ISSN 0883–6884
; no. 162)
    Includes bibliographical references and index.
    ISBN 0–313–29656–1 (alk. paper)
    1. United States—Military policy. 2. Russia (Federation)—
Military policy. 3. Security, International. 4. World
politics—1989– I. Title. II. Series.
UA23.C5427   1995
355'.033573—dc20   95–7511

British Library Cataloguing in Publication Data is available.

Library of Congress Catalog Card Number: 95–7511
ISBN: 0–313–29656–1
ISSN: 0883–6884

First published in 1995

Greenwood Press, 88 Post Road West, Westport, CT 06881
An imprint of Greenwood Publishing Group, Inc.

Printed in the United States of America

The paper used in this book complies with the
Permanent Paper Standard issued by the National
Information Standards Organization (Z39.48–1984).

10 9 8 7 6 5 4 3 2 1

Contents

Contents

Tables

Collective Insecurity

Introduction

In the final days of November 1994, the United Nations and the North Atlantic Treaty Organization (NATO) played out their fitful string in Bosnia. Bosnian and Croatian Serbs closed the ring on Bihac, one of the United Nations' six declared safe havens in Bosnia. The United Nations denied permission to NATO to conduct a campaign of air sorties against Bosnian Serb forces burning villages within the Bihac pocket. As the United Nations fiddled, Europe burned. It seemed unbelievable that the collective powers of the UN Security Council, or of NATO, could not muster the wherewithal either to deter or to defeat Serbian incursions into territory previously agreed to by all parties as sanctuary.

The reasons for UN and NATO inaction had to do with political paralysis, not lack of military capability. The NATO governments were democracies, whose publics and parliaments had no taste for intervening in Bosnia's internal ethnic and national wars. The United Nations was caught up in its own conflict between two of its objectives: peaceful settlement of disputes and imposition of peace on those who otherwise refuse to agree. Faced with the demand for NATO military escalation against Serbian forces to restore peace, Britain and France responded that escalation would threaten the viability of their peacekeeping forces in Bosnia. The U.S secretary of defense perhaps pronounced the last rites for UN and NATO credibility in Bosnia with his November 27, 1994, statement on U.S. television that the battle for Bosnia was essentially over, and in favor of the Serbs.[1]

In a separate television interview the same day, Secretary of Defense William Perry gave a candid appreciation of the U.S. military estimates for what it would cost, in numbers of troops and casualties, for a multinational force, presumably including Americans, to intervene and stabilize former Yugoslavia. Perry told reporters that it would require ground forces of several hundred thousand personnel deployed in the immediate theater of operations, and he added that casualties from fighting would be high. Looking into the camera and at the assembled reporters, he deliberately and pointedly added, "We [meaning the Clinton administration] are not about to do that."[2]

The futility of UN and NATO buck-passing on Bosnia was, in part, a reflection of the post–Cold War paradox of international security. The Cold War United Nations was deadlocked by the Security Council vetoes of the Americans and Soviets, reflecting their bipolar competition for global political and military preeminence. The end of the Cold War and the demise of the Soviet Union opened the door to cooperation between Russia and its Security Council partners in support of UN peacekeeping. However, the United Nations carried a structural limitation from its founding into the new world order. The United Nations was built as an organization of state governments, constituted to deal with the problem of interstate war and other threats to peace and security. The largest challenge facing the United Nations after 1990 was not interstate war, but violence within territorial states. This violence was rooted in political controversies related to ethnonationalistic and religious civil wars, environmental deterioration, proliferation of nuclear and other weapons of mass destruction, mass starvation and malnutrition, and other agenda items for which Cold War reflexes were clearly inappropriate.[3]

Not all of these issues posed security problems for the United States, Russia, and other great powers, but some did. A new context for security and defense decision making clearly had arrived with the departure of the Cold War and the disestablishment of Soviet military power. NATO and the Soviet Union had imposed on Europe a security glacis that prevented not only the outbreak of a major war but also the development of small wars that could escalate into a major regional conflict. For example, as long as Yugoslavia remained a unitary state under the firm grip of national communists, its ethnic and religious differences were submerged within a larger political community. When the communists lost their grip on Yugoslavia and on other states in Southern and East Central Europe, nationalism filled the power vacuum. First Slovenia, then Croatia, and finally Bosnia declared themselves to be independent states with unique ethnic bases of legitimacy.

In Algeria and in Egypt, nationalists clashed with Islamic fundamentalists. Nationalism was one of the major forces driving the Soviet Union toward a breakup into 15 former Soviet republics, now independent states seeking territorial integrity and political sovereignty. Three of those states, in addition to the Russian Federation, had nuclear weapons: Ukraine, Belarus, and Kazakhstan. Civil wars marked efforts to stabilize government authority in Azerbaijan, Moldova, Georgia, and other former Soviet republics contiguous to Russia along the arc of Russia's "near abroad." Ethnic, including tribal, disputes previously thought to be confined to the third world appeared in East Central and Western Europe, including ethnic Hungarians in Romania, Basques in

Spain, and foreign guest workers of various ethnic backgrounds in newly reunited Germany.

A new "rational map" of threats to U.S. and allied security was needed, but theorists and policy makers in the latter Bush and early Clinton administrations struggled to assemble such a map. Eventually it was agreed that the threat of global war from a reborn Soviet Union belonged to fiction, but Russia remained a great power with nuclear weapons and with domestic politics of an uncertain cast. Regional rivalries between states possessing or seeking weapons of mass destruction (including nuclear weapons) and ballistic missiles for weapons delivery included rivalries between Israel and Syria, Iran and Iraq, India and Pakistan, China and India, and Israel and Iraq (temporarily stripped of its nuclear and other weapons of mass destruction by UN resolution following the Gulf War of 1991). Following the paradigm applied to the successful expulsion of Saddam Hussein from Kuwait, the United States proposed under Bush and Clinton a contingencies strategy for dealing with regional conflicts.

The problem was that there were many more contingencies than one could reasonably plan for. In addition, the U.S. defense budget was, under Bush and Clinton, in a serious decline, dropping by fiscal 1997 to a point in real dollars (discounted for inflation) below pre–World War II peacetime levels. The U.S. forces remaining were not inconsiderable, and given the Soviet demise, the United States remained *primus inter pares* among global military powers. But this was not a position of hegemony: the United States could lead, but not dictate, policy to its allies and, with the assistance of allies, only selectively compel potential adversaries to do its bidding. Because not all contingencies could be planned for, those involving major U.S. regional allies or strategic interests (so-called major regional contingencies) generated basic military planning scenarios.

Much of the collective international disorder attendant to the end of the Cold War was not based on war between states but on war within states. The breakdown of political legitimacy drove governments toward compromises with nationalist opposition or to draconian, even dictatorial, measures to establish firm rule. As order broke down, militaries or militias took charge, in some cases outside the reach of government. Privatized forces under the control of privateers or warlords appeared, for example, in Mogadishu, Somalia, to impede U.S. and UN efforts in humanitarian relief. Similar forces appeared in the republics of the former Soviet Union, for example, in Moldova's Trans-Dniester region. Guerrilla *mujaheddin* armed by the United States in the 1980s to wage holy war against the Soviet occupiers of Afghanistan now appeared in Tajikistan, armed and for hire. In the former Soviet republic of Georgia, President Shevardnadze was forced reluctantly in 1994 to call upon Russian forces in order to prevent a complete breakdown of civil authority into internecine warfare.

If warlords threatened to take over Somalia, drug lords held sway in cooperation with Shining Path Maoist guerrillas in parts of Peru inaccessible to government control. The arrival of capitalism in Russia, together with the sudden breakdown of social controls formerly embedded in the Communist party and Soviet state, led to an explosion of Russian criminal gangs. Threatening the very integrity of the Russian political process by bribery, intimidation, and murder (including the 1994 shooting of a member of Russia's Parliament), Russia's several thousand *mafiyas* were a state within a state. Reminiscent of Chicago in the 1920s but on a broader scale, Russia's criminal gangs stepped in to provide order where ordinary internal security forces were weak or corrupt. Russia's military, meanwhile, had all it could do to find housing and prevent its weapons stores from being sold off on the black market.

In short, the very notion of polity, of a legitimate political order with consensual support of its citizens, was being stripped down from the state to the substate level. Nor was this all. An equal, but opposite, force was pulling at state sovereignty and legitimacy from another direction. This force opposed to statism included, for example, the transnational power of multinational corporations, including banks and other financial institutions; the power of interstate and international political communities, including the European Union and the United Nations; the influence of international ideologies, such as Islamic fundamentalism; and the pervasiveness of global communications media, making impossible the isolation of any regional conflict from the rest of the world.

The immediate prospect was, therefore, one of numerous small and bitter wars but, unlike the "low intensity" conflicts of the nineteenth century, conflicts made visible to a world community. This immediate visibility of small wars conferred on them a symbolism and centrality that was certain to cause problems for Western academics, military planners, and policy makers. The twentieth century study of war had been skewed toward the major coalition wars based on national mobilization and campaigns across many theaters of operation. As Ian Beckett has noted, "While low-intensity conflict has most frequently been the actual practical soldiering experience of Western soldiers in the nineteenth and twentieth centuries, it is the dream of what French soldiers knew as *la grand guerre* that has commanded the attention of theorists and of historians in turn."[4]

It is significant that the U.S. political system and, in particular, its media and congressional Monday morning quarterbacks of presidential foreign policy have insufficient understanding of low intensity or unconventional conflicts. Vietnam is their standard of reference, but Vietnam was a complicated mélange of conventional and unconventional war with deeply historical and cultural as well as immediately political causes. Even so, it had some aspects of the prototypical small war, and those aspects were hard, if not impossible, for Americans to cope with. Irregular units, without uniforms and using hit-and-run tactics, fought at night and disappeared by day. Americans were forced either to cede control of areas to the Viet Cong or to wage war against the entire population of the surrounding countryside, self-defeating as it was. Nothing apparently was learned from the previous French experience in Indochina or, for that matter, from previous U.S. experience in counterinsurgency (against native Americans in the nineteenth century or against Philippine insurrections in the early twentieth century).[5]

Most regrettable was the intellectual failure on the part of U.S. thinkers about insurgency and revolution, then and now. Formula based assessment and menu driven thinking have survived in assessments of U.S. experience in low intensity conflicts from Vietnam through Somalia. Ignoring variation in the particular cultures and historical experiences of third world countries, U.S. Cold War leaders and analysts assumed that there were standard formulas by which revolutions could be made to succeed. It was necessary only to invert the standard Maoist or other formulas for revolutionary success in order to bring about successful counterinsurgency.[6]

If there is no single, fungible template for revolution or counterrevolution, it follows that the degrees of freedom for nonstate actors to upset the international status quo are likely to increase. The United States, therefore, does not want to be caught in the position, with or without allies, of defending every existing order of things on the grounds that stability is itself a virtue. Not every instability is threatening to U.S. security interests, and some instabilities are the natural result of years of mass frustration with leaders' political ineptitude. Some situations will defy either unilateral or multilateral solution, by whatever combination of external politics or force. In Somalia in 1994, a reluctant UN Secretary-General Boutros Boutros-Ghali finally decided to run up the UN flag. He asked U.S. help in extricating the last of the UN peacekeepers from that besieged country. Without an effective government and prone to unrestrained warlord violence, Somalia in 1994 provided a test bed for the wisdom of nonintervention.

The framework that forms the basis for this study is as follows. In the first two chapters, I focus on the development of U.S. security policy during the Cold War and its unexpected denouement in U.S. leadership of the multinational coalition against Iraq in 1990 and 1991. I argue that U.S. policy evolved, not altogether as planned, from postwar collective defense to incipient collective security with the end of the Cold War, the demise of the Soviet Union, and the challenge of regional conventional wars and unconventional conflicts taking center stage. Some of the dilemmas that this evolution has created unexpectedly for U.S. policy are explored in later chapters. The Cold War may allow for the reduction of U.S. defense expenditures but not for the apparent willingness of others to depend upon U.S. leadership for world order.

U.S. leadership on behalf of future world order assumes a willingness on the part of others to follow and to share responsibilities and burdens more equally than in the Cold War past. In chapters 3 through 5, we look at some of the more important determinants of Russia's security in the future international environment. These, among other factors, will determine whether the environment is favorable or unfavorable for U.S. collective security leadership. In Chapter 3, I discuss the problem of military transition in Russia. Soviet military doctrine allowed for the combination of a defensive state policy with an offensively minded military establishment and operational art. Post-Soviet Russia can draw on both offensive and defensive traditions in pre-Soviet military art. A defensive military force posture, primarily suited to the protection of Russia's borders and for peacekeeping in its near abroad of contiguous former Soviet republics, is feasible provided Russia can hold its armed forces together and keep them accountable to democratic political authority.

One indicator of Russia's tendency toward or away from military defensivism is Russia's post–Cold War participation in international peacekeeping. Russia's peacekeeping potential is the topic of Chapter 4. Russian peacekeepers already have been deployed in former Soviet republics adjacent to Russia's borders, from Armenia to Tajikistan. About 500 Russians were serving with the UN Protection Force in Bosnia at the time of this writing. There could be even more potential for exporting Russian peacekeepers to global trouble spots, even outside the UN framework. Russia, in need of hard currency and having many unemployed and dehoused former Soviet officers, could make bilateral deals with other governments to supply peacekeepers for hire. On the other hand, obstacles stand in the way of a larger role for Russia in multinational peacekeeping, including the indeterminacy of Russia's future as a democracy and the instability of Russian military politics.

In Chapter 5, I consider the extent to which the United States and Russia can reduce their dependency on the Cold War overhang of strategic nuclear weapons. These arsenals, large and redundant during the years of U.S.-Soviet confrontation, are even more inappropriate for both states' future policy objectives. Arms control negotiations between Washington and Moscow now have the potential to lower significantly the numbers of strategic weapons deployed by both sides. Welcome news as this is, it leaves open the question of how far reductions can go before international stability is jeopardized and the nuclear preeminence of the United States and Russia, considered a Cold War stabilizer, is threatened. In addition, the Russian military, already in a parlous condition because of budget cuts, political dissidence, and mission malaise, may resist any agreements perceived as one-sidedly disarming of their already deficient military capabilities.

Indications in our data analysis are that the United States and Russia can safely reduce to START II levels (3,000 to 3,500 warheads on each side) or below before either side's retaliatory power is lacking in either necessary size or flexibility. Reductions down to 1,000 warheads or so for both the United States and Russia could still preserve a stable deterrent relationship, although neither will be motivated to go much below START II levels unless the arsenals of other nuclear powers (Britain, France, and China) are constrained. Some autolimitation by those other three members of the acknowledged "nuclear club" is now in progress, and Britain, France, and China could enter the twenty-first century with strategic nuclear arsenals of several hundred warheads. A necessary caution for the United States and Russia, if reductions below 1,000 warheads are undertaken, is that, at these drastically reduced levels, flexible response and survivability of some force components become difficult to guarantee.

It is also far from obvious that Russia can maintain anything approaching strategic nuclear parity with the United States even if forces are gradually and symmetrically reduced. Russia's military-industrial complex is in disarray, and border-secessionist wars will occupy most of the time of Russia's military planners. Containment of illegal nuclear seepage (of technology and know-how) will be Russia's more immediate challenge, compared with nuclear weapons modernization. Nuclear weapons–grade material has already found its way onto the international black market, and the U.S. Congress has forced the Department of Defense to cough up special appropriations for Russian nuclear dismantlement, storage, and transport.

In Chapter 6, we consider the peace paradox that the Cold War has bequeathed to its successor international environment: apparent permissiveness for more frequent and more successful use of collective security, but more danger of escalation and nuclear weapons spread. Unconstrained nuclear weapons spread is simply incompatible with collective security: on this, almost all parties agree. Even nuclear weapons spread only to a few ambitious regional hegemons becomes difficult to make compatible with collective security, however. Collective security demands an altruistic willingness on the part of a coalition to run serious military risks against alleged malefactors who threaten peace and security. The risk acceptance of states for multinational peace enforcement against regional hegemons, such as Iraq, may depend very much on the availability of weapons of mass destruction to those regional overachievers. In addition, because a little deterrence goes a long way, it follows that nuclear weapons, which allowed the Americans and Soviets to dominate the Cold War international system, may be more useful in the future as "equalizers" for international trouble-makers. Confronted with a regional aggressor armed with tactical nuclear weapons and short or medium range ballistic missiles, would states coalesce and rapidly send countervailing forces in the face of aggression?

Chapter 6, in short, points to a problem of post–Cold War escalation management made more complex by greater degrees of freedom on the part of highly weaponized actors and tentatively bonded coalitions. Chapter 7 digs into the problem of nuclear proliferation more specifically and more deeply. It turns out, though, that there are two schools of thought about nuclear weapons spread. One school holds that nuclear weapons spread is actually compatible with international stability: the dispersion of nuclear weapons should cause no more international perturbation than did the acquiring of nuclear weapons by the original Big Five. Another school, to the contrary, holds that nuclear proliferation is dangerous even in small doses and, in larger quantities, may bring down the house. The danger is not the Armageddon of U.S.-Soviet nuclear exchanges feared during the Cold War years. The nuclear danger now is that the spread of weapons of mass destruction and long range delivery vehicles occurs without the U.S.-Soviet nuclear condominium of the past four decades to encourage restraint. In addition, the realist theories on which the "optimistic" view of nuclear weapons spread is based are themselves vulnerable on some of their assumptions most pertinent to the new world order. These vulnerabilities include the large variety of military command and control systems out there into which nuclear or other mass destruction weapons might be put. Vulnerabilities also include the potential for military usurpation of civil responsibilities in states now seeking to acquire, or already having acquired, nuclear and chemical weapons.

Chapter 8 considers the problem of military persuasion, of which coercive diplomacy, deterrence, and operations other than war are examples. Introducing a theoretical framework for the discussion of military persuasion, it then discusses in particular detail the prospectus for U.S. adjustment to a new world order in which operations other than war are normative, not exceptional. It turns out that such a world will strain professional militaries, including the U.S. one, and governments to rethink the connection between strategy and policy. Few show any inclination to do so, coping on a daily basis with crises and targets of opportunity.

For the U.S. armed forces, some experts feel that operations other than war threaten a virtual identity crisis. Other experts disagree, pointing to a long tradition of U.S. military involvement in civil affairs and nation building. The U.S. military track record in this regard is better on the domestic front than it has been in military operations designed to support foreign policy. Operations other than war strain the mind sets of the most traditional military components, such as regular infantry, and enhance the significance of Special Operations Forces and others trained for unconventional missions and conflicts. The top of the U.S. military command structure has, on the basis of limited post–Cold

War evidence, shown some reluctance to be involved in multinational peacekeeping operations without guarantees that the U.S. military chain of command will remain intact throughout and that an exit strategy for U.S. armed forces will be outlined before the fact of military intervention.

The concluding chapter summarizes main findings and offers some prospectuses to help anticipate the major problems faced by U.S. policy makers and military planners in the world after the Cold War. An environment of threat, uncertainty, and budgetary decline poses for the U.S. armed forces the dilemma that they must lay stronger claims to missions other than victory through combat. Overdosing on noncombat missions can distract an officer corps from its principal responsibility: the mastery of battle. Nevertheless, the political reality is that U.S. and other policy makers will insist upon military participation in crisis management, in peace operations, and in civic action. The challenge of military adaptation to a larger menu of policy requirements in the next century is already apparent.

NOTES

1. *Philadelphia Inquirer*, November 28, 1994, p. A12.

2. Television interview with Secretary of Defense William Perry, November 27, 1994, witnessed by the author.

3. Paul Kennedy, *Preparing for the Twenty-first Century* (New York: Random House, 1993), esp. Part I.

4. Ian Beckett, "Low-Intensity Conflict: Its Place in the Study of War," in *Military History and the Military Profession*, eds. David A. Charters, Marc Milner, and J. Brent Wilson (Westport, Conn.: Praeger Publishers, 1992), pp. 121–30.

5. Sam C. Sarkesian, *Unconventional Conflicts in a New Security Era: Lessons from Malaya and Vietnam* (Westport, Conn.: Greenwood Press, 1993), esp. pp. 95–122 discusses U.S. Vietnam experience. See his characterization of U.S. military strategy, pp. 104–5.

6. D. Michael Shafer, *Deadly Paradigms: The Failure of U.S. Counter-insurgency Policy* (Princeton, N.J.: Princeton University Press, 1988), pp. 104–34; 276–90.

I

U.S. DEFENSE POLICY IN THE COLD WAR

1

U.S. Military Strategy from 1945 to 1990: From Collective Defense to Collective Security

From the end of World War II until the demise of the Soviet Union, U.S. military strategy was dominated by the requirements for collective defense. The identity of the most plausible security threat to U.S. and allied interests had a clear and singular address in Moscow. The United States committed itself to defend Western Europe against Soviet aggression by stationing unprecedented numbers of U.S. troops on European soil in peacetime and by threatening prompt nuclear retaliation in case conventional defenses failed.

This chapter reviews how U.S. Cold War strategy for collective defense based on nuclear dependency moved gradually toward a strategy emphasizing collective security and high technology conventional weapons.[1] The destination of 1990–91 was not necessarily pre-planned in the origins of U.S. Cold War strategy, nor was it excluded. Allied wartime agreements between 1943 and 1945 opened the door to postwar security collaboration among the five great powers, but U.S.-Soviet global competition caused collective security to be placed in suspended animation. When Gorbachev's declining and desperate Soviets acquiesced to UN resolutions calling for the liberation of Kuwait from Iraq, the U.S. ready blueprint for air-land battle was applied with devastating effect against Iraqi military forces, command systems, and other targets.

BIPOLARITY AND U.S.-SOVIET CONFLICT

The international system of the Cold War was an unexpected outcome of an unexpected war. Between World War I and World War II, the United States had sought to disconnect itself from any responsibility for collective security or for preserving the balance of power in Europe. U.S. armed forces were demobilized from their World War I peaks. However, this effort at interwar military self-effacement already had been compromised by several factors. First, the U.S. imperialist experience in the aftermath of the Spanish-American War gave to Americans a heady sense of world engagement, however selective that engagement might be. Second, European security concerns would not go away from U.S. national interests. To the contrary, during the 1930s, the two became inextricably linked. The major significance of Franklin Roosevelt's election to the presidency was not apparent at first blush; triumphed by his partisans as an economic savior, his actual innovation was to brilliantly guide an isolationist Congress and polity toward European engagement.

Given the size and competency of its military establishment during the 1930s, the United States could not extend deterrence on behalf of the status quo in Europe and Asia against rising hegemonies in Berlin and Tokyo. The League of Nations proved to be feckless. The power vacuum that resulted when Britain and France only belatedly grasped the ring of antifascist resistance had to be filled from outside Europe. Russia was a possible source of rescue, but Hitler's initial diplomatic moves had neutralized Stalin as an opponent until Germany was ready to deal with Russia. As France crumbled and Britain scrambled to evacuate Dunkirk, U.S. political leaders were forced to confront their responsibility for global political order. The Japanese attack in December 1941 influenced the timing of U.S. national awakening, but the content of that awakening had already been settled.

Forced to rearm on a scale unprecedented before or since, Americans were divided in their assumptions about the probable shape of the postwar world and of U.S. civil-military relations within that world. Some maintained that wars were caused by renegade states and perverse ideologies. Once these states and ideologies had been defeated and discredited, a return to normalcy in U.S. overseas commitments and in the size of the U.S. military establishment could be expected. Others who saw the causes for World War II as more complicated doubted that the United States could extricate itself from postwar responsibility for world peace. President Roosevelt and his advisors, clearly in sympathy with the internationalist viewpoint of postwar global engagement, expected that the United States and other great powers, including the Soviet Union, could cooperate through the United Nations to deter irruptions of world peace.[2]

This expectation was to be disappointed, and bitterly so. There are various explanations for why events turned out so much against the optimism of U.S. wartime leaders. Most important for the discussion here was the immediate postwar distribution of global military power. The bipolar international system that followed the collapse of Axis military power left the United States and the Soviet Union in a position of uniquely global reach. It became the perception of U.S. and Soviet Cold War leaders that world politics was a constant sum game in which the winnings of one side would have to take place as a consequence of the other's losses.[3] As suspicion hardened into hostility during crises over Greece and Turkey, Iran, Czechoslovakia, and Berlin, President Truman was persuaded that only diplomatic firmness and military preparedness would deter further Soviet adventurism. The Truman doctrine and the Marshall Plan declared U.S. universal and regional interests in keeping friendly regimes outside the Soviet political orbit, but Truman was not prepared to pay the defense costs for these expanded commitments until the outbreak of war in Korea in 1950.

The U.S. postwar military establishment was not returned to a status similar to that awaiting the U.S. armed forces after World War I. Although more than 10 million men were demobilized as rapidly as possible, the Truman administration did not foresee the peacetime period ahead as one of pacific deterrence through international organization and U.S. disengagement, as had been the expectation of President Woodrow Wilson following World War I. Instead, the United States committed itself to oversee the postwar reconstruction of Japan and Germany, the former as a political democracy and the latter according to the four-power division of the pie agreed to during wartime conferences. Germany was permanently divided and rearmed, but not before the United States confronted the need for the rearmament of Europe along with the economic construction of it.

The rearmament of free Europe had to be undertaken with some sensitivity to U.S. and European sensitivities: U.S. political neuroses about overseas commitments in peacetime, and European sensitivities about being dominated by U.S. guns and capitalism. The solution for incorporating Western Europe within a U.S. strategic protectorate was the North Atlantic Treaty Organization (NATO), a voluntary alliance of unprecedented scope and inclusiveness in peacetime Europe. NATO grew up along with the maturing of the U.S. nuclear arsenal and the hardening of Cold War lines between the Soviet sphere of interest and the Western one. Eventually the Soviet side copied NATO's approach and organized the Warsaw Pact as a belated answer to NATO's European rearmament, although decisions were not taken by democratic consent within the pact as in NATO.

The extension of U.S. peacetime defense commitments to Western Europe, followed by the stationing of permanent U.S. garrisons there, was a political-military strategy for Cold War competition. However, it was also a strategy for freezing the status quo in the center of Europe, thereby reducing the risk of inadvertent war between the United States and the Soviets.[4] NATO was to contain the independent proclivities of the British, French, and Germans to fight with one another as a byproduct of its importance for deterring Soviet attack. Although not fully appreciated even now, NATO's political role was as important as its military one. Most U.S. foreign policy influentials did not anticipate an actual shooting war in Europe during the late 1940s or early 1950s. As George F. Kennan had anticipated, what was more probable was the slow squeeze of Kremlin pressure against U.S. and allied interests both directly, as in the Berlin crisis of 1948, and through surrogates, as in Korea in 1950.

Prior to the outbreak of the Korean War, the Truman administration had a hard sell for military buildup, including a rapid expansion of the U.S. nuclear arsenal. NSC-68, a high level policy study calling for major U.S. rearmament in view of an imminent Soviet military threat to Europe and Asia, had been completed shortly before the eruption of North Korea's forces across the thirty-eighth parallel in June 1950.[5] U.S. defense spending shot across the previous ceilings imposed by the Truman administration, and the Chinese entry into the war only convinced many Americans that a Sino-Soviet bloc now threatened U.S. global interests. However, Korea was an improbable war for which U.S. strategic planners had scarcely prepared. Expecting a global war against the Soviet Union begun in Europe, planners had given little consideration to the possibility of U.S. involvement in limited wars supported by the Soviet leadership but fought by other governments and forces.

Korea posed strategic and policy-making dilemmas in Washington. The Truman administration's decision to fight a limited war was controversial on several grounds. Field commander Douglas MacArthur chafed at political restrictions on military operations. Truman neglected to ask for a formal declaration of war against North Korea or against China after Chinese troops later entered the fighting on the Korean peninsula. The war was fought under the auspices of a UN collective security operation. Because the precedent had been set for commitment of U.S. forces to limited war without a congressional declaration of war, the precedent would be repeated to disastrous effect in Vietnam. Nor was the U.S. intervention in Korea exemplary of truly multilateral collective security operations, because it was, in fact, a U.S. military operation terminated according to U.S. requirements. Thus, it provided no model for future uses of U.S. military power on behalf of collective security missions (a subject developed to greater depth in a later section). To the contrary, the Korean War led to the militarization of containment and to the hardening of Cold War fault lines between the communist and capitalist worlds.

The Korean War also allowed U.S. defense spending to reach a new peacetime plateau, peaking in fiscal 1953 at about $330 billion (in fiscal 1990 dollars). This total was not achieved again during the Cold War, even during the Vietnam escalation or the Reagan defense expansion of the 1980s, although, at its apogee, Vietnam defense spending came close. Table 1.1 presents summary figures for defense outlays from slightly prior to World War II through 1990.

TABLE 1.1
U.S. Cold War Military Expenditures for National Defense, Selected Years

Fiscal Year	DoD Outlays as Percent of Federal Outlays	DoD Outlays as Percent of GDP
1950	27.5	4.4
1960	45.0	8.2
1970	39.4	7.8
1980	22.5	5.0
1990	23.1	5.3

Source: Les Aspin, *Annual Report to the President and the Congress* (Washington, D.C.: U.S. Government Printing Office, 1994), Appendix B, p. B-3.

Cold War military budgets declined from Korean War levels as a result of Eisenhower's "New Look" policy emphasizing nuclear deterrence. Expenditures rose again during the Kennedy-Johnson years, to a near record $323 billion in fiscal 1969. A large build down during the Nixon-Ford years followed U.S. disengagement from Vietnam and congressional and public disillusionment with defense expenditures. Fiscal 1976 defense outlays were the lowest since before the Korean War. Budgets moved upward for defense thereafter, gradually during the Carter years and dramatically during the Reagan administration.

These oscillations in defense outlays also reflect the ambivalence of leaders and planners about the requirements for extended deterrence (of threats or attacks against U.S. allies). During the Cold War years, the United States accepted unprecedented levels of peacetime commitment to European allies or to other strategic countries located in critical regions. Extended deterrence could not be supported by conventional military power alone, and in Eurasia, the size of Soviet ground forces loomed large. Therefore, nuclear deterrence was relied upon not only for protection of the U.S. homeland but also for the dissuasion of regional aggressors who might threaten U.S. European or other protectorates. Increased nuclear reliance would have important implications for U.S. strategy, force structure, and budgets throughout the Cold War years.

NUCLEAR WEAPONS AND MUTUAL DETERRENCE

The paradox of nuclear weapons was that they made the U.S. homeland vulnerable to destruction without invasion for the first time. At the same time, they gave the United States the retaliatory power to strike back at any aggressor, inflicting unacceptable damage. Therefore, a perceived sense of imminent vulnerability to possibly devastating surprise attack went hand in hand with a conviction on the part of leaders that mutual deterrence would guarantee strategic stasis. This vulnerability-invulnerability paradox left some persons confident in U.S. security based on the threat of nuclear retaliation. Other persons were equally confident that nuclear weapons would cancel themselves out and that meaningful military competition between the United States and the Soviet Union would occur below the nuclear threshold.[6]

The arrival of the atomic bomb did not lead to an immediate restructuring of U.S. military strategy around the touchstone of nuclear deterrence. The U.S. nuclear stockpile was relatively small when Truman left office, and control of nuclear weapons in peacetime remained with the Atomic Energy Commission. Leading U.S. policy planners feared in 1950 that, without a large U.S. conventional and nuclear buildup, comparative U.S.-Soviet force building trends worked against continued U.S. security. For example, Paul H. Nitze, director of policy planning for the Department of State, contended that U.S. military weakness meant that the United States must [avoid becoming involved in general hostilities with the USSR" until a "position of strength" could be created.[7] The development of thermonuclear weapons and the eventual availability of nuclear weapons in abundance led the Eisenhower administration toward a New Look strategy that emphasized deterrence by threat of nuclear punishment instead of deterrence by means of conventional combat capability. Although later administrations would seek a less nuclear dependent set of military options, U.S. strategy thereafter was always under the shadow of nuclear plenty and, once the Soviet Union approached strategic nuclear parity, military gridlock.

The Korean War had seen the United States commit combat forces overseas without a congressional declaration of war. The judgment of the Truman administration had been that a formal declaration of war was neither necessary nor desirable. Nuclear weapons posed another kind of challenge to established civil-military relations.[8] The National Security Act of 1947 had established a national military establishment headed by a secretary of defense and responsible for the administration and combat performance of all U.S. arms of service, including the newly independent Air Force. Amendments to the National Security Council (NSC) in 1949 created the office of the secretary of defense and removed service secretaries from cabinet rank. Defense reorganization is considered at greater length below, but the preceding points about the initial unification of the Department of Defense and the assumptions on which that unification was built are pertinent for the present discussion.

For reasons well-understood by the framers of the U.S. Constitution and accepted by most nineteenth and twentieth century presidents, the United States could not have a presidential military force. The armed forces belonged to the people and, to this end, were subdivided into active duty forces, reserve forces (trained service reserves and individual ready reserve pools), and unorganized militia. The U.S. Congress had rejected universal military training prior to the Korean War despite

President Truman's strong support. The U.S. Constitution lodged the power to declare war in the Congress because the authors of that document distrusted executive power acting without legislative oversight, but the framers also required a congressional declaration of war for another reason: it would empower the president to conduct a war on behalf of the entire aroused nation in arms. Public opinion was thought to be the bedrock on which effective commitment of U.S. forces had to be based, and congressional assent to war was deemed improbable unless broad public support was available.[9]

Nuclear weapons called into question this carefully circumscribed relationship created by the Constitution between the executive and legislative branches of the U.S. government. They did so in two ways. First, they made necessary the avoidance of total war. Because it was easier for the public to perceive that total war was more threatening than limited war, presidents found it harder to make the case for those kinds of wars that the nuclear constraint would permit. Second, nuclear weapons promised unprecedented destructiveness in a short time. Especially once the Soviet Union had acquired a strategic nuclear retaliatory force capable of destroying many targets in the continental United States, the United States had to devise warning and assessment systems and create a nuclear decision-making process which, by implication, circumvented the constitutional luxury of a declaration of war. In case of Soviet nuclear attack against targets in the continental United States with ballistic missiles launched from land or sea, the U.S. effective warning would be measured in minutes rather than hours.

The constitutional bypass created to deal with this situation of unprecedented danger was that the president was recognized as commander in chief and that this status permitted him to retaliate against surprise attack without immediate congressional authorization. The Congress had other ways of reviewing and controlling the development of U.S. nuclear weapons programs and military budgets, too. Therefore, the legislative branch was not frozen out of the process of force acquisition and general military-strategic planning. However, the arcana of nuclear weapons target planning and the packaging of strategic and other nuclear options remained largely within the compass of the executive branch during the Cold War years.

By itself, this might have been regarded as an unavoidable necessity, but the nuclear habit of presidential initiative unencumbered by legislative oversight spilled over into Cold War presidential approaches to other security and defense issues. It was no surprise that maintaining a state of permanent military preparedness raised the status of the Pentagon relative to other cabinet departments, which themselves grew in stature on the coattails of Cold War presidential power. In addition, the play of power within the national security community in response to activist presidents, to the visibility of Cold War crises, and to the possibility of prompt nuclear surprise attack was important in its own right. As discussed in the next section, the implications of instant readiness for deterrence and for total war were far-reaching for defense reorganization. This section emphasizes the implications of the strategic paradigm shift from mobilization to deterrence for military strategy.

Nuclear weapons affected the means of defense preparedness and the expectation of surprise attack, but they did not provide usable forces in battle. Therefore, Cold War presidents and their advisors confronted the problem of what to do if deterrence failed. This problem was diverted partly by the expectation of "extended" deterrence: nuclear weapons would deter any Soviet conventional attack against NATO Europe or other vital U.S. interests. However, there were several problems with extended deterrence of this sort. First, not all Europeans wanted it; the French, for example, quite vociferously rejected any reliance on U.S. nuclear protection. Second, the absolute character of nuclear weapons did not lend themselves to military separatism: self-defense by threat of nuclear retaliation was bound up intimately with notions of sovereignty. Third, presidents wanted usable options in time of crisis so they could up the ante by using coercive measures short of war, as President Kennedy showed by his choice of blockade during the Cuban missile crisis of 1962.

Because nuclear weapons implied separate sovereignties, they complicated NATO alliance cohesion unless NATO Europeans were prepared to play only the role of U.S. military satellites. West European economic recovery subsequent to the Marshall Plan and the creation of the European Community led to assertive self-confidence within NATO deliberative bodies for policy consultation and for military planning. By the 1960s, U.S. military strategy had to be marketed aggressively if it were to be adopted consensually by the United States' NATO European allies. In 1967, NATO settled on a declaratory doctrine, flexible response, which carried it to the end of the Cold War. It was a political success wrapped in a military enigma. Europeans were allowed to believe that flexible response was something other than graduated escalation, whereas U.S. expositors contended that graduated escalation was exactly what flexible response was all about. Although NATO represented singular success in the area of peacetime military planning and coordination, under the stress of actual crisis or war, the political diversity of its member states could have prevented consensual response to any Soviet challenge. Fortunately for NATO, such a challenge was not provided by Moscow.

DEFENSE REORGANIZATION

The preceding section noted that nuclear weapons and the possible outbreak of large scale conventional war in Europe forced U.S. military planners to shift from a mobilization to a deterrence paradigm in force and policy planning. The requirement to be ready for instantaneous response and global military operations meant that both plans and budgets would have to be coordinated across service lines. This caused civilians in the office of the secretary of defense to interfere in decisions about military procurement and war planning to an extent without precedent in peacetime U.S. history.

The battles over planning, programming, and budgeting systems during the McNamara years in the Pentagon do not require retelling. The political controversy during those years was not really about budgeting techniques but was about preferred strategy, doctrine, and prerogatives in determining force size. During the latter years of the Eisenhower administration, it was recognized that separate service planning for nuclear retaliation was not acceptable. The single integrated operational plan was established by McNamara's predecessor as a method for the coordination of Navy and Air Force strategic target planning. It followed that the same model might be extended to general purpose forces: defining objectives and asking what mixes of forces, regardless of service ownership, would most effectively and efficiently fulfill those objectives.

McNamara and his associates knew that the battle between the office of the secretary of defense and the services over conventional forces programs would be more difficult than that over nuclear.[10] Nuclear weapons lent themselves to tight presidential control: release would be obtained only in the gravest circumstances. Conventional forces readiness and structure were other matters, and military leaders felt, with some justification, that they were the resident experts on war fighting with armies, navies, and air forces apart from nuclear deterrence. Civilians in the McNamara Pentagon doubted openly that there was any such thing as military science or military art and disparaged combat experience as a necessary constituent of fruitful policy analysis. Although the military services outlasted some of McNamara's more ambitious exertions into their domains, his lasting impact on defense decision making was to exploit the National Security Act of 1947 and the subsequent amendments of 1949, 1953, and 1958 to make the office of the secretary of defense the most powerful of cabinet departments.

Nonetheless, the post-McNamara secretaries of defense would have their hands full. One source of trouble was the already-mentioned tradition of decentralized military decision making within each service. Another was the growth of presidential power and the derivative raising in stature of the president's advisor for national security affairs. The first person to hold this title formally was McGeorge Bundy in the Kennedy administration, and the significance of the NSC advisor and his staff grew proportionately as the Cold War demands for U.S. preparedness thrust presidents into the cockpit of military decision making. Not all of Bundy's successors necessarily enhanced the power and prerogatives of the NSC advisor, but one who surely did was Henry

Kissinger. As NSC advisor to President Nixon, Kissinger became the
president's *eminence grise* for all matters of security and foreign policy,
eventually eclipsing Secretary of State William Rogers and finally
preempting his job.[11]

Kissinger's NSC apparat represented a threat not only to the
Department of State but also to the Pentagon. In defense of the
Pentagon, it must be said that Kissinger was a formidable and relent-
less bureaucratic opponent whose grasp of policy and power mindedness
in Washington were uncommon. Kissinger also profited during Nixon's
second term from that president's preoccupation with domestic policy,
especially with Watergate. However, Kissinger's special talents for self-
aggrandizement foraged into two areas of great military sensitivity:
crisis management and arms control. In addition, the failed U.S. military strategy in Vietnam was all too apparent by the time Nixon took
office, and the U.S. program of phased withdrawal for U.S. forces from
South Vietnam, termed "Vietnamization," required the orchestration of
military and diplomatic instruments to exploit coercive diplomacy in
reverse.

Laird's and Schlesinger's Pentagon fought off the NSC about as well
as any bureaucrats could have, but the legacy left by Kissinger was an
empowered NSC with the prerogative to exert control over the coordination of all matters touching upon foreign and defense policy. Once
power had flowed in the direction of NSC, presidents no longer had the
choice of reinstituting a weak NSC organization and depending upon
cabinet departments to take up the slack. Reagan attempted just this
solution at the outset of his first term, and it failed. The NSC emerged
during the Reagan administration as the locus for highly sensitive
covert operations, in part because the Central Intelligence Agency
wanted to avoid congressional investigations related to covert action
and in part because the expectations of experienced bureaucrats were
that NSC was the place to get things done.

The tendency to empower NSC reappeared during the Bush administration. Brent Scowcroft, formerly NSC advisor in the Ford administration, accepted the same position under George Bush. NSC
retained its status as a second policy planning and crisis management
department for national security affairs. Scowcroft served as Bush's
most articulate expositor of U.S. security policies, confident that
defense management would be carried out according to the president's
wishes by long-time Bush political colleague Dick Cheney. However,
one important legacy from the Reagan to the Bush administration
had been congressional passage of defense reform in the form of
the Goldwater-Nichols legislation. This added to the power of the
chairman of the Joint Chiefs of Staff, who became the principal advisor
to the president and the secretary of defense on matters of military
strategy and force structure. The joint staff was also reorganized and
made more responsible and responsive to the chairman. In addition,

Goldwater-Nichols mandated that future officers aspiring to general or flag rank must have career-defining experiences wearing "purple" in specified joint assignments. Finally, the Goldwater-Nichols legislation mandated that the various commanders in chief of the U.S. military unified and specified commands (LANTCOM, PACOM, CENTCOM, and so forth) be given more weight in the process of developing combat and crisis management plans.[12]

Throughout the Cold War history of defense reorganization, one could, with some justification, divide policy makers, military professionals, and scholarly observers into two schools of thought: those who were structural optimists and believed that defense reorganization was actually related to improved policy outcomes and bureaucratic pessimists, who rejected the possibility of any direct connection between structural reorganization and better defense policy.[13] In defense of the optimists, one could point to McNamara's introduction of planning, programming, and budgeting systems and its avoidance of waste and duplication in some high technology, expensive service programs. In defense of the optimists, one could also cite the Goldwater-Nichols legislation and its apparently favorable implications for the conduct of U.S. defense planning and war-fighting strategy during the Gulf Crisis and War from August 1990 through February 1991. Pessimists could argue, to the contrary, that the reach of McNamara's reforms frequently exceeded their grasp, as in the eventual demise of the TFX (tactical fighter — experimental). Pessimists could also note that "servicism" remained, even after the Goldwater-Nichols reforms, an unavoidable barrier to jointness in planning and procurement: command and control systems usable by more than one service provide excellent illustrations of the pervasiveness of single service opportunism.[14]

PERSONNEL POLICY AND MILITARY DOCTRINE

The U.S. military experience of the Cold War years was marked by unprecedented beginnings and endings with regard to personnel policy and military doctrine, beginnings and endings that were related. The early Cold War years saw conscription carried over into the peacetime armed forces in the form of selective service. This went hand in hand with the concept of permanent preparedness for global war. The Army was, of course, more dependent than the Navy (including Marines) or Air Force on conscription. Large forces permanently stationed in Europe, Korea, and elsewhere served as tripwires to deter Soviet attack on U.S. allies. U.S. strategy for global war during the Truman administration, given the relative scarcity of nuclear munitions and delivery vehicles compared with forces available to Truman's successors, did not envision an air-atomic offensive against the Soviet Union as capable of fulfilling U.S. wartime objectives by itself. It was assumed in late 1940s war plans that air-atomic attacks by both sides would be followed by protracted conflict between Soviet and opposed armed forces in Europe and worldwide.

The availability during the Eisenhower administration of larger numbers of nuclear weapons supported the shift to a declaratory strategy for general war of massive retaliation. Although administration officials eventually were forced to retreat from this formulation in cases of less than total war, for global war against the Soviet Union, Eisenhower defense planning relied mainly upon promptly delivered and massive air atomic offensives. Special study committees such as the Gaither committee pointed to the need for a larger menu of military responses, and Army officials chafed at the allocation of defense resources within arbitrary ceilings and under planning assumptions favoring Air Force and Navy procurement. NATO's declared objective of 96 active duty and reserve divisions was far beyond any commitment its members were actually willing or able to provide. Thus, reliance on nuclear weapons for extended deterrence became all the more necessary as a result of allied as well as U.S. domestic budgetary priorities.

The Army emerged from the 1950s as the fourth wheel of a defense establishment whose preferred military doctrines favored the more technical and less manpower intensive arms of service. Under the Kennedy administration, things would soon change. Kennedy preferred the strategy that became known as "flexible response," calling for improved U.S. conventional forces for crisis response, forward presence, and, if necessary, actual war fighting in order to raise the nuclear threshold in Europe. This last rationale was pushed hard within NATO by McNamara, to the detriment of alliance solidarity on doctrine until the French departure from NATO's military command structure in 1966 and the promulgation of flexible response in 1967. Flexible response arguably allowed a greater role for the ground forces in U.S. military doctrine and force planning, but by the time flexible response became official NATO doctrine, the lines between Cold War "East" and "West" had solidified, and neither side seemed interested in even limited probes against the other. The outcome of the imbroglio over the Berlin crisis of 1961 and the Cuban missile crisis of 1962 had been to establish a minidetente between the superpowers on matters of high politics and security, especially on the likelihood that either side would instigate even a crisis in Europe, let alone a war.

If strategic stasis reigned in Europe, Khrushchev's insistence that wars of national liberation could be unleashed against third world regimes supportive of U.S. policy called forth a burst of doctrinal innovations from the Kennedy administration. Special operations and low intensity conflict studies led to an emphasis on subconventional warfare, psychological operations, and nation building as constituent elements of U.S. military strategy.[15] However, only a fringe of the armed forces officer corps, such as the Green Berets, committed themselves to careers along these lines. The more traditional arms of service lacked serious interest in special operations and regarded their counter-insurgency brethren with undisguised distaste. As the U.S. commitment to Vietnam escalated well beyond the engagement of special operations forces and intelligence operatives, conventional military mind sets displaced the political side of the political-military equation on which special operations had been predicated. U.S. conventional forces in Vietnam, on the evidence, fought well against North Vietnamese conventional forces and Viet Cong units when the latter were willing to stand and fight pitched battles.

However, it became apparent by 1968 even to the Department of Defense that the United States could not win the counterinsurgency or propaganda wars at an acceptable cost: Johnson's resignation and Nixon's phased disengagement followed. Many arguments can be started in bars as to whether U.S. conventional or unconventional military strategy failed in Vietnam. The present discussion bypasses that temptation and emphasizes the implications of counterinsurgency displacement, by conventional strategy, for military personnel policy. Having decided that escalation from limited commitment to a major U.S. military campaign in South Vietnam was necessary, President Johnson, nonetheless, sought to balance the requirement for military escalation against his other priorities in domestic politics, especially his cherished Great Society programs recently passed by Congress. Johnson's "guns and butter" policy filled the armed forces ranks of enlisted personnel by expanded conscription of young persons while forgoing the option to mobilize the organized reserve forces. The result of this approach was to create nationwide dissent against the war, first across U.S. college campuses and then to wider audiences.

The draft, more than anything else, had brought the U.S. military escalation in Vietnam to a stopping point. When U.S. Commander-in-Chief William Westmoreland asked for several hundred thousand additional troops in 1968, then-Secretary of Defense Clark Clifford suggested to Johnson that he pull the plug. Johnson did so, announcing his intention not to seek another term of office and thereby conceding the failure of U.S. policy and strategy in Vietnam. However, Johnson left the nation with a major force and policy commitment to a war that would continue without complete U.S. disengagement until 1973 and with war between Vietnamese until 1975. With military disengagement from Vietnam went another look at U.S. conscription policy, and the Gates commission recommendation to end conscription was adopted and ordered into effect beginning in 1983. In effect, the United States had come full circle to its pre–twentieth century peacetime standard of raising armed forces by voluntary enlistment (except for the U.S. Civil War, when both sides drafted).

The onset of the all-volunteer force coincided with post-Vietnam doctrinal revisionism. The Nixon administration changed the 1960s strategy of being able to fight two and one-half wars simultaneously to one and one-half wars, and Nixon emphasized that U.S. support for besieged allies would stop short of involving U.S. ground forces. Voluntary enlistment dictated a strategy of selective rather than ubiquitous military engagement. Selective engagement also was facilitated by the full-blown emergence of U.S.-Soviet detente during the 1970s and Sino-U.S. rapprochement. It was perceived by U.S. foreign and defense policy elites that diplomatic containment of Moscow's ambitions was more cost effective than overpromising of U.S. military involvement in regional conflicts. U.S. and Soviet leaders worked to stabilize the Middle East and to create new expectations about their mutual interests in avoiding nuclear war and inadvertent military escalation. In addition, under the direction of Chief of Staff General Creighton Abrams, Army planners during the early 1970s configured the "total force" concept so that future presidents could not avoid substantial reserve call-ups during any national mobilization for war.[16]

The Carter administration ended its term of office on a sour note in U.S.-Soviet relations: the invasion of Afghanistan caused Carter to ask that the U.S. Senate suspend consideration of the SALT II treaty he had negotiated. In addition, Carter called for the creation of a rapid deployment force for prompt intervention in the Middle East/Persian Gulf: this force eventually would grow into the central command, which U.S. Army General Norman Schwartzkopf would take into battle against Iraq in 1991. However, Carter's belated acknowledgment of the seriousness of Soviet military potential did not lead to a full court press with U.S. military forces against perceived Soviet vulnerabilities. Carter maintained the path of selective engagement of U.S. military power previously established under Nixon and Ford. Thus, Carter was disinclined to call for a return to conscription, and Reagan was even less interested in doing so.

Although some describe the Reagan administration as a period of U.S. overcommitment to counterinsurgency or insurgency wars, Reagan's advisors were stronger on anticommunist rhetoric than they were committed to bailing out hapless dictators or overthrowing leftist regimes. Reagan preferred to direct U.S. commitments toward counterterrorism and covert action at the low end of the conflict spectrum and U.S. investment toward conventional high technology supportive of "air-land battle" between the Warsaw Pact and NATO at the higher end of conventional military options. The all-volunteer force, so badly underfunded that it could scarcely meet its recruitment goals during the 1970s, fared better in the 1980s after enlisted and officer compensations were raised significantly by Congress. Congress also supported the administration's emphasis on firepower intensive as opposed to manpower intensive military strategies, although the Department of Defense and services emphasized the need to make firepower smarter through precision guided munitions, improved capability for electronic warfare, and eventual applications of sensors and weapons based on other physical principles.

Reagan's high-tech strategic focus extended even into the heavens, where he assumed his proposed strategic defense initiative eventually would yield deployments of space based battle stations and other accoutrements of postnuclear deterrence This vision also seemed to require technology intensive, not manpower intensive, forward planning, and the vision of massive manpower wars was pushed even farther from planning consciousness. A war that began in Europe might, according to Reagan planning guidance, extend into a world war, but U.S. and allied NATO strategy did not envision a repeat of any conflict as extended in time as World War II. NATO's campaign on the central front in Europe would be based on conventional deep strikes, aided by modernized sensors, battlefield computers, and precision weapons, and it would be designed to disconnect the tail of the Soviet offensive from its teeth.[17]

The modernized U.S. air-land battle template also remains interesting for its subsequent application to the Persian Gulf War against Iraq in 1991.[18] Here, U.S. military planners who contemplated how to prevail in a war between NATO and the Warsaw Pact and who were confounded by the commingling of conventional and nuclear forces in Europe found a more amenable theater of operations for the application of U.S. military power. A five-month period of grace for military buildup in Saudi Arabia did no harm to U.S. readiness for war in January 1991, and U.S. air-land battle doctrine played successfully before a packed house. (Additional comments on the military-technical aspects of the Desert Storm air war appear below.)

The results of the Gulf War of 1991 seemed to vindicate not only U.S. conventional military strategy and technology but also the decision in favor of the all-volunteer force taken decades earlier. Columnist Charles Krauthammer, celebrating the "unipolar moment" in which the United States had allegedly found itself by virtue of the collapse of the Soviet Union, noted that:

In 1950 the U.S. engaged in a war with North Korea: it lasted three years, cost 54,000 American lives, and ended in a draw. Forty-one years later, the U.S. engaged in a war with Iraq: it lasted six weeks, cost 196 American lives, and ended in a rout. If the Roman Empire had declined at this rate, you would be reading this in Latin.[19]

However, experts recognized the ironical character of the vindication of U.S. strategy, because the air-land battle doctrine had been intended for a force structure that was obviously not going to be preserved intact into the post–Cold War era. The United States might not even be able to repeat Desert Storm by 1997 with forces drawn down considerably from 1990 levels even according to the Bush plan of 1991, which Congress might choose to modify. In addition, the Congress and some political-military strategists in the executive branch were also planning to employ U.S. military capability for nontraditional or noncombat missions, including operations designed to preserve sanctuary from attack for besieged ethnic or national populations (such as operation Provide Comfort for the Kurds in Iraq). The Bush strategy for more traditional uses of U.S. military power emphasized the performance of forward presence and crisis response missions intended for regional contingency operations outside of Europe, not for global warfare or for large interstate wars in Europe.

A U.S. military strategy based on regional contingencies may be as controversial as the containment strategy that preceded it: implementation of a contingency oriented strategy involves complicated political, economic, and military decisions in the years ahead.[20] Declining U.S. defense budgets will create difficult trade-offs among the desired goals of preserving force size, modernizing weapons, and C3 (command, control and communications), maintaining readiness for crisis response, and preserving sustainability for protracted conflict. Because of constrained U.S. resources, U.S. forces will be dependent upon international coalitions for the conduct of major contingent operations, as they were in Desert Shield and Desert Storm. In addition, "to the extent that deterrent strategies form part of the response to today's threats and challenges, they will increasingly be implemented *multilaterally* and *economically*."[21] Beyond resource constraints, Desert Storm also suggests a qualitative dilemma for U.S. military planners. Precision guided munitions, improved communications and command/control, and reconnaissance-strike complexes will make possible, in theory, the selective targeting of enemy military assets while minimizing collateral damage.[22] In practice, as opposed to theory, the economies and social fabrics of third world states may be so fragile that the "precision" possible in high technology warfare is irrelevant to those on the receiving end. In addition, coalition air attacks within and outside of the Kuwaiti theater of operations used a preponderance of other than "smart" munitions, as Table 1.2 shows.

Thus, efforts to maintain specific political and military limitations in war and to derive from those limitations carefully laid down strike plans could fail unavoidably and to the detriment of coalition management.[23] In addition, the one-sided outcome of the Gulf War of 1991 caused a hubris about the potential of U.S. air power alone to win wars or to terminate crises.[24] The Air Force–commissioned Gulf War Air Power Survey noted that, in some respects, the coalition was unable to obtain desired damage expectancies against preferred targets, including mobile Scuds, Iraqi nuclear capabilities, and Iraqi command, control, and communications.[25] In addition, problems of interservice command and control were not absent from Desert Storm. Tensions developed between U.S. ground forces commanders and the Joint Forces

TABLE 1.2

Munitions Employed in Desert Storm Air War (Selected List)[a]

Munitions	Air Force	Navy	Marines	Total
General purpose bombs				
Mk-82 (500 lb)	59,884	10,941	6,828	77,653
Mk-83 (1,000 lb)		10,125	8,893	19,081
Mk-84 (2,000 lb)	10,467	971	751	12,289
Mk-117 (B-52)	43,435			43,435
CBU-52 (fragmentation bomb)	17,831			17,831
CBU-87 (combined effects munition)	10,035			10,035
CBU-89/78 (Gator)	1,105	148	61	1,314
Mk-20 (Rockeye)	5,345	6,814	15,828	27,987
Laser-guided bombs				
GBU-12 (laser/Mk-82)	4,086	205	202	4,493
Air-to-surface missiles				
AGM-114 Hellfire (AH-64 and AH-1W)[b]		30	159	3,065 (Army — 2,876)
AGM-65 (Maverick), all models	5,255		41	5,296

Notes:

[a]The selected munitions displayed in this table are those that were primarily, although not exclusively, used in the Kuwaiti theater of operations by coalition forces. Other types of laser-guided bombs and air-to-surface missiles were used in the war, but not primarily in the Kuwaiti theater of operations.

[b]Navy and Marine Corps also fired 283 BGM-71 TOW munitions from helicopters.

Source: Abbreviated Summary of the Gulf War Air Power Survey (Carlisle Barracks, Pa.: U.S. Army War College, 1993), pp. 14–33.

Air Component Commander Lieutenant General Charles A. Horner, who was responsible as commander of Central Command's Air Force component. General Norman Schwartzkopf sought to centralize control of coalition air power under one component commander, and Schwartzkopf and Horner favored target attack priorities not shared by Marine Corps and Army commanders. As the Gulf War Air Power Survey noted:

In the dispute over the best use of precision bombing in the KTO (Kuwaiti Theater of Operations) . . . Schwartzkopf made decisions which displeased his ground commanders and caused grumbling about the JFAAC's execution of those decisions. Not only did Schwartzkopf emphasize bombing Republican Guards rather than frontline forces, but he shared Horner's enthusiasm for "tank plinking" (the destruction of tanks with precision guided bombs) — an enthusiasm that was not shared by Generals Franks (Lt. Gen. Frederick Franks, USA) and Boomer (Lt. Gen. Walter Boomer, USMC). For their part, the JFAAC's air campaign planners complained that targets nominated by ground forces were often out of date and had already been disabled by previous air attacks.[26]

As the use of sophisticated information gathering, processing, and distributing systems grows, so do the dependency of commanders on those systems and the vulnerability of the entire operational plan if the high tech command, control, communications, and intelligence systems are destroyed. Modern communications technology also subverts traditional, hierarchical notions of control. During the Gulf War of 1991, for example, U.S. military staffs in Colorado relayed warnings of Iraqi Scud launches directly to Tel Aviv and Riyadh; members of the Joint Chiefs of Staff and civilian policy makers had the CNN backchannel to supplement communications directly with the field.[27] The difficulty of bomb damage assessment during the Gulf air war shows that, notwithstanding the availability of high tech reconnaissance systems and data fusion centers, war remains mostly in the domain of uncertainty.[28]

CONCLUSIONS

Bipolarity and U.S.-Soviet hostility forced U.S. security policy during the Cold War into a collective defense framework, contrary to the expectations of the victorious World War II allies. Collective security had to await the end of the Cold War and the defenestration of communist power in Russia. However, the plunge into a collective security function taken by the United States with UN blessing in 1990 and 1991 was not necessarily normative for the future. The Iraqi case of blunt aggression against Kuwait offered none of the ambiguity of other challenges to stability for which Security Council consensus on ends and means might be harder to obtain.

U.S. anticipation of global war against the Soviet Union for 40 years led to a nuclear dependent security posture that provided for deterrence but left open the question of priorities among actual war fighting capabilities. The war in Vietnam caused rethinking of the balance between conventional and unconventional strategy by U.S. planners, although lessons about unconventional conflicts are not always retained in the military memory bank. A higher profile for the U.S. military in multinational peace operations implies that the roles of unconventional forces and the sociopolitical aspects of military doctrine will receive greater emphasis in the future, compared with the past.[29]

NOTES

1. I am using the terms "collective defense" and "collective security" in a functional sense, which may not correspond to legal distinctions. For example, the coalition war against Iraq in 1991 was authorized by the United Nations under Article 51 for collective self-defense, not under Chapter VII peace enforcement. A functional distinction between collective defense and security is more appropriate here.

Collective defense is exclusive: it is based on alliances formed in peacetime and prepared to respond to aggression from a specified, particular threat. Collective security is inclusive: ad hoc groupings of responsive states are formed to deal with cases of aggression whatever their sources. Later chapters discuss collective security as it relates to military operations other than war, such as peacekeeping or peacemaking.

2. Gaddis Smith, *American Diplomacy during the Second World War, 1941–1945* (New Haven, Conn.: Yale University Press, 1965), esp. pp. 59–80.

3. These developments can be traced in John Lewis Gaddis, *The United States and the Origins of the Cold War, 1941–1947* (New York: Columbia University Press, 1972), esp. pp. 282–352; Adam Ulam, *The Rivals: America and Russia since World War II* (New York: Viking, 1971).

4. For pertinent documentation, see Walter Lafeber, *America, Russia and the Cold War, 1945–1975* (New York: John Wiley and Sons, 1976). On the development of U.S. Cold War policy, see Gaddis, *The United States.* For Soviet policy, see Vojtech Mastny, *Russia's Road to the Cold War: Diplomacy, Warfare, and the Politics of Communism, 1941–45* (New York: Columbia University Press, 1979).

5. John Lewis Gaddis, *The Long Peace: Inquiries into the History of the Cold War* (New York: Oxford University Press, 1987), p. 114.

6. Robert Jervis, *The Meaning of the Nuclear Revolution* (Ithaca, N.Y.: Cornell University Press, 1989); Lawrence Freedman, *The Evolution of Nuclear Strategy* (New York: St. Martin's Press, 1981).

7. Paul Nitze, "A Project for Further Analysis and Study of Certain Factors Affecting Our Foreign Policy and Our National Defense Policy," Project Control Papers, U.S. Air Force Historical Research Center, Maxwell AFB, Alabama, September 15, 1954, cited in Marc Trachtenberg, *History and Strategy* (Princeton, N.J.: Princeton University Press, 1991), p. 112.

8. See Peter Douglas Feaver, *Guarding the Guardians: Civilian Control of Nuclear Weapons in the United States* (Ithaca, N.Y.: Cornell University Press, 1992), esp. pp. 3–28.

9. This case is argued in Harry T. Summers, *On Strategy: A Critical Analysis of the Vietnam War* (New York: Dell, 1982), Chap. 1.

10. For an account from the perspective of McNamara's staff, see Alain C. Enthoven and K. Wayne Smith, *How Much Is Enough?: Shaping the Defense Program, 1961–1969* (New York: Harper & Row, 1971), esp. pp. 117–64; see also William W. Kaufmann, *The McNamara Strategy* (New York: Harper & Row, 1964).

11. Evolution of the National Security Council is discussed in John Prados, *The Keepers of the Keys: A History of the National Security Council from Truman to Bush* (New York: William Morrow, 1991).

12. For assessments of Goldwater-Nichols, see Robert J. Art, *Strategy and Management in the Post–Cold War Pentagon* (Carlisle, Pa.: U.S. Army War College, Strategic Studies Institute, 1992); Les Aspin and William Dickenson, *Defense for a New Era: Lessons of the Persian Gulf War* (Washington, D.C.: U.S. Government Printing Office, 1992).

13. For a sampling of expert assessments, see Robert J. Art, Vincent Davis, and Samuel P. Huntington, eds., *Reorganizing America's Defenses: Leadership in War and Peace* (New York: Pergamon Brassey's, 1985).

14. Art, *Strategy and Management in the Post–Cold War Pentagon*, pp. 26–27.

15. A critique of U.S. experience is provided in D. Michael Shafer, *Deadly Paradigms: The Failure of U.S. Counterinsurgency Policy* (Princeton, N.J.: Princeton University Press, 1988); see also Douglas S. Blaufarb, *The Counterinsurgency Era: U.S. Doctrine and Performance, 1950 to the Present* (New York: Free Press, 1977). For evaluations of U.S. experiences with covert action, see John Prados, *Presidents' Secret*

Wars: CIA and Pentagon Covert Operations Since World War II (New York: William Morrow, 1986); Roy Godson, ed., *Intelligence Requirements for the 1980s, Vol. 4: Covert Action* (Washington, D.C.: National Strategy Information Center, 1983). An assessment of the impact of low intensity conflict on U.S. military professionalism appears in Sam C. Sarkesian, *Beyond the Battlefield: The New Military Professionalism* (New York: Pergamon, 1981), Part II, Chaps. 4–7.

16.   Harry G. Summers, Jr., *On Strategy II: A Critical Analysis of the Gulf War* (New York: Dell, 1992), pp. 72–73.

17.   John G. Hines and Phillip A. Petersen, "NATO and the Changing Soviet Concept of Control for Theater War," in *The Soviet Challenge in the 1990s*, ed. Stephen J. Cimbala (New York: Praeger, 1989), pp. 65–122.

18.   Summers, *On Strategy II: A Critical Analysis of the Gulf War*, pp. 139–50.

19.   Charles Krauthammer, "The Unipolar Moment," in *Rethinking America's Security*, eds. Graham Allison and Gregory F. Treverton (New York, W. W. Norton, 1992), p. 298. U.S. battle deaths in Korea actually totalled about 34,000: total deaths raised the number above 54,000.

20.   The point is emphasized in Michael J. Mazarr, Don M. Snider, and James A. Blackwell, Jr., *Desert Storm: The Gulf War and What We Learned* (Boulder, Colo.: Westview, 1993), pp. 162–68.

21.   Ibid., p. 175.

22.   The term "reconnaissance-strike complexes" originated in Russian/Soviet military discourse to describe combinations of increasingly accurate conventional munitions, improved target identification and location, and enhanced control and communications systems for directing the employment of munitions against selected targets. See V. G. Reznichenko, I. N. Vorob'iev, and N. F. Miroshnichenko, *Taktika* [Tactics] (Moscow: Voenizdat, 1987), p. 24, which notes: "In the opinion of foreign specialists, reconnaissance-strike (fire) complexes are the most effective form of high precision weapon. High precision reconnaissance resources and high precision weapons are coordinated by an automated control system making it possible to carry out reconnaissance and destruction missions practically in real time." The issue continues to preoccupy the Russian military, although it will struggle to maintain the military-industrial base for future modernization. See John Erickson, "Quo Vadis? The Changing Faces of Soviet/Russian Forces and Now Russia," in *The Soviet Military and the Future*, eds. Stephen J. Blank and Jacob W. Kipp (Westport, Conn.: Greenwood, 1992), pp. 33–58.

23.   According to one source, "various offices in the Pentagon are battling for control of a dramatic new initiative for nonlethal warfare. By using blinding lasers and chemical immobilizers to stun foot soldiers and munitions with "entanglement" warheads to stop armored vehicles on land or ships at sea, it is hoped by some that the United States could some day fight a war that did not involve death, or at least few deaths" (Mazarr, Snider, and Blackwell, *Desert Storm*, p. 172). Life imitates art or, at least, simulation.

25.   Some 1,500 strikes were conducted against Iraqi ballistic missile capabilities, of which 15 percent (about 215 strikes) included attacks against mobile launchers. According to the Gulf War Air Power Survey, "the actual destruction of any Iraqi mobile launchers by fixed-wing coalition aircraft remains impossible to confirm." Despite coalition attacks on leadership and command, control, and communications targets, the Iraqi command and communications system "turned out to be more redundant and more able to reconstitute itself than first thought." The redundancy, advanced status, and elusiveness of Iraq's nuclear program led the United Nations to conclude that Desert Storm had no more than "inconvenienced" Iraqi plans to field atomic weapons. See *Abbreviated Summary of the Gulf War Air Power Survey* (Carlisle Barracks, Pa.: U.S. Army War College, 1993), pp. 14–27. The study was

commissioned by the then-Secretary of the U.S. Air Force, Donald Rice, in 1991 and directed by Eliot A. Cohen, Johns Hopkins University.

26.   *Abbreviated Summary of the Gulf War Air Power Survey*, pp. 14–43.

27.   Eliot A. Cohen, "The Mystique of U.S. Air Power," *Foreign Affairs* 73 (January 1994): 118.

28.   Ibid., p. 119.

29.   For expansion of this point, see Sam C. Sarkesian, *Unconventional Conflicts in a New Security Era: Lessons from Malaya and Vietnam* (Westport, Conn.: Greenwood, 1993), esp. pp. 194–95.

2

A Voyage of Discovery: Bush Strategy and Civil-Military Relations

The Bush administration provides an interesting and potentially fruitful case study of U.S. civil-military relations. First, the Bush years straddle the Cold War and the post–Cold War worlds. Second, the Gulf War of 1991, fought under Bush's leadership, was the first post–Cold War conflict based on a regional contingency. Third, the process of strategy making and force building under Bush has come in for significant controversy, including claims that professional military influence on policy was excessive.

This discussion revisits the strategy-making process under Bush and the role of military advice in that process, in five stages. First, background pertinent to the international and domestic settings facing Bush and his national security team is noted. Second, the initiative of former Joint Chiefs of Staff (JCS) Chairman General Colin Powell and others in strategy and force structure planning is reviewed. Third, the dominant scenarios on which Bush's strategic planning was based are revisited. Fourth, the role of civil-military relations and military advice in the Gulf War is considered. Fifth, an assessment of whether professional military advice under Bush was excessive or otherwise miscast is attempted.

THEORETICAL PERSPECTIVE AND BACKGROUND

Military organizations, more than most, have a significant interest in stable environments. Rapid environmental change, as in a greatly increased threat perception, raises the prospect of surprise attack or defeat in battle. A changed environment threatens both the existing

The original version of this chapter was presented at the Conference on U.S. Civil-Military Relations, U.S. Army War College, Carlisle Barracks, September 13–14, 1994. I am grateful to Don Snider for his comments and suggestions pertinent to this study.

"treaties" or organizational distributions of resources, power, and prestige and the role perceptions and career orientations of military and other professionals.[1] New bargains and revised role expectations create turbulence among policy makers and commanders. The "masks of war" worn by each service, in terms of its preferred doctrine, strategic concepts, and organizational ethos, are more subject to critique by domestic forces or subversion by foreign enemies when revised or ambiguous threat assessments are substituted for older and more comfortable ones.[2]

Soon after taking office, the Bush administration realized that a changed international environment demanded rethinking of Cold War requirements for strategy and force structure. The strategy of the Cold War was driven by planning scenarios centered on global conflict against the Soviet Union. U.S. force structure was based on the requirements for fighting a nuclear war or a major conventional war in Europe. As the Soviet empire disintegrated and its military successor Russia veered erratically toward democracy, a Soviet-centered global war machine obviously was no longer either necessary or desirable from the standpoint of strategic thinking or optimal U.S. force structure.

It was not so obvious how to get from here to there. The new international order was not taking any definite shape in the transition years from 1989 through 1992. Regional hegemonies continued to threaten U.S. vital interests or U.S. allies. Europe, less threatened by attack from without, was divided by turbulence within, especially in former Yugoslavia. The proliferation of nuclear and other weapons of mass destruction, together with the spread of ballistic missiles to third world countries, argued against complacency and raised the potential threat to international stability. The new international environment presented a series of "fuzzy" threats to replace one very concrete one.

Previous defense reorganizations had settled the issue of centralized control on the administrative side of the Pentagon.[3] The powers of the secretary of defense relative to those of the individual service secretaries were progressively enhanced by the defense reorganizations of 1949, 1953, and 1958. On the professional military side, centralization was less successful. The JCS, until the Goldwater-Nichols reforms of 1986, operated as a consensus-seeking committee and offered little in the way of sharp strategic options and advice for the secretary or the president.[4] The Goldwater-Nichols Department of Defense Reorganization Act of 1986 strengthened the office of the chairman, JCS, and gave additional authority over service components to the unified and specified commanders in chief (CINCs) who have responsibility for operating wartime forces.[5] It remained an open question whether any particular JCS chairman could take advantage of Goldwater-Nichols to force the JCS to produce a truly unified national military strategy, as opposed to a compromise among particular service strategies.[6]

The Bush administration inherited the Reagan force buildup and, therefore, found itself with excessive force structure for the post–Cold War world. However, a new strategy could not simply reduce forces across the board: the world had undergone a change in kind, not just in degree. What faced U.S. defense planners by 1990 was not a shrunken version of the old Soviet armed forces with the same planning guidance, but a realigned Eurasian political landscape. A single security dilemma "from the Bering sea to the Bering sea"[7] had been fractured into multiple security dilemmas, mostly outside of Europe and involving many regimes governed by autocrats with grievances against their regional neighbors. The door was open to new approaches to strategy and force structure planning.

It can be argued that changes in defense strategy and policy that took place under President Bush and Secretary of Defense Richard Cheney were far-reaching. In the main, these tectonic shifts in the premises for U.S. defense planning and budgeting have carried forward into the Clinton administration, reappearing, for example, in Secretary of Defense Les Aspin's Bottom-Up Review. Among the more important Cheney-Aspin changes in defense planning parameters are those listed in Table 2.1

LEADERS AND CHANGE

The appointment of General Colin Powell as chairman, JCS, brought to that office a change oriented and dominant personality. Powell took seriously the mandate given to the chairman by the Goldwater-Nichols reforms. The JCS were responsible for producing a national military strategy, not just a compendium of service strategies. Powell became the driving force in bringing about this unified national strategy. Powell prodded and pushed the JCS toward zero based rethinking of U.S. military requirements. The JCS chairman's well-honed political skills also anticipated what would come out of the office of the secretary of defense (OSD) — policy reviews overseen by Under Secretary of Defense for Policy Paul Wolfowitz. What emerged was as unified a product of the JCS as any U.S. president or defense secretary had ever seen.

Powell could have taken either of two approaches to a unified strategy. Strategy could have been based on a revised threat assessment. From a newly sized threat, a newly designed strategy and force structure would be deduced. Powell chose not to go in this direction. One reason might have been that in 1990, as the strategy began to take shape, the Soviet Union was still in existence and Gorbachev was still clinging to power. Gorbachev's objectives never included the abolition of the Soviet Union nor the demise of communism in Russia. The possibility, however unlikely, of a reconstituted Soviet threat could not be dismissed. Even without a revived Soviet threat, the

TABLE 2.1
New Perspectives in Defense Planning and Budgeting under Bush and Cheney and Carried Forward into Clinton Bottom-up Review

I. Redefinition of U.S. national security interests and objectives
   United States was forced to rethink fundamentals of strategy and did so in several authoritative policy directives.

II. Russia no longer a global military threat
   A. Cheney and Powell estimates reduce Russians to regional threat that still bears watching.
   B. Aspin Bottom-Up Review not as concerned with Russia as regional threat but agrees that it no longer constitutes global threat.
   C. Because Russia is no longer a global military threat, reduced insurance coverage against a reemergence of that threat can be purchased. Strategic warning will be measured in years, and capabilities for a renascent global threat can be reconstituted if necessary.

III. Environmental or milieu shaping
   A. The United States is now concerned with milieu or environmental shaping in at least three ways:
      1. encouraging regional stability
      2. encouraging peaceful change within and among states
      3. reducing incentives for others to seek superpower status
   B. Cheney and Aspin, consistent with A, above, have argued for preserving significant U.S. forward presence in important regions and for continued assertive nonproliferation and counterproliferation policies.

IV. Realism in threat assessment
   A. The Department of Defense is more willing to assume in the present and in the future, compared with the past, that potential adversaries will be less capable than the United States in weapons systems, personnel, and other combat related indicators.
   B. At the same time, the tightness of Clinton projected budgets through fiscal 1999 leaves little slack above adequacy for two almost simultaneous major regional contingencies.[8]

V. Fighting to win
   A. As apparent in the Bush strategy for Desert Storm and implicit in Clinton strategy documents, the United States now expects to win any war in which it becomes engaged. This is in contrast to the Cold War NATO/Europe oriented strategies of holding or restoring the border or buying conventional forces adequate to raise the nuclear threshold.
   B. Many military persons doubt that this insistence upon winning carries forward into the instincts of President Clinton, although they concede that it was conveyed from the Bush to the Clinton Pentagon. The roots of this fight-to-win lie further back, in the United States' frustrating experience in Vietnam and military reluctance to become involved again without a willingness on the part of political leaders to pursue victory.

VI.   Building-block forces
      The Department of Defense has now conceptualized and institutionalized
      the use of building-block forces for major regional contingencies (MRCs)
      and lesser regional contingencies (LRCs).
      A. The MRC building block includes:
          1. 4–5 Army divisions
          2. 4–5 Marine expeditionary brigades
          3. 10 Air Force tactical fighter wings
          4. 100 Air Force heavy bombers
          5. 4–5 Navy carrier battle groups
          6. special operations forces
      B. The LRC building block involves:
          1. 2 Army light divisions
          2. 1 Marine expeditionary brigade
          3. 1–2 Navy carrier battle groups
          4. 1–2 composite tactical fighter wings
          5. special operations forces
          6. various support units

VII. New military missions
      A. Operations other than war assumed centrality in Bush defense planning
          and have received even greater visibility under Clinton. These include
          peace operations of all varieties, unilateral and multilateral.
      B. Military cautionary flags about U.S. participation in multinational
          peacekeeping or peace enforcement operations were raised under Bush
          and elevated under Clinton. One result was the Clinton policy on
          reforming multilateral peace operations (May 1994), which asserted
          stringent criteria for U.S. military participation in those operations and
          mandated exclusive command of U.S. forces by the U.S. chain of
          command.

Source: Adapted from Paul K. Davis, "Planning Under Uncertainty Then and Now:
Paradigms Lost and Paradigms Emerging," in *New Challenges for Defense Planning:
Rethinking How Much Is Enough*, ed. Paul K. Davis (Santa Monica, Calif.: RAND
Corporation, 1994), pp. 31–33. I have omitted some items and revised or expanded
upon others in the original list, and I am solely responsible for the present format.

shape of other threats was difficult to foresee under post–Cold War
conditions.

Powell and the JCS, therefore, chose to base force planning on
something other than threat assessment. Planning was based on a
conceptual foundation known as the "base force." The base force was
that minimum force with which the United States would have to meet
in order to continue to function as a global superpower. It was predicated on Powell's conviction as early as 1989 that the changes taking
place in the Soviet Union were irreversible.[9] In this decision, he was
moving faster than either Secretary of Defense Dick Cheney or Under
Secretary of Defense for Policy Paul D. Wolfowitz was then prepared to
go.

The fundamental force components of the base force were announced as the strategic force, including offensive and defensive long range nuclear missiles and bombers; the Atlantic force; the Pacific force; and the contingency force.[10] The contingency force was the newest element. Borrowing from the former strike command and rapid deployment force, the contingency force was to be available for quick response to any theater of operations. It also was to provide deployable conventional military power in areas not covered by the Atlantic and Pacific forces, such as South America and sub-Saharan Africa. A schematic of the proposed base force is presented in Table 2.2.

Powell's base force concept was actually the culmination of rethinking about U.S. strategy that had begun in the JCS as early as 1988. The joint strategic capabilities plan for fiscal year 1989–90, prepared in spring 1988, concluded that a deliberate Soviet attack against NATO Europe was improbable. The more probable threats, according to this study, were regional, conventional wars outside of Europe and with low probability of Soviet intervention.[11] Support for strategy reformulation also appeared in the efforts by the JCS Strategic Plans and Policy Directorate (J-5) from 1988 through 1990 to revisit U.S. thinking about mobilization readiness and warning. Under the direction of Lt. General George Lee Butler (future head of Strategic Command), J-5 convened the roundtable on warning in 1989 and 1990. The discussions in the roundtable on warning identified the problem of multiple warning patterns that applied to regional as well as global conflict. Reconceptualization of the problem of warning dovetailed with General Butler's own evolving strategic overview that the Cold War was indeed over, that communism had irretrievably failed, and that the world was entering an era of multipolarity.[12]

The base force concept also evolved from efforts of the Program and Budget Analysis Division (PBAD) of the Force Structure, Resource and Assessment Directorate to consider the impact of budget reductions on U.S. force structure. Beginning in the fall of 1988, PBAD held regular discussions with Office of Management and Budget and congressional staffers. Anticipating a fiscal climate more adverse than that assumed in OSD, PBAD began its own study of force reduction options in October 1988. It completed "Quiet Study I" and "Quiet Study II" under JCS Chairmen Crowe and Powell respectively. Quiet Study II anticipated a shift in emphasis in U.S. defense planning from the East-West confrontation in Europe to regional contingencies outside of Europe.[13]

The Bush administration decision to build down U.S. military capabilities was in contrast to the strategy inherited from Reagan. As the Bush administration assumed office in 1989, the inherited strategy was global in orientation and focused on deterrence of Soviet aggression. It required a very credible nuclear deterrent and large conventional forces, many deployed outside the United States to create "forward defense" along the perimeter of Soviet influence.[14] The inherited

TABLE 2.2
U.S. Force Packages, Bush Base Force

	Army	Navy	Marines	Air Force
Atlantic Forces				
Europe	2 divisions	1 CVBG	MARG in Mediterranean; MPS	3 wings
CONUS	4 active, 6 reserve, (+2 cadre) divisions	5 CVBGs and support ships	2 MEBs (+ 1RC)	2 active; 11 reserve wings
Pacific Forces				
Korea	1 division	1 CVBG	1 MAGTF (TBD)	1–2 wings
Japan			1 MEB	1–2 wings
Hawaii and Alaska	1 division (light)	5 CVBGs and support ships	1 MEB	1 wing
CONUS				
Contingency Force	4 divisions	Forces from Atlantic and Pacific; 8 SL-7s and rest of RRF	Forces from Atlantic and Pacific; 8 SL-7s and rest of RRF	7 wings intertheater airlift
	SOF	SOF	SOF	SOF

| Strategic Nuclear Forces | 18 Trident submarines | 500 Minuteman III ICBMs; bombers (B-52H, B-1, and B-2 mix)* |

Notes:
  *Bush plan originally included 50 MX (Peacekeeper ICMB).
  Abbreviations — CVBG, carrier battle group; MAGTF, Marine air-ground task force; MARG, Mediterranean amphibious ready group (Marine expeditionary unit); MEB, Marine expeditionary brigade; MEF, Marine expeditionary force; MPS, maritime prepositioning ships; RC, reserve component; RRF, ready reserve fleet; SOF, special operations forces; TBD, to be determined.

Source: Lawrence J. Korb, "The Impact of the Persian Gulf War on Military Budgets and Force Structure," in *After the Storm: Lessons from the Gulf War*, eds. Joseph S. Nye, Jr., and Roger K. Smith (Lanham, Md.: Madison Books/Aspen Strategy Group, 1992), p. 230. Based on testimony of Admiral David E. Jeremiah, vice-chairman of the U.S. Joint Chiefs of Staff before the House Armed Services Committee, March 12, 1991.

strategy called for increased defense spending from fiscal year 1990 to 1994 of 2 percent real growth per year. In contrast to the inherited strategy, the Bush strategy was based on four central strategic concepts: forward presence, crisis response, reconstitution, and strategic deterrence and defense. The last of these was the only carryover concept from the Cold War.[15]

The base force concept presupposed budget cuts over a five-year period no greater than about 25 percent of 1990 levels in total obligational authority. The force reductions called for in the Bush plan are enumerated in Table 2.3.

TABLE 2.3
Reductions in U.S. Military Forces, 1990–97 (1991 Bush Plan)

	1990	1997	Percent Reduced
Active Forces			
Ground forces			
Army divisions	18	12	33
Marine brigades	9	7	22
Naval forces			
Aircraft carriers	13	12	8
Carrier air wings	13	11	15
Ships	545	448	18
Air forces			
Tactical fighter wings	24	15.5	35
Strategic forces			
ICBMs	1,000	550	45
SLBMs	608	432	29
Bombers	228	181	21
Reserve forces			
National guard divisions	10	6	40
Marine brigades	3	3	0
Carrier air wings	2	2	0
Tactical fighter wings	12	11	8

Source: Statement of General Colin Powell, Subcommittee on Defense, House Committee on Appropriations, September 25, 1991, revised in U.S. Congressional Budget Office, *The Economic Effects of Reduced Defense Spending* (Washington, D.C.: Congressional Budget Office, 1992), p. 4.

The impact of the Bush base force plan on projected service force levels, active and reserve, is shown in Table 2.4. It turned out that Congress was generally agreeable with the recommended cuts in active duty forces but was more resistant to proportionate reductions in reserves.

TABLE 2.4
Military Personnel Levels in 1991 and 1997, by Service and
Component, under Bush Base Force Plan
(in thousands)

Service and Component	1991	1997	Percent Change
Active			
Army	725	536	−26
Navy	571	501	−12
Marines	195	159	−18
Air Force	511	430	−16
Total Active	2,002	1,626	−19
Selected Reserve			
Army National Guard	441	338	−23
Army Reserve	300	229	−24
Navy Reserve	151	118	−22
Marine Reserve	44	35	−20
Air National Guard	118	118	0
Air Force Reserve	84	82	−3
Total Selected Reserve	1,138	920	−19

Source: Martin Binkin, *Who Will Fight the Next War? The Changing Face of the American Military* (Washington, D.C.: Brookings Institution, 1993), p. 134.

THE SCENARIO DRIVERS IN BUSH STRATEGY

Bush strategy making was atypical by post–World War II standards in several ways. First, there was no raucous and loud congressional debate about the ends and means of strategy. Debates about the ends of policy and the purposes of U.S. military strategy at the beginning of the Cold War were prolonged and difficult. Debates at the end of the Cold War were barely noticeable. Second, strategy was more difficult to connect to threat assessment than at any time from 1947 to 1990. Third, the declining threat perception influenced Congress by focusing its attention on domestic issues. Even the Gulf War did not change this congressional emphasis on domestic issues very much because of its rapid and successful conclusion.

These conditions abroad and at home gave Powell and the JCS a great deal of leeway in developing strategy and war plans. However, the absence of a driving threat assessment made it difficult to find a conceptual pivot for the new strategy. Because there were many regions, there could be many regional contingencies.[16] The international system seemed open ended with respect to the kinds of challenges it might pose, but none of those challenges threatened either the national survival of the United States nor that of its NATO allies. Strategy making became an exercise in planning for the unknown. One could, as Bush planners did, imagine more or less probable contingencies, but there was no scientific method by which to attach probabilities to these contingencies. Because anything could happen, anything had to be planned for. The 1994–99 "Defense Planning Guidance Scenario Set" attempted to bring some order to this chaos by outlining seven hypothetical situations that might lead to U.S. military involvement:

1. Military forces of Russia and Belarus invade Lithuania. NATO responds, including about 12 U.S. Army divisions. NATO forces prevail in 89 days of combat that includes three weeks of "very high intensity" warfare.

2. Rearmed Iraq invades Kuwait and continues into Saudi Arabia. A U.S.-led coalition again defeats Iraq, in 54 days, with almost five U.S. Army divisions and a Marine expeditionary force committed to the victorious side.

3. North Korea launches a surprise attack on South Korea with the objective of reunification. The United States assists South Korea with more than five Army divisions and two Marine expeditionary forces, winning after 91 days of combat.

4. The United States acts against a coup in Panama that would otherwise close the canal. Airborne and amphibious operations include two airborne brigades, two Ranger battalions, and a Marine amphibious brigade. The United States wins in eight days of midintensity war.

5. As the result of a coup in the Philippines, several hundred U.S. workers at Subic Bay Naval Base are taken hostage. U.S. armed forces prevail in seven days of midintensity war by mounting three simultaneous landings with a Ranger regiment, airborne infantry brigade, amphibious brigade, and a brigade or more of light infantry. (The United States later relinquished this base, making this specific scenario obsolete.)

6. Simultaneous attacks by Iraq and North Korea, as in numbers 2 and 3, above. The United States first fights Iraq before turning to Korea. A U.S.-led coalition defeats Iraq in 70 days and North Korea in an additional 157 days.

7. The worst case of "resurgent/emergent global threat," a revived and hostile Russia, is ready by the year 2001 to start a second Cold War or to initiate a major global war. The United States reconstitutes its previously built down military capabilities after a year of debate.[17]

The principal scenario driver for the Bush defense planners was the MRC. An MRC was, for example, another North Korean invasion of South Korea or an Iraqi attack on the oil fields of Saudi Arabia. Contingency planning for these scenarios assumed that the more rapidly deployable elements among U.S. forces would arrive first to hold the ring. Successive waves of reinforcements then would be sent as the situation required. The likelihood was that no more than a single MRC operation would tax U.S. leaders at a time. Nevertheless, Bush defense planners allowed for the possibility that two might occur simultaneously. They could get away with this as a planning assumption as long as the United States retained leftover Cold War forces that were obviously oversized for dealing with regional aggressors outside Europe.

U.S. experience in the Cold War suggested that either an immediate and obvious threat to vital U.S. strategic interests or a tangible threat to the U.S. economy would be necessary to build popular and congressional support for military action outside Europe. An attack on Saudi oil fields fulfilled both requirements, and an attack on a Saudi neighbor that included a plausible threat against the kingdom's oil reserves also would suffice. On the other hand, the danger in this scenario was that, by the time that the threat became apparent and an actual attack had been launched, it might be too late to stop it. The United States would then have to use force for compellence, or the undoing of an aggressor's gains already accomplished.[18]

Bush planning for this scenario can be said to have anticipated to some degree the outlines of Saddam Hussein's coercion against Kuwait in 1990 and his subsequent attack in August of that year. However, there was less prescience in the evaluation of political intelligence about Saddam's intentions than there was in the central planning scenario for regional aggression in Southwest Asia. Political intelligence about Iraqi intentions was colored by favorable assumptions based on U.S.-Iraqi cooperation during the Iran-Iraq war of the 1980s. Although Saddam gave plenty of evidence of hostile intent toward Kuwait and other gulf neighbors during the early months of 1990, his actual commitment to military action if his political demands went unmet was doubted by senior U.S. policy makers until the very day of his attack.

Whether the Bush proposed or Clinton reduced forces could, in the time period 1995–97, cope with two nearly simultaneous major regional contingencies was a matter of some controversy among defense analysts and policy makers. Lawrence J. Korb, former assistant secretary of defense under Reagan and Brookings Institution defense analyst, compared the size of forces deployed to the Persian Gulf under Desert Storm with the Bush base force and with his own version of an adequate, but reduced, base force II. The results are depicted in Table 2.5.

One implication of Table 2.5 is that the United States could conduct another Desert Storm between 1995 and 1997 and an additional regional contingency operation, provided the appropriate numbers of reserve forces were mobilized. This leaves open the question of how ready reserve forces would be, especially "roundout" combat brigades for active Army divisions. Gulf War experience was not especially encouraging.[19] Admittedly, Guard and other reserve forces are not as combat ready as active duty forces; therefore, they make poor constituent elements for rapid deployment. However, reserve combat units organized around a single function, requiring fewer combined arms exercises than combat brigades in order to prepare for battle, and various supply and support units deployed quickly and effectively during Desert Shield.[20] Mixed experience with Guard and reserve forces in Desert Shield and

TABLE 2.5
Bush Base Force Compared with Desert Storm
Deployments and Alternative (Korb Base Force II)

	Bush Base Force	Korb Base Force II	Desert Storm
Ground divisions	22 (46)	17 (59)	10 (31)
Tactical air wings	26 (39)	20 (50)	10 (28)
Aircraft carriers	12 (50)	9 (67)	6 (43)
Carrier air wings	13 (46)	10 (60)	6 (40)
Ships	450 (22)	350 (29)	100 (20)
Personnel	2.6 million (21)	2.0 million (28)	550,000 (18)

Note: Numbers in parentheses give the size of forces deployed to the Persian Gulf during the Gulf War of 1991 as percentages of the total current or proposed force. For example, the ground divisions deployed for Desert Storm equaled about 31 percent of the 1991 total active and reserve forces available. The same divisions would have constituted about 46 percent of the Bush Base Force and about 59 percent of Korb's Base Force II.

Source: Lawrence J. Korb, "Real Defense Cuts — and the Real Defense Issues," *Arms Control Today*, May 1992, p. 7.

Desert Storm showed that the relationship between the Guard and reserve and active forces would be a continuing civil-military relations controversy even after Clinton assumed the presidency.

CIVIL-MILITARY RELATIONS AND THE GULF WAR OF 1991

The Bush administration had to work to build support for Desert Storm on two fronts: among members of the international coalition that was organized against Iraq and within the U.S. domestic body politic. The second task was the harder. As the Desert Shield phase of U.S. military buildup took place in the autumn of 1990, various military experts testified before Congress against going to war and in favor of continued economic sanctions against Iraq.[21] Public attitudes toward the option of offensive military action to expel Iraq from Kuwait were ambivalent. Americans regarded Saddam Hussein as a less than admirable symbol of statesmanship, and the Bush administration capitalized on this and exploited it. On the other hand, Americans worried about the consequences of a costly war of attrition against Iraq's large ground forces.

Theater commander Norman Schwartzkopf's originally submitted plan for a four-phase offensive campaign, including straight-up-the-middle ground offensives against fortified Iraqi defenses near the Kuwaiti border, was reviewed, and rejected, by higher Army and JCS echelons.[22] More important, the instincts of the president were all against a massive war of attrition and in favor of the maximum use of

U.S. and allied power against strategic targets. Bush said repeatedly during the fall of 1990 that, if war were resorted to, it would not be "another Vietnam." Saddam apparently mistook this for simple bravado about the expected outcome. He did not hear one part of the message that Bush intended. It would not be another Vietnam because, regardless of what planners recommended, Bush was determined to fight in a way that minimized U.S. and allied losses.

Two things were required in order for Bush to accomplish U.S. political and military purposes in this fashion. First, the war would have to be terminated quickly. Second, firepower, especially air delivered firepower, would have to be substituted for manpower. The second component was very traditional and consistent with what scholars have described as the "American way of war."[23] However, it was also clear to U.S. planners that simply dumping air ordnance on Iraq would not necessarily redound to a U.S. political or military victory. Vietnam had shown that the coercive aspects of air power were much more difficult to employ than its purely destructive aspects. Air power could be used against a country like Iraq to destroy many things, but whether that destruction could influence decisively the opponent's intentions was another matter.

The significance of the commander-in-chief's role in the U.S. constitutional system of government was all-important in the actual formulation of U.S. Gulf War strategy. Bush clearly had in mind his political objective: to expel Iraq from Kuwait. He set this objective firmly in place in August 1990 and would not deviate from it. For this he was criticized subsequently, but it permitted his military planners a fixity of purpose and held together an improbable political coalition, including a majority of Arab powers. Bush was decisive about his political and military objectives, but he left to Colin Powell, the JCS, and the CINCs, especially Schwartzkopf, the operational details. There was certainly enough room for argument, even then.

The Air Force was doctrinally and organizationally inclined to see the Gulf War as an opportunity to validate its theory of victory by strategic air power. However, the Gulf air campaign had a different emphasis compared with the U.S. and allied air power theories of the 1920s and 1930s: instead of attacks centered on industrial production or national morale, the Desert Storm air campaign sought to disorganize the brain and central nervous system of the Iraqi regime.[24] Air staff planners tasked by Powell and Schwartzkopf developed a list of strategic target classes whose prompt destruction was intended to cripple Iraq's ability to fight. These target classes included Iraqi air defenses, political and military command and control, electrical power, and nuclear, chemical, and biological weapons facilities. Of top priority for air planners was to obtain command of the air in order to obtain three principal advantages. First, knocking out Iraq's air defenses and airfields would clear the way for coalition attacks against other targets.

Second, the possibility of Iraqi offensive attacks against coalition forces would be reduced or eliminated. Third, Iraqi reconnaissance would be prevented from discovering later coalition strategic movements, such as the flanking attack from ground forces shifted westward at the outset of the ground war.[25]

These operational or tactical expectations about the effectiveness of air power were accompanied, in the minds of U.S. air war planners, by the expectation that Saddam's regime might fall under the sustained weight of coalition air power. The demise of Saddam's leadership might happen in either of two ways, according to this widely believed but carefully held theory. First, Saddam and his principal aides might themselves be underneath a bomb dropped on Iraqi military command bunkers or political leadership centers.[26] Second, the Iraqi military, foreseeing no favorable outcome to the war, might act to depose Saddam Hussein in order to bring about war termination while the bulk of their fighting power was still intact.

These were not unreasonable expectations on the part of U.S. air planners, but they were hopeful ones. The theater commander and JCS were convinced that without at least some ground warfare, there could be no decisive capitulation by Iraqi forces. Bombing could blind and destroy Iraqi capability, but driving Iraqi forces out of Kuwait required that the tail of Saddam's military capability in southwestern Iraq be disconnected from its spear point. Only then would isolated units see the inevitable need to surrender in droves, as they did once this coalition ground campaign began to succeed.

Air planners could claim a very successful campaign, but controversy took place within the theater command and between the U.S. theater command and Washington. Air planners and Schwartzkopf wanted to prolong the air war until tactical air bombardment of Iraq's elite armored units had reduced their effectiveness in support of continued activity in the Kuwaiti theater of operations. Thus, the central command air planners and the CINC concurred that many tactical sorties should be assigned to strikes against Iraqi armored units, or "tank plinking." U.S. ground forces corps commanders objected to this order of priority. Several Army corps commanders contended that priority in air strikes should go to close air support, especially to attacks against enemy artillery.

The expectations of U.S. air planners that air attacks could destroy Iraq's nuclear, biological, and chemical weapons and weapons facilities were overly optimistic. Postwar UN investigation revealed that the Iraqi nuclear program, for example, was far more extensive than coalition planners had realized. Wartime attacks had dented only a fraction of it.[27] In addition, U.S. air planners were not as successful as they had expected to be in attacking Iraq's Scud missiles. Mobile Scuds proved difficult to find and difficult to strike, because by the time intelligence about their original firing positions had been analyzed and transmitted to strike aircraft, the missiles had changed position.[28] Cloud cover and clever use of decoys by the Iraqis only made matters worse. The Iraqi Scuds presented a complex problem of civil-military relations for U.S. foreign policy and for coalition military strategy. The numbers and results of Iraqi Scud attacks in the gulf War are summarized in Table 2.6.

TABLE 2.6
Targets and Results of Iraqi Scud Attacks, Gulf War 1991

	Targets		
Result	Saudi Arabia	Israel	Bahrain
Total fired	48	40	3
Missed target area	11	15	1
Intercepted by Patriot	34	11	0
Hit target	0	13	0
Debris hit	7	7	0
Missed country	3	1	2

Source: Norman Friedman, Desert Victory: The War for Kuwait (Annapolis, Md.: U.S. Naval Institute Press, 1991), p. 365.

The political impact of the Scuds falling on Israeli cities was potentially catastrophic to the war effort. Bush's effort to hold together the Arab participants within the anti-Iraq coalition was dependent upon keeping Israel out of the war. U.S. strategy was especially dependent on maintaining access to Saudi air and supply bases for strikes against Iraq. The emphasis on preventing Scud attacks spilled over from the government of Israel to the international media. In turn, this required the central command, at the behest of Washington, to divert far more attacks against Scuds that the actual military threat posed to U.S. and allied forces otherwise would have justified.

Other aspects of U.S. civil-military relations and of the U.S. policy-making process influenced the conduct of the Gulf War. The administration was sensitive to the charge that attacks against military or command targets in Baghdad would injure innocent civilians. Widespread loss of civilian life in Iraq apparently unrelated to wartime military objectives could have compromised international and U.S. public or congressional support for the war. After attacks against the Al Firdos command bunker entombed many civilians who had taken shelter there (whether at the behest of Iraqi leaders or on their own was unclear), Washington placed some previously authorized target categories off the approved list for downtown Baghdad. This had a familiar ring of Lyndon Johnson's selection of tactical bombing targets; had the war been more prolonged or more two-sided, such restrictions might have become more controversial.

U.S. military advice on the conduct of the Gulf War was consistent with the pattern found in most Cold War cases of military intervention or escalation. Political generals in Washington were concerned about access to policy makers but not necessarily predisposed to favor the use of force over other options. Field commanders were less concerned about military influence on the policy process and more worried about the propensity of top policy makers to intervene in operational and tactical decisions.[29] Bush strategy making was a closely held process, befitting the president's insistence upon consensus or "collegiality." Once war policy had been decided upon, the theater commander was given great discretion over operational and tactical decisions. Only the case of the "great SCUD hunt" stands as a possible exception to the otherwise delegative cast of theater war strategy.

BUSH STRATEGY MAKING: LAPSED CIVILIAN CONTROL?

The Indictment

The Bush strategy and security policy-making process inevitably came under scholarly examination. Some military historians have already taken aim at the Bush administration on the issue of civil-military relations. In an article entitled, "Out of Control: The Crisis in Civil-Military Relations" in the Spring 1994 issue of *The National Interest*, Richard H. Kohn argues that Colin Powell's influence on Bush strategy and policy was excessive.[30] According to Kohn, Powell developed a set of concepts to realign the entire U.S. military establishment and promoted his own vision of a new national military strategy without any real authorization from his civilian superiors. In essence,

General Powell — not the President, nor the National Security Council, nor the Department of Defense — thought through a new national security policy for the country, one based on his own political and international forecasts about Soviet collapse, de-communization in Eastern Europe, German unification, accelerated arms reductions, lessened tensions, and a new focus by the United States on regional conflicts rather than worldwide confrontation with the Soviet Union.[31]

Military historian Russell F. Weigley, in a review of the operation of the principle of civilian control in U.S. military history, suggests that civilian control of the armed forces "faces an uncertain future."[32] Weigley argues that the U.S. officer corps did not become truly professional, by developing shared expertise, corporateness, and sense of responsibility, until the Civil War.[33] From the Civil War through the end of World War II, he contends, the military meekly acquiesced to civilian dominance of strategy and force planning decisions. This pattern held even for decisions that were costly in terms of military effectiveness and strategic soundness. The Cold War, according to Weigley, changed the relationship between officers and civilian policy makers. Unprecedented commingling of military and civilians at the highest policy levels "reduced the distanced respect of the military for the civil authorities that rendered the military almost excessively self-deprecating" as late in the game as the time of U.S. preparation for war against Japan in 1940 and 1941.[34]

In addition, military resentment at apparently illogical restraints on operations imposed by civilians during the Vietnam War led to a post-Vietnam military assertiveness about the kinds of interventions that were appropriate for the U.S. armed forces. Powell's willingness to participate in the public debate on this issue draws criticism from both Kohn and Weigley. In a *New York Times* Op-Ed column under his signature and in various interviews during 1992, Powell argued against U.S. military intervention in Bosnia on the grounds that military force was best used to achieve a decisive victory. According to Powell, the limited use of force in Bosnia would be self-defeating.[35] Weigley is critical of Powell's temerity and of his perspective. Of the latter, Weigley comments:

It is not an assertion of professional military knowledge to state, as General Powell did in his own article in the *Times*, that "Decisive means and results are always to be preferred, even if they are not always possible." Limited military force may well be preferable for policy reasons to the employment of force overwhelming enough to offer possibly decisive victory but also posing the risk of expanding an existing conflict by its own very order of magnitude. Bosnia might reasonably be considered to offer the kind of situation where limited force is to be preferred to unlimited.[36]

Russell Weigley is uncommon among military historians in his sensitivity to the problem of escalation, and he undoubtedly is correct to warn that massive intervention in Bosnia might have been counterproductive to U.S. policy objectives in 1992. Nevertheless, the willingness of Powell to offer advice about limited versus unlimited means is not necessarily a breach of civilian control over the military. Powell's superiors should have been asking the JCS for advice about the feasibility of various options, limited or otherwise, in Bosnia. Powell's interviews and Op-Ed pieces were reruns of the same advice he was giving to the Bush administration. In essence, the public was being made aware of professional military hesitation about commitment of force to Bosnia without a clear strategy for victory, however victory might have been defined.

A More Visible Policy Debate

Instead of seeing this as a departure from civilian control, historians should see it as a necessary corrective from the tendency of Cold War presidents and defense secretaries to rely on closely held strategy-making decisions vulnerable to "groupthink."[37] The inertia of U.S. strategy in Vietnam resulted, in part, because military doubts about the feasibility of escalation with U.S. combat forces after 1965 were self-suppressed or were otherwise made invisible to Congress and to the public. Unless one argues that the public and Congress have no role in strategy making, military reservations about piecemeal escalation belong in public view. The desirability of escalation decisions is more clearly a "civilian" than a "military" matter, to be sure, but for the public and for the Congress, the feasibility of intervention at acceptable cost is part of their judgment about its desirability. Neither most of the U.S. public nor a majority of members of Congress turned squishy on Vietnam escalation until the infeasibility of winning the war at a politically acceptable cost became apparent.

The Cold War changed the nature of U.S. civil-military relations not only in terms of the relationship between uninformed and civilian elites but also with respect to the engagement of the public and Congress in decisions regarding the use or threat of U.S. military force. Congress always had been legally responsible for raising and supporting armed forces and for declaring war, but in peacetime practice prior to the Cold War, this meant a few, well-informed congressional leaders, not Congress at large. Cold War peacetime defense expenditures, and the resulting pervasiveness of the Department of Defense in communities throughout the United States, made more members of Congress aware of, and attentive to, issues of military policy. Also, the enormity of the Cold War defense establishment had a similar effect on the visibility of military issues to the public.

At least three other Cold War forces raised the visibility and controversiality of military policy decisions, compared with earlier U.S. peacetime periods. First, the growth of national media, especially electronic media, coverage of politics increased public levels of awareness and enhanced popular sense of efficacy about influencing military policy debates. Second, the expansion of congressional staffs allowed members of Congress to develop countervailing professional expertise to that housed in the Pentagon, Office of Management and Budget, or the White House. Third, the threat of nuclear war and the experience of mass vicarious participation in nuclear crisis management made any use of force with the potential for escalation one of high drama and great visibility.[38] These forces suggest that the line between acceptable and unacceptable military participation in war policy debates has moved as a result of U.S. superpower status and greater public and congressional awareness of the military role in policy decisions. In Huntington's terms, U.S. subjective civilian control of the military has not disappeared, but it may have been transmuted into a more hothouse environment.[39]

Among secretaries of defense prior to Cheney, Kohn admires Robert McNamara. The McNamara years witnessed, according to the former Air Force historian, a reimposition of civilian control over the military that had lapsed in the latter 1940s and 1950s. McNamara used bureaucratic procedures and management by objectives to connect policy, strategy, and force structure planning. Power flowed from the services to OSD because McNamara "ignored or dismissed military advice, disparaged military experience and expertise, and circumvented or sacked generals and admirals who opposed him."[40] Kohn is not the first to hold up the McNamara style of defense management as exemplary.[41]

On the other hand, the McNamara years also might be cited to argue that an improved management style does not necessarily translate into better military strategy. Under McNamara's allegedly superior approach to management, U.S. military strategy crashed and burned. The relationship was not a coincidence. Ignoring professional military advice about strategy and turning to disciplines outside of politics and history for models of war, the McNamara Pentagon mistook the war in Vietnam for a competition in limited risk taking.[42] Related to this, the Johnson administration also neglected to mobilize the reserves and the U.S. home front for war, with the result that an aroused and confused public and congressional opinion finally forced a U.S. withdrawal and a South Vietnamese defeat.

Should Powell and the JCS be faulted, as Kohn implies, for engaging in what is the essence of their professional business: the design of strategy for victory in war? It is the responsibility of the president and the Congress, as advised by cabinet members and others, to decide whether and why the United States should fight, and it is the business of the defense secretary to see that the tools of war are efficiently employed in accord with policy objectives. As important as the political decision for war or the management of defense resources might be, they are decisions apart from the essence of strategy. The essence of strategy is the commander's ability to anticipate the military moves of his opponent and to preempt them with moves of his own, inflicting decisive defeat on opposed forces with minimal losses to friendlies, or, as Clausewitz said, "the employment of the battle as the means toward the attainment of the object of the War."[43]

No one can deny that Powell was very assertive in strategy making and in force structure planning, the latter a role in which professional military and civilian judgment are deliberately mixed. It is equally the case that the empowerment of Powell was not a coincidence but was exactly what Congress called for in passing the Goldwater-Nichols reform legislation. Congress was fed up with the inability of the pre-1986 JCS to provide national, as opposed to service oriented, professional military advice. Congress, therefore, legislated that the chairman of the JCS should be an actor with independent political clout, apart from the JCS as a committee. Congress anticipated that the chairman of the JCS would take the lead in strategy formulation, or Goldwater-Nichols was nothing more than an exercise in symbolic reassurance. In short, Congress became exasperated with amateur hour in strategy formulation and demanded a change.[44]

Clausewitz Redux

The most mistaken indictment of Powell's role in Bush strategy mak-ing is the contention by Kohn that Powell, "turning the age-old Clause-witzian formula about war being an extension of policy on its head," insisted that political objectives must be carefully matched to what is achievable with military means.[45] This critique mistakes Clausewitz's views of the relationship between military means and political ends. Clausewitz expected commanders to speak with the utmost candor to their heads of state about the goodness of fit between available forces and the political or military objectives set for wartime operations. He also noted that the military effort that a political object calls forth will vary with the character of the states concerned.

According to Clausewitz, the same political object may produce "totally different effects upon different people, or even upon the same people at different times."[46] Thus, a war preceded by the arousal of mass political passions will approach nearer to its abstract and most destructive form, and in such a war, "so much the nearer will the military and political ends coincide."[47] On the other hand, the weaker the motives and passions of states engaged in a war, the more divergent is the political object from the aim of an ideal war. Finally, Clausewitz notes that the political object "must accommodate itself to the nature of the means"; changes in these means of war may require modification of the political objective, although the latter has a prior right to consideration.[48]

The significance of Clausewitz's observation about the relationship between military effort and character of states, including their propensities for popular arousal to national causes, is that the U.S. government cannot sustain military intervention for very long without popular support. In addition, Clausewitz's statement about the rela-tionship between military means and political object in war simply asks policy not to demand what armed forces cannot deliver. Powell's hesitation for the Gulf War unless sufficient forces were made available and unless popular support was apparent for military action shows a correct, not an incorrect, reading of Clausewitz.

Richard Betts found, in his study of U.S. Cold War decision making, that military advice was most influential on decisions for intervention or escalation when it was both direct and negative (Table 2.7).[49]

TABLE 2.7
Levels and Directions of Military Influence

	Negative	Positive
Direct	1	4
Indirect	2	3

Source: Richard K. Betts, *Soldiers, Statesmen and Cold War Crises* (New York: Columbia University Press, 1991), pp. 11–12. This schematic version is based on the original text.

"Negative" in this context means that military advisors recommended against the use of force or against escalation. The second most influential pattern of military advice for escalation and intervention decisions was indirect and negative. In this pattern, officers did not recommend explicitly against the use of force but presented alternatives in such a way that force seemed comparatively unattractive. In the third pattern, indirect and positive military influence, information or options provided by the military encouraged civilian decisions for intervention, although military advice was not accepted. The fourth and least influential pattern of military advice was direct and positive, when the military explicitly recommended the use of force or escalation.[50]

According to Betts' taxonomy, Powell's influence on Bush strategy leading up to Desert Storm begins in the indirect-negative category and ends in the direct-positive cell. Powell's influence on the timing and character of the Gulf War offensive follows, not leads, Bush's own initiatives. The difference between single decisions for or against intervention or escalation and broader decisions about strategy and policy formulation is important here. In the second category of decisions, the professional military, and Powell in particular, were more influential under Bush than they were under some of his predecessors. Nevertheless, it remains significant that, in the several months immediately following Iraq's invasion of Kuwait, Powell was dovish and Bush was impatient with a lack of military options to expel Iraq from Kuwait.

CONCLUSION

Bush strategy making was characterized by conceptual innovation under the stress of a rapidly changing global environment. New domestic and foreign policy environments called for new political thinking. Goldwater-Nichols defense reform legislation mandated that the chairman, JCS, become the strategist in chief as part of the role of principal military advisor to the president. Another domestic factor forcing new thinking about force structure was the anticipated reduction in U.S. defense budgets after the Cold War.

The international environment changed along with the domestic. The end of the Soviet Union and the likelihood of regional contingencies required new thinking about force structure and strategy. Powell's and OSD's responses to these new environments demonstrate a search for conceptual framework for military planning, not usurpation by the military or a lapse of civilian control. Military influence on issues of security context, or the broad planning guidance for future decisions, was greater than military influence on decisions for or against the use of force. Operational and tactical decisions were delegated to the military chain of command, especially after war began, but policy decisions remained presidential and highly personal under Bush.

NOTES

1.   Illustrative cases of U.S. national security policy decision making that confirm both points are provided in Warner R. Schilling, Paul Y. Hammond, and Glenn H. Snyder, eds., *Strategy, Politics and Defense Budgets* (New York: Columbia University Press, 1962).

2.   Carl H. Builder, *The Masks of War: American Military Styles in Strategy and Analysis* (Baltimore, Md.: Johns Hopkins University Press, 1989).

3.   Vincent Davis, "The Evolution of Central U.S. Defense Management," in *Reorganizing America's Defenses: Leadership in War and Peace*, eds. Robert J. Art, Vincent Davis, and Samuel P. Huntington (Washington, D.C.: Pergamon Brassey's, 1985), pp. 149–67.

4.   See William J. Lynn, "The Wars Within: The Joint Military Structure and Its Critics," in *Reorganizing America's Defenses: Leadership in War and Peace*, eds. Robert J. Art, Vincent Davis, and Samuel P. Huntington (Washington, D.C.: Pergamon Brassey's, 1985), pp. 168–206; Robert W. Komer, "Strategymaking in the Pentagon," in *Reorganizing America's Defenses: Leadership in War and Peace*, eds. Robert J. Art, Vincent Davis, and Samuel P. Huntington (Washington, D.C.: Pergamon Brassey's, 1985), pp. 230–54; Samuel P. Huntington, "Organization and Strategy," in *Reorganizing America's Defenses: Leadership in War and Peace*, eds. Robert J. Art, Vincent Davis, and Samuel P. Huntington (Washington, D.C.: Pergamon Brassey's, 1985), pp. 207229. Historical perspective on the Cold War performance of the JCS is provided in Lawrence J. Korb, *The Fall and Rise of the Pentagon: American Defense Policies in the 1970s* (Westport, Conn.: Greenwood Press, 1979).

5.   Goldwater-Nichols also formally designated the chairman, JCS, as the president's principal military advisor, gave the CINCs a larger role in defense resource planning, and mandated that joint service experience was a prerequisite for any officer seeking flag or general officer rank. C. Kenneth Allard, *Command, Control and the Common Defense* (New Haven, Conn.: Yale University Press, 1990), pp. 3, 247–48.

6.   It is, according to one expert source, unrealistic to expect that unified or specified commanders will be isolated from service influences in the future, nor would it necessarily be desirable. One objective of Goldwater-Nichols and related reforms was to make more congruent the service-dominated weapons development process with the warfighting perspectives of CINCs. See Allard, *Command, Control and the Common Defense*, p. 248.

7.   I acknowledge Ed Kolodziej for this felicitous expression.

8. As Kevin Lewis notes, during the Cold War, the United States planned routinely for canonical major conflicts with the Soviet Union but found itself fighting in wars that are now called MRCs. The historical record indicates that "we consistently underestimated or misestimated the true requirements of these other contingencies," but we coped because of our large, surplus force posture planned for a global war against the Soviet Union. Without those surpluses in the post–Cold War world, our estimates of the requirements for MRCs must be correct. See Kevin Lewis, "The Discipline Gap and Other Reasons for Humility and Realism in Defense Planning," in *New Challenges for Defense Planning: Rethinking How Much Is Enough*, ed. Paul K. Davis (Santa Monica, Calif.: RAND Corporation, 1994), pp. 101–34, esp. p. 103.

9. Lorna S. Jaffe, *The Development of the Base Force, 1989–1992* (Washington, D.C.: Office of the Chairman, Joint Chiefs of Staff, Joint History Office, 1993).

10. James John Tritten, *Our New National Security Strategy: America Promises to Come Back* (Westport, Conn.: Praeger, 1992), p. 30.

11. Jaffee, *Development of the Base Force*, p. 2.

12. Ibid., pp. 7–8. General Butler did not become J-5 director until August 1989.

13. Ibid., p. 10.

14. Don M. Snider, *Strategy, Forces and Budgets: Dominant Influences in Executive Decision Making, Post–Cold War, 1989–91* (Carlisle, Pa.: Strategic Studies Institute, U.S. Army War College, 1993), p. 3.

15. Ibid., p. 4.

16. As noted in one assessment, "A series of contingency plans for each possible regional crisis is by itself neither a strategy nor a satisfactory substitute for military strategy." Michael J. Mazarr, Don M. Snider, and James A. Blackwell, Jr., *Desert Storm: The Gulf War and What We Learned* (Boulder, Colo.: Westview, 1993), p. 162.

17. Scenario summaries are from Martin Binkin, *Who Will Fight the Next War? The Changing Face of the American Military* (Washington, D.C.: Brookings Institution, 1994), pp. 140–41.

18. This is exactly the situation in which the United States found itself after Saddam's rapid conquest of Kuwait in August 1990. On the concept of compellence, see Thomas C. Schelling, *Arms and Influence* (New Haven, Conn.: Yale University Press, 1966).

19. Part of the reason for this was that roundout brigades, which are National Guard combat brigades that bring incomplete active duty divisions up to full strength, were not recalled by the Department of Defense until November 1990. The required predeployment training could not be completed before the war ended. See Mazarr, Snider, and Blackwell, *Desert Storm*, pp. 53–54.

20. Ibid., p. 52.

21. Including immediate past-JCS Chairman Admiral William Crowe. General Powell also initially favored a containment strategy of economic strangulation against Iraq but eventually gave way in the face of clear evidence that Bush had ruled out that option. See Bob Woodward, *The Commanders* (New York: Simon and Schuster, 1991), pp. 38–40, 303; Rick Atkinson, *Crusade: The Untold Story of the Persian Gulf War* (Boston, Mass.: Houghton Mifflin, 1993), p. 122.

22. Woodward, *The Commanders*, pp. 304–7.

23. Russell F. Weigley, *The American Way of War: A History of United States Military Strategy and Policy* (New York: Macmillan, 1973).

24. GWAPS, *Summary Report*, p. 236.

25. Thomas A. Keaney and Eliot A. Cohen, *Gulf War Air Power Survey: Summary Report* (Washington, D.C.: U.S. Government Printing Office, 1993), Vol. 6, p. 41.

26. Woodward, *The Commanders*, p. 291.

27. GWAPS, *Summary Report*, pp. 78–79 discusses U.S. prewar intelligence estimates about Iraq's nuclear program and postwar findings by UN inspectors. A graph of coalition strikes by target categories appears in the same volume, p. 65. See also, in the same volume, Figure 16, p. 80, for a summary graph of coalition strikes against NBC targets. The Gulf War Air Power Survey *Summary Report* concluded that "Overall, the United States did not fully understand the target arrays comprising Iraqi nuclear, biological, chemical, and ballistic missile capabilities before the Gulf War" (p. 79).

28. *Abbreviated Summary of the Gulf War Air Power Survey* (Carlisle Barracks, Pa.: U.S. Army War College, 1993), pp. 14–28.

29. Richard K. Betts, *Soldiers, Statesmen and Cold War Crises* (Cambridge, Mass.: Harvard University Press, 1977), p. 11.

30. Richard H. Kohn, "Out of Control: The Crisis in Civil-Military Relations," *The National Interest*, 35 (Spring 1994): 3–17.

31. Ibid., p. 10.

32. Russell F. Weigley, "The American Military and the Principle of Civilian Control from McClellan to Powell," *Journal of Military History* 57 (October 1993): 27–58.

33. These criteria for defining military professionalism are drawn from Samuel P. Huntington, *The Soldier and the State: The Theory and Politics of Civil-Military Relations* (Cambridge, Mass.: Belknap Press/Harvard University Press, 1957).

34. Weigley, "The American Military and the Principle of Civilian Control," p. 56.

35. For example, Colin L. Powell, "Why Generals Get Nervous," *New York Times*, October 8, 1992, p. A35, cited in Weigley, "The American Military and the Principle of Civilian Control," p. 28.

36. Weigley, "The American Military and the Principle of Civilian Control," p. 29.

37. Irving L. Janis, *Groupthink* (Boston, Mass.: Houghton Mifflin, 1982), esp. pp. 97–130 on Vietnam.

38. One reason why U.S. decision making in the Cuban missile crisis of October 1962 may have turned out so successfully was that Kennedy and his advisors were able to obtain press cooperation in avoiding the atmosphere of crisis until the president was ready to take the initiative by announcing the blockade. See Graham T. Allison, *Essence of Decision: Explaining the Cuban Missile Crisis* (Boston, Mass.: Little, Brown, 1971).

39. Huntington, *The Soldier and the State*, pp. 80–84.

40. Kohn, "Out of Control," p. 6.

41. See, for example, William W. Kaufmann, *The McNamara Strategy* (New York: Harper & Row, 1964).

42. Harry G. Summers, Jr., *On Strategy: A Critical Analysis of the Vietnam War* (New York: Dell, 1984), esp. pp. 74–76; see also Deborah Shapley, *Promise and Power: The Life and Times of Robert McNamara* (Boston, Mass.: Little, Brown, 1993), esp. pp. 338–39.

43. General Carl Von Clausewitz, *On War*, Vol. I, translated by J. J. Graham (London: Routledge and Kegan Paul, 1966), Book III, Chap. I, p. 165.

44. See the pertinent references in Allard, *Command, Control and the Common Defense*, pp. 3, 247–48.

45. Kohn, "Out of Control," pp. 11–12.

46. Clausewitz, *On War*, Book I, Chap. I, p. 12.

47. Ibid., pp. 22–23.

48. Ibid., p. 23.

49. Betts, *Soldiers, Statesmen and Cold War Crises*, p. 11.

50. Ibid., pp. 11–12.

II

RUSSIAN ARMS AND AIMS IN THE NEW WORLD ORDER

3

Military Transition in Russia: Can Defensive Doctrine Prevail?

During most of its Soviet period, Russian military doctrine and military strategy emphasized the decisive character of the offensive in war.[1] It was asserted by numerous Soviet military writers that, although the political objectives of the Soviet Union in world politics were basically defensive, the offensive form of warfare was superior to the defensive. Only the offensive held out the possibility of rapid and decisive victory over the enemies likely to confront the Soviet Union in battle. Even if the Soviet armed forces were forced onto the defensive in the initial period of war, a decisive counteroffensive should be organized as soon as possible in order to expel the invader and push the fighting back onto his territory.[2] Although the Gorbachev era from 1985 to 1991 witnessed some renewed interest on the part of Soviet military theoreticians in defensive military doctrine, the political turbulence of those years gives no indication whether the doctrinal slant toward "defensive sufficiency" and the like has taken permanent root in the mind sets of future Russian commanders.

In this chapter, we consider whether the political and military context expected to obtain in post–Cold War Europe is favorable to the development and viability of defensive military doctrine, especially for Russia. Russia faces enormous obstacles in preventing the professional dissolution of its armed forces because of political disintegration or economic stagnation or both. Yet, a future Europe with a defensively minded Russian military is more secure against post-Bolshevik reactionism, and it is also more reassured against its own worst fears of political instability prompted by sources outside Russia. Russia plays heavily into European security despite the indeterminacy about her

Portions of this chapter appeared in Stephen J. Cimbala, "Non-offensive Defense and Strategic Choice: Russia and Europe After the Cold War," *Journal of Slavic Military Studies* 6 (June 1993): 166–202.

future intentions and capabilities, much as she did immediately prior to and after the Napoleonic wars.

STRATEGIES, DOCTRINES, AND POLICY CHOICES

The development of nonoffensive defenses is not a new topic for Europeans. European strategic thinkers and others dissatisfied with the military postures of the Cold War years studied various alternatives for individual or coalition defenses based on territorial self-defense or on other concepts excluding surprise attack and large-scale conventional offensives.[3] The "solutions" to regional stability offered by superpower extended deterrence and offensively poised conventional forces did not commend themselves, especially to the nonaligned states of northern Europe. Even North Atlantic Treaty Organization (NATO) member states produced leading advocates of nonoffensive defenses, and some U.S. and European analysts were willing to endorse nonmilitary, in addition to nonoffensive, defenses as the basis of regional security. The development of interest in nonoffensive defenses was significant not only as an alternative to the superpower-oriented bloc politics of the Cold War but also as an alternative to those states that sought to transcend Cold War military postures but distrusted supranational solutions, in the form of politically powerful multilateral institutions. Such states as Sweden and Switzerland offered different forms of nonoffensive defense while reserving to themselves the right to decide when and where their forces would be committed to battle.

During the Cold War, the idea that members of NATO or the Warsaw Pact might turn to nonoffensive defenses contradicted preferred NATO and Soviet planning guidance. It was all very well for the Swiss, for example, to plan for territorial homeland defenses on the assumption that Switzerland might escape direct attack or invasion. However, this solution would not do for those states whose territory would certainly be violated by invaders once war began on the central front that separated NATO and pact forces. The vulnerability of much of Germany to a Soviet strategy of rapid penetration and encirclement of vital areas seemed also to diminish the credibility of nonoffensive defenses for states bound to NATO and close to the Cold War firing lines. Finally, the presence of U.S. and allied NATO nuclear weapons of various ranges deployed within the probable area of battle almost guaranteed levels of destruction that would preclude the effectiveness of any defensive strategy based on attrition, which nonoffensive defense schemes often were.[4] Other political obstacles, both domestic and foreign, seemed to stand in the way of major actors, such as France or Germany, adopting nonoffensive defense concepts as the basis for national defense or for their contributions to coalition defense. These political obstacles included the possibility that, faced with NATO Europeans adopting self-oriented nonoffensive strategies beneath the alliance umbrella, the

United States might return to fortress itself and allow Europeans to nonoffensively defend themselves into surrender.

Regardless of the pros and cons of nonoffensive defense as seen from the Cold War perspective, the future European environment may be more conducive to the implementation of nonthreatening defensive alignments and reduced security dilemmas. The security dilemma is a construct that refers to the propensity for one state's search for greater security to cause another state to feel more insecure, because of being threatened by the first state.[5] States' intentions in force building or in mobilizations may be benign and not, in their own minds, designed to destabilize the existing equilibrium in a particular region or in the system as a whole. However, the stability of any particular balance of power among states is determined by their perceptions of one another's intentions as much as by the "reality" of state intentions that an objective observer might describe. The security dilemma suggests that there is a significant difference, for the inferences that leaders will draw about the probable intentions of potential adversaries, between those force deployments and modernizations that appear preparatory to attack compared with those that appear to have been motivated by defensive, that is, self-protective, goals.

Doctrinal Choice

The difference between forward leaning or offensively oriented and rearward looking or defensive conventional force postures is not always obvious. More than the counting of men and arms is required. Some concept of the opponent's operational doctrine (or maxims for the conduct of battle should deterrence fail) is a necessary supplement to weapons and troop inventories if states are to draw accurate conclusions about the intentions of others. Intentions cannot be separated from capabilities; the capabilities that a state thinks it has will influence its definition of acceptable policy and war aims. Capabilities also will affect bargaining strategies during a crisis or in peacetime. The fact that the United States had apparent nuclear superiority relative to the Soviet Union during the Cuban missile crisis was an important part of the context for decision making by President John F. Kennedy and his advisors.

States may choose to adopt a defensively oriented strategy, or circumstances may force one on them. Stalin was incapable of preempting Hitler between 1939 and 1941. The Soviet leader, therefore, sought to placate Hitler while he bought time to improve Soviet defensive capabilities. Even improved capabilities would not have substituted for lack of good intelligence about the German army's style of war.[6] Despite premonitory information from the conduct of the German campaigns in Poland in 1939 and against France in 1940, Soviet forces were insufficiently prepared mentally as well as physically to combat the *blitzkrieg* strategy designed by Hitler's generals. France offered an example of a state that based its strategy on the offensive prior to World War I, with apparent lack of success. Between the world wars, French planning, cognizant of World War I experience, based its strategy for future war on a defensively oriented concept based around the Maginot line and other fortifications. The concept was a not-unreasonable extrapolation of World War I experience into a future war, but it was proved wrong. The Germans simply went over and around the line, striking at the heart of France by concentrating their main force through the Ardennes. Although the defensively oriented concept was not necessarily a bad theoretical basis for French prewar planning, it demanded a better system for command and control and improved capabilities for timely reinforcement of threatened sectors. These capabilities could not be improved in the midst of the pounding administered to French defenders by German tactical fighters and armored spearheads.[7]

The German Schlieffen plan for World War I also has been subjected to retroactive criticism that faults the plan excessively. The plan, or, rather, Schlieffen's various drafts of it, provided for a strategy of annihilation, striking a decisive blow against the French armies through a massive encircling movement executed by the right wing of advancing German forces. The strategy has been criticized for being offensively oriented to excess, whereas the French pre–World War II strategy has been criticized for overemphasis on the defensive.[8] However, both strategic concepts were influenced by the perceived constraints of domestic and foreign policy. Expectations about alliance commitments or defections, military organizational biases and institutional role perceptions, and intelligence appreciations of probable enemy strategy all figured into the German offensive World War I and the French defensive World War II conceptual frameworks for military planning. That the armed forces attached to those concepts proved inadequate in battle does not necessarily prove that the concepts were flawed, only that neither World War I Germany nor World War II France could field forces that would guarantee the successful enactment of their preferred concepts once pitted against the strategy and forces of the opponent.

Other examples could be summoned to show, as well as these two cases do, that the relational quality of war precludes a valid assessment of prewar plans based on postwar outcomes. Good plans can fail badly, and bad plans can succeed against the odds. In World War II, the Germans fought on the Western and Eastern fronts with much greater operational and tactical efficiency than did any of their opponents. The efficiency was expended in a lost cause, for want of adequate grand strategy. Hitler's grand strategy allowed the formation of a decisive winning coalition against Germany. Hitler's strategy was the antithesis of Bismarck's strategy in the nineteenth century, which isolated potential enemies of Germany from one another in a variety of short-term agreements. Because Bismarck was able to keep Germany's most competent potential adversaries from making common cause, the armed forces of the German general staff did not have to rely on a strategy as offensively biased as the Schlieffen plan.[9] The departure of Bismarck left uncertain political guidance to the German general staff, which filled the vacuum with a war plan that seemed to satisfy operational requirements, if not grand strategic ones.

Annihilation versus Attrition

According to noted Russian military theorist A. A. Svechin, a strategy of annihilation or destruction required an "extraordinary victory" based on one operation or on several coordinate operations with the goal of "the complete disorganization of the enemy's manpower and its complete destruction, splitting every link between his intact fragments and capturing communications that are most important for the armed forces rather than the country as a whole."[10]

In contrast to a strategy of annihilation or destruction, a strategy of attrition involves the creation of a protracted military stalemate, often on several fronts, in order to wear down the opponent's military strength and to weaken his resolve to continue fighting. According to Svechin, the "weary path of a strategy of attrition, which leads to the expenditure of much greater resources than a short destructive strike aimed at the heart of the enemy, is in general chosen only when a war cannot be ended by a single blow."[11] Offsetting its lack of promise for a rapid and decisive victory, an attrition strategy favored a defender with superior mobilization potential and economic resources. Svechin's analysis of the Soviet condition in the early 1920s, relative to the military and economic potential of Soviet enemies, was that a strategy of attrition based on large territory and superior mobilization potential was preferable for Russia to a strategy betting everything on prompt offensives.[12] For Russians, a strategy of attrition, however improvised it was, prevailed against Bonaparte's invasion in 1812. Napoleon's campaign of annihilation, as did Hitler's, came to nothing against the vastness of Russia and the inability of invaders since the reign of Peter the Great to subject the vital areas of western Russia to hostile control.

A strategy of attrition is risky for a small state without allies facing a large invader. A rapid campaign of annihilation will appeal to the larger state.[13] However, the Finns, much to the disappointment of Stalin, executed a strategy of delay and denial in 1939 and 1940 before the Soviets were forced to throw overwhelming forces against them. One might argue for this example that the Soviet strategy was not one of annihilation of Finland's military power or political system but was a strategy of limited aim to induce Finnish cession of strategic territory for the defense of Leningrad. Stalin obtained this objective at the price of military institutional and party embarrassment. Finnish resistance revealed not only the tenacity of that state's outnumbered armed forces and the improvisational skills of Marshal Mannerheim but also the lackluster preparedness of Soviet commanders for the larger war that was eventually coming. Stalin's purge trials were paid for on the shores of Lake Lagoda and later, in larger coin, on the Western front.

Soviet lack of preparedness for Hitler's invasion is well-known, although Soviet sources are not agreed on the reasons for it. The best known Soviet critiques of Stalin's political decision making, related to Soviet preparedness for the German invasion, are unsparing of the dictator and his advisors, including his military ones. A large Soviet literature devoted to the topic of the "initial period of war" attempted to unravel the reasons for the nearly decisive defeats inflicted on Soviet border and other forces in the early months of Hitler's attack.[14] During the period of glasnost set in motion by Gorbachev, "new thinkers" among Soviet military writers asserted, along with highly regarded authors from the general staff, that, prior to *Barbarossa*, the Soviet armed forces lacked an adequate concept for conducting defensive operations on a strategic scale.[15]

If the point about the lack of sufficient awareness for the necessity of strategic defense in the initial period is fairly taken, it provides a perspective that loses none of its relevance for the Russian military planner of the 1990s and beyond. The western borders of Russia, after the separation of the Baltic republics from Soviet control, are now even closer to Moscow and St. Petersburg than they were on June 22, 1941. A strategically defensive military posture for the Russian armed forces would be a logical derivative of the widely discussed concepts of "defensive sufficiency" and "reasonable sufficiency."[16] The Russian armed forces, if not tied down policing border and ethnic disputes in the remaining republics of the former Soviet Union, would present, with or without nuclear weapons, a formidable challenge to any invader from the west. Democratization of the states on the western border of Russia makes it even less likely that a forward leaning Russian military strategy, based on annihilation instead of attrition, will be necessary. Svechin's argument that an attrition oriented strategy was preferable for a state with Russia's territorial vastness and underdeveloped economy resonates with strategic prescience more than half a century later.

On the other hand, the broad strategic choice between annihilation and attrition applied mostly to total wars among great powers. Future challenges to Russian security might come from less-than-great-power border states with designs on Russian or other Commonwealth territory. Interethnic and regional conflicts within the Russian federation or between Russians and other nationals outside Russia might spill over into interstate war. For example, separatist and Russian nationalist sentiment have combined to produce conflict in the trans-Dniester region of Moldova for several years: this conflict had the potential to involve Russia, Ukraine, and Romania in military actions during some of its more active phases in 1992.[17] Interethnic nationalism and separatism certainly are forces that must be contained if the Commonwealth and Russia are to survive. For Russian defense planners, the worst-case situation is not only the problem of interethnic containment and regional strife but also the potential combination of these with foreign invasion. For that reason, the broad choice between offensively or defensively oriented strategic military options remains highly pertinent.

Ideal Types of Strategy

In his study *Conventional Deterrence*, John Mearsheimer set out three ideal types of strategy: attrition; blitzkrieg, another expression for annihilation; and limited aim.[18] The strategy of limited aim describes a campaign more than it does a war, but it is a useful collective for those military operations that have as their motive the accomplishment of improved positions for postwar bargaining or very restricted territorial gains. For major wars involving large arms of service in more than a single theater of operations, the dichotomy between attrition and annihilation strategies holds up well. Mearsheimer's contribution to the distinction includes his pointing away from the meaningless distinction alleged to exist between attrition and "maneuver" strategies; maneuver is more appropriately characterized as an ability that armies must have under either an attrition or an annihilation strategy.

In a study of Germany's pre–World War I grand strategy, Dennis Showalter argued that the conceptual framework for German military planning prior to World War I could be characterized as one of total war for limited aims.[19] This seemingly paradoxical appraisal he drew from his analysis of German policy and strategy in the Franco-Prussian War and from subsequent strategic planning by the German general staff under the direction of Helmuth von Moltke (the elder). Von Moltke's military strategy after German unification ruled out the likelihood that Germany could inflict total defeat on the field forces of France and Russia simultaneously or sequentially. He envisioned an offensive-defensive strategy on two fronts that would present to either France or Russia an impossible scenario for victory in battle, the better to deter them individually or jointly. The German general staff departed from this planning guidance under Schlieffen when political conditions, without Bismarck, changed for the worse. However, even the Schlieffen plan in its various incarnations, as described by Ritter and other experts, did not necessarily entail the annihilation of Germany's opponents on all fronts or the complete destruction of France's field forces. Instead, the prompt surrender of many of France's intact forces once they had been encircled and Paris was besieged was the preferred outcome of the Western campaign as envisioned by Schlieffen and his successor, von Moltke (the younger).

Historians have correctly noted that pre–World War I military planners mistakenly foresaw a short war and that the actual war of attrition that resulted was poorly planned for. World War I illustrates the complexity of the issue of attrition versus annihilation in several directions. As Michael Howard has noted, neither Germany nor Britain in World War I had as a preferred war aim the total elimination of the opponent from the group of major powers on the world stage.[20] Each sought to inflict military losses on the other in order to change its intentions and imperial reach, but neither entered the war with the intent to remake the internal regime of the loser or to destroy fully its capacity for national self-defense. Military technology dictated a prolonged war of attrition on the Western front, as did the alliance entanglements that discouraged defections from the carnage by any single state despite its growing losses. World War I became a war of attrition unexpectedly, shattering prewar plans based on short war assumptions and destroying societies and governments rested shakily on that premise.

CAMPAIGNS OF ATTRITION

If it is correct that a strategy of annihilation can support a defensive grand strategy of marginal adjustment to the status quo, can a strategy of attrition be used in support of the maximum political objective of total conquest and defeat of opposed armed forces and regimes? The strategy employed by the Union in the U.S. Civil War exhausted the manpower and resources of Confederate armed forces and laid waste to the social and economic structure that supported those armed forces. Grant's Wilderness and Cold Harbor campaigns were archetypical examples of attrition, but his victory at Vicksburg exploited the opportunities for maneuver and surprise that the larger theater of operations in the west made possible. Vicksburg is among many campaigns that give the impression that battles fought over large territories involve more opportunity for maneuver and for an offensive thrust that strikes a decisive blow against the unprepared defender. However, the choice of attrition or annihilation strategy is not dictated only by the geographical extent of the fighting. U.S. strategy against Japan and Germany in World War II was basically a strategy of attrition, crushing the opponents under the endless stream of logistics and fresh personnel supplied by the world's strongest economy.

Attrition strategies are distinguished from annihilation and other rapid victory strategies by their assumption that war will be protracted and unavoidably costly. Because war is assumed to involve more than one important phase, attrition strategies for fighting on land can be based on defenses that are assumed impenetrable and immediately repelling or on those that are designed for flexible absorption of attackers and gradual expulsion of the attacker from the defender's territory. The French Maginot line was thought to be impregnable, and, in fact, the Germans did not plan to run over it but planned to circumvent it. An interesting "thought experiment" is what would have happened had the Maginot line been extended to cover the entirety of the French and Belgian vulnerable fronts. In any event, the French strategy was to wear out German attackers who fruitlessly threw their forces against the Maginot line. This first and stalemated phase of the war was to be followed by a protracted counteroffensive into Germany using the combined armies of Britain and France. It was envisioned by French planners that this process of counteroffensive against Germany would require great losses on both sides and consume great quantities of societal resources. Therefore, total mobilization capacity for a war of long duration was judged to be more significant than the capability for counterattacks and counteroffensives in the initial period of war. The French defensive concept was a logical one for the war that France hoped to fight but not for the kind of war that the German armed forces launched in May 1940.[21]

Russia's latter nineteenth- and early twentieth-century war planning was bedeviled by the emotional attachment of some quarters to the fortresses in western Russia (Congress Poland). Some Russians had a "Maginot" mentality about these fortresses, which were obsolete and in danger of being overrun in the early stages of any attack eastward by Germany. Symbols of Russian commitment to forward defense of the outer reaches of the empire, the fortresses became the subjects of fierce controversy among general staff defense planners, war ministers, and various other actors in the tsarist policy-making process. Among the partisans for preserving the fortresses at any cost were the "grand dukes" who interfered repeatedly in military planning and personnel issues. The costs of maintaining the fortresses diverted Russian military resources that would, almost certainly, have been better used. As critics had predicted, in the event of war, the fortifications were quickly reduced by the modern field artillery that was brought to bear against them, and they contributed nothing to retarding the devastating thrusts of German offensives in 1915.[22]

Although Russian pre–World War I fortifications and French Maginot line defenses proved inadequate given the technologies and strategies that defeated them, neither French nor Russian emphasis on defense in the initial period of a major war was illogical. Each sought to take advantage of its perceived strengths and to offset its apparent weaknesses. For Russia in 1914, planners recognized that Germany might make its main thrust eastward against Russia or westward against France. If the main German attack were eastward against Russia, plan "G" would mobilize and deploy the greater part of Russia's ready forces against Germany, leaving a comparatively smaller force deployed against Austria. If, as was thought to be more likely by the Russian and French general staffs, the bulk of Germany's forces were initially directed westward against France, then the greater share of Russia's already mobilized defenses would be deployed against Austria (plan "A").[23] Mobilization plans called for significant deployments in both directions and for prompt offensives against both Austria and Germany, with the aim of rapidly transferring the conduct of battle onto enemy territory.[24] However, Russian general staff pessimists doubted whether prompt offensives against Germany in East Prussia would be successful and recognized that any two-front war would almost certainly strain the total fighting capacity and resources of the empire.

French military leaders between the world wars recognized that any strategy for prompt offensives against Germany would be doubtful of success. Although they were aware of the necessity for mechanization and motorization of the armed forces to keep pace with the technology of their probable enemies, French armed forces planners did not adjust their theory of war to take into account the extreme possibilities for exploiting this technology. Neither did the German general staff, in the main. However, faced with Hitler's insistent demands for a victory strategy without a war of attrition that would bleed Germany into economic stasis, innovators in the Wehrmacht proposed the attack through the Ardennes, which disrupted French command and control and defeated French field armies. The French theory of war was logical on the basis of World War I experience and on the assumption that "normal" usage would be made of newly mechanized and modernized forces on both sides.

Offensive strategies can pay large dividends if the attacker catches a defender unprepared or if the attacker's strategy is superior to that of the defender. On the other hand, to take the offensive is to gamble that Clausewitz's friction or Machiavelli's *fortuna* will work in your favor and against your opponent. Military analyst Trevor N. Dupuy studied 42 selected battles from 1805 to 1973, including the most significant campaigns fought in Western Europe in that space of approximately one and one-half centuries.[25] Of these 42 battles, 28 attackers and 14 defenders were successful. Twelve of 13 numerically inferior attackers succeeded. In addition, 24 victors were numerically inferior, and only 18 numerically superior, to their opponents. Dupuy's summary of some of those battles, including the force sizes and attacker/defender outcomes, is presented in Table 3.1.

Russian World War II strategy was based on attrition in the initial period of the war against Germany. How much this was a matter of choice, as opposed to necessity, is still a subject of debate among Soviet historians. Soviet armed forces eventually regrouped from their initially disastrous campaigns, reconstituted powerful offensive forces, and launched successful campaigns of annihilation against German defenders on the Eastern front.[26] A delaying strategy forced upon an underprepared or outperformed defender is not necessarily a strategy of attrition. Thus, the strategy employed by Fabius Maximus against Hannibal in 217 B.C. was improvised under duress. It succeeded in denying to the attacker a decisive battle of annihilation, so it accomplished one denial aim, which is a necessary, but insufficient, condition for fulfilling the requirements of a strategy of attrition.[27] An attrition strategy, properly conceived, seeks to wear out the war-making capacity and military tenacity of the attacker, not just to buy time for the defender to regroup. Some recipes for "mobile defense" on NATO's central front and other mobile defense schemes proposed as part of non-offensive defense postures in Cold War Europe elided this distinction between a true strategy of attrition and any mobile defense.

TABLE 3.1
Outcomes for Attackers and Defenders in Selected Battles, 1805–1973

Battle	Date	Attacker	Force	Defender	Force
Austerlitz	1805	French*	75,000	Allies	89,000
Auerstadt	1806	Prussians	50,000	French*	30,000
Borodino	1812	French*	130,000	Russians	120,000
Dresden	1813	French*	100,000	Allies	150,000
Leipzig	1813	Allies*	300,000	French	180,000
Ligny	1815	French*	77,000	Prussians	83,000
Waterloo	1815	Allies†	129,000	French†	72,000
Buena Vista	1847	Mexicans	16,000	United States*	16,000
Cerro Gordo	1847	United States*	8,500	Mexicans	12,000
Shiloh	1862	Confederates	40,335	Union*	62,642
Antietam	1862	Union	80,000	Confederates*	45,000
Fredericksburg	1862	Union	106,000	Confederates*	77,500
Chancellorsville	1863	Union	161,000	Confederates•	57,352
Gettysburg	1863	Confederates	75,000	Union*	88,289
Chattanooga	1863	Union*	56,359	Confederates	46,165
Cold Harbor	1864	Union	107,907	Confederates*	63,797
Koennigratz	1866	Prussia*	220,000	Austria	215,000
Sedan	1870	Prussia*	190,000	French	110,000
Frontiers	1914	Germany*	1,200,000	Allies	1,400,000
Tannenberg	1914	Germany*	187,000	Russia	160,000
Marne	1914	Allies†	1,200,000	Germany†	900,000
Masurian Lakes	1914	Germany*	288,600	Russia	273,000
Champagne II	1914	French	500,000	Germany*	190,000
Gorlice-Tarnow	1915	Germany*	175,000	Russia	300,000
Arras	1917	British	276,000	Germany*	120,000
Aisne II (Nivelle)	1917	French	1,000,000	Germany*	480,000
Meuse-Argonne	1918	United States*	600,000	Germany	380,000
Flanders	1940	Germany*	2,500,000	Allies	3,000,000
Crete	1941	Germany*	20,000	Anglo-Greek	41,000
Barbarossa (Group Kliest)	1941	Germany*	132,000	Soviet Union	150,000
Malaya	1941–42	Japan*	60,000	Britain	130,000
El Alamein	1942	Britain*	177,000	Axis	93,000

Battle	Date	Attacker	Force	Defender	Force
Stalingrad	1942	Soviet Union*	1,000,000	Germany	800,000
Kursk-Oboyan**	1943	Germany*	62,000	Soviet Union	90,000
Anzio (U.S. 45th Inf. Div.)	1944	Germany	41,974	United States*	20,496
Velletri (U.S. 1st Armored Div.)	1944	United States	14,620	Germany*	12,327
Metz (U.S. XX Corps)	1944	United States	60,794	Germany*	39,580
Ardennes (U.S. 4th Inf. Div.)	1944	Germany*	10,000	United States	8,634
Iwo Jima	1945	United States*	68,000	Japan	22,000
Sinai, Six Day War	1967	Israel*	54,993	Egypt	100,000
West Bank, Six Day War	1967	Israel*	45,650	Jordan	43,300
Golan, Six Day War	1967	Israel*	40,450	Syria	60,000

*Victorious side.

†Where both sides were attacking, attacker-defender designations refer to their final dispositions or posture (for example, Waterloo and Marne).

**The Battle of Kursk was actually a major Soviet victory and a turning point in the war against Germany. The reference above is to only one aspect of that battle, the German 48th Panzer Corps sector for the first seven days of battle and prior to the arrival of a new Soviet army group.

Source: Adapted with abridgment from Trevor N. Dupuy, *Numbers, Predictions and War: Using History to Evaluate Combat Factors and Predict the Outcome of Battles* (Indianapolis, Ind.: Bobbs-Merrill, 1979), pp. 14–15.

A strategy of attrition requires a reasonably large territory relative to the forces attempting to seize and capture it, a relative balance of forces not too lopsided in favor of the attacker, and a capacity for reconstitution of losses by the defender to replace armies, fleets, and tactical air forces lost in the initial period of war. The Swiss do not have a lot of territory, but they have territory that is difficult for invaders to hold and to occupy. Russia's historic disadvantage in making an attrition strategy work was the open access to the vitals of her country provided by endless plains and steppes. A parade of invaders from east and west drove Muscovy to expand until the tsars had more secure borders, which, in the event, added to the insecurity of their neighbors, including the Turks, the Japanese, and the Germans, among others. One of the difficulties with proposals for a delaying or attrition oriented strategy for the defense of West Germany from 1945 to 1990 was the lack of territorial breadth in that country relative to the ranges of modern Soviet weapons and to the presumed speed of any Warsaw Pact offensive in Central Europe. Subtraction of France from the NATO military command structure only added difficulty to any plan for a delaying and denial oriented defense of the Federal Republic of Germany without a prompt counteroffensive into Eastern Europe.

CAMPAIGNS OF ANNIHILATION

Just as there are multiple variations of an attrition strategy as dictated by geography, climate, numbers of forces on the opposed sides, and so forth, so are there also many variations of offensively oriented annihilation strategies. In modern times, a decisive campaign of annihilation may be directed, primarily, against the enemy's armies, government, or people at large. However, most conquerers have preferred to subjugate defeated populations rather than to exterminate them, because the extraction of economic wealth from the defeated state usually requires at least some cooperation from its remaining citizens. Even if directed at the opponent's government, a strategy of annihilation does not necessarily require the physical destruction of that government. It suffices to get that government to call off its armed forces from further resistance to the inevitable. A considerable risk for a strategy of annihilation directed against the enemy's government is that it may work too well. If the enemy has significant field forces remaining to carry on the fight and the government dissolves before effectively commanding those forces to stand down, the formal surrender by the loser may be followed by a protracted campaign of resistance without official approval. Proponents of a strategy of annihilation need to keep in mind that tactical defeat, tactical surrender, and strategic surrender are different realities. Tactical defeat implies that the field forces are no longer capable of putting up effective resistance to the opponent's armed forces. Tactical surrender occurs when the condition of tactical defeat is officially acknowledged by military commanders. Strategic surrender occurs when one government capitulates to another, officially renouncing its war aims and, on occasion, its very existence.[28]

For the most part, strategies of annihilation have been directed against the field forces of the opponent. The assumption has been that once they have been defeated, terms can be imposed at will on the loser's government and population. It follows from this that advocates of a strategy of attrition will seek to trade space for time and remove many of their forces away from their borders and into the interior of their country. For example, from the time of the Franco-Prussian War until the outbreak of World War I, the relative proportion of Russian forces stationed near the western frontier in tsarist Poland relative to the number of active and reserve formations located in the interior of the empire was a matter under constant review by the general staff and war ministry.[29]

From Obruchev through Danilov, Russian war planners faced the problem that the Polish salient provided both a danger and an opportunity. If the Austrians and the Germans could coordinate their efforts and mount a combined offensive from East Prussia and Galacia, the encirclement and crushing of Russian forces in Congress Poland might deal a decisive blow to the tsar. Among other things, a wave of rebellion for independence might be let loose among Poles. However, the Polish salient also allowed Russia extra time in the event of a war against Germany. Provided that the forces sacrificed in the initial period of war could be replaced with others capable of maintaining a provisional defensive cordon around the vitals of interior Russia, reserves eventually could retake the lost territories after the German offensive had reached its culminating point. The expectation that Russian armies would, if attacked from the west, simply retreat into their interior, denying the enemy a victorious strategy of annihilation, was one reason why von Moltke (the elder) eventually decided in favor of an offensive defense in two directions as the basis for general staff war planning.

For most of the nineteenth and twentieth centuries, strategies of attrition have not appealed to professional military planners, nor to the apostles of daring operational art. Blitzkrieg became a twentieth-century synonym for the rapid and decisive defeat of opposed forces by artful maneuvering of armored and tactical air forces. Blitz strategies certainly offer more glamour than "sitz," and they may make possible victory at a lower cost than an extended and brutal campaign of slaughter would do. However, not all annihilation strategies are blitzkriegs. Blitzkrieg is a strategy for the disruption of an enemy's command and control system more than it is a strategy for the physical destruction of his armies. Annihilation strategies, including those based on blitzkrieg operations, accept maximum risk for maximum gain. If they fail, they are apt to fail badly. Hitler's strategy in 1940 defeated France but not England. England's survival until the United States entered the war ensured Hitler's eventual defeat. Japan's attack against Pearl Harbor was designed to inflict a stunning operational blow that would induce U.S. strategic pessimism against an all-out war on Hirohito's empire and in favor of a *modus vivendi* with Japanese imperialism in the Far East. This misestimate of U.S. tenacity cost Japan its empire and regime.

The Cold War threat of a Soviet campaign of annihilation, by means of a theater-strategic offensive against NATO Europe, dissolved along with the Warsaw Pact and the Soviet Union. The Russian Federation seems almost driven toward a strategy of nonoffensive defense in some form, if nonoffensive defense means any strategy that is more attrition than annihilation oriented. However, it may be a mistake to suppose that Russia will evolve a strategy of attrition without a very competent counteroffensive component.[30] Faced with reunited Germans, free Poles, and liberated Baltic republics, Russia's western frontier poses serious potential vulnerabilities as nuclear weapons inventories are drawn down to token levels or eliminated entirely. Therefore, the Russians could maintain a residual nuclear force of 2,000 to 3,000 nuclear charges and long-range delivery vehicles, no longer directed against the United States but, instead, devoted to deterrence of any territorial revisionism against their western, southern, and eastern borders. Nuclear weapons in a bipolar world were the principal components of offensively oriented strategies of annihilation. In Europe after the Cold War, nuclear weapons may be the weapons of last resort that provide the ultimate power of attrition to dissuade against any temptation to strategies of annihilation.

If the strategy of Russia evolves in this direction, toward a conventional and nuclear force posture that is rearward regarding instead of forward leaning, Russian military power could serve as a bulwark of stability on the Eurasian continent. This evolutionary trend in Russian military power would merely return Russian military planners to the decision context faced by their general staffs in the latter nineteenth and early twentieth centuries. A multipolar power system that allowed for flexibility of alignment and for the separation of peripheral wars from central European conflicts created a favorable political and military context for defensively oriented strategies of attrition instead of offensively oriented campaigns of annihilation. As alliances became more committing and mobilization timetables more rigid in the years immediately preceding the outbreak of war, speed and weight of blow in the initial period of war received more emphasis from military planners than did the capacity for sustainability and reconstitution. As World War I turned out, sustainability counted for more, and Russia's premature and ill-prepared offensives against Germany cost her dearly in the early stages of fighting.

For current and future U.S. and European defense planners, one lesson of nineteenth- and twentieth-century experience is that attrition or reconstitution strategies must be based on the potential to bring to bear superior maritime power and industrial war potential if things go badly in the first weeks or months of war. A strategy of attrition by means of reconstitution presupposes that the defender has the superior industrial, technological, and social potential to defeat any combination of adversaries that may assemble from the outset of war to its denouement. Reconstitution also assumes that the industrial and postindustrial base for rebuilding forces can be kept from enemy hands. If reconstituted, rather than ready, U.S. forces, excluding nuclear weapons, become the overseas guarantors of peace and stability for Europe, then a novel experiment in the nuclear age is being tried: extended deterrence conveyed by means of delayed, rather than prompt, retaliation.

The credible threat of attrition as a deterrent has not been thoroughly studied nor fully tested in crisis management. Crisis management in the nuclear age, under the umbrella of U.S.-Soviet nuclear preeminence, mostly has been about the avoidance of surprise attack and preemption through deliberate or inadvertent escalation. Future crisis management in a more denuclearized world may need to place greater reliance on the credible threat of escalation by attrition:

facing potential disturbers of the peace with protracted coalition warfare that would exhaust their resources and slowly destroy their armies. The strategy of deterrence by threat of attrition, short of nuclear escalation, should certainly be among the salient military-strategic menu items for U.S. military planners. The U.S. homeland faces no serious threat of military invasion, and continued friendship with post-Soviet Russia eliminates the problem of large-scale nuclear attack. As the world's only conventional military superpower, the United States can rely on mobilization and reconstitution for global or major regional war, with a saving remnant of forward presence and rapid response forces available to it and to NATO for contingencies short of major war. One could argue that U.S. experience in Desert Storm has been misread by those who assume that the victorious campaign against Iraq was a textbook campaign of annihilation. The Iraqi field forces and command and control infrastructure certainly were subjected to rapid and decisive strikes once war had broken out. However, the rapid operational victories of January and February 1991 were made possible only after an uninterrupted buildup of five months, subsequent to almost a decade of the most extensive peacetime modernization of U.S. armed forces during the Cold War years.[31]

FUTURE WAR AND DEFENSIVE MILITARY STRATEGY

If attrition based strategies are to serve as tools of crisis management in Moscow, Russia must estimate correctly how any future war might begin. With regard to the timing of mobilization and concentration of forces, Soviet and other major power twentieth-century war planners essentially have assumed one of four possible cases:

1. Most or all of the major powers' forces are mobilized and concentrated prior to the outbreak of war.

2. Major power forces are partially mobilized before war begins, with completion of mobilization thereafter.

3. One state attacks to attain operational-tactical advantage while its opponents are still mobilizing and concentrating.

4. One state attacks to achieve strategic surprise before opponents can mobilize and concentrate.[32]

Soviet military planning during the 1920s essentially was based on variations 1 and 2, and during the 1930s assumptions vacillated between numbers 2 and 3. Germany's blitzkrieg into the western Soviet Union in 1941 represented the most memorable example of variation 4 for the Soviet armed forces and perhaps will rise in significance for future Russian ones. The ultimately destructive form of variation 4, successful strategic surprise in the initial period of war, would be a nuclear surprise attack on an unprepared defender whose retaliatory power was preemptively destroyed. Mutual assured destruction turns this form of strategic surprise into a self-defeating proposition.[33]

Defensive strategic models for conventional deterrence, in addition to those proposed by Kokoshin and Larionov, surfaced during Gorbachev era military policy and strategy discussions. One new model was based on a publication in 1989 of the alleged defensive plan for the group of Soviet occupation forces in Germany, designed in 1946.[34] Of more relevance to future Russian defensive strategies within a multipolar system are models based on Soviet experiences and planning during the 1920s and 1930s. One model recreates the assumptions of the international setting during most of the 1920s and until 1935, arguing for some similarities between then and now. This model includes newly independent East European states bordering Germany and Russia and a militarily constrained but potentially stronger Germany in the center of Europe.[35] A second model based on analogies with earlier multipolar systems is based on Soviet strategy from about 1935 to 1941. Soviet planners during this period were faced with the need to develop, within the context of a politically defensive grand strategy and while facing a growing threat perception, a military strategy that would provide for larger and more capable armed forces and a more mature system for accomplishing the transition from peace to war.[36]

Despite last minute efforts that were impeded by doctrinal confusion, delayed force rebuilding, and truncated strategic rethinking, Stalin's war planners were the victims of his decision for nonprovocation over preparedness. Insufficiently prepared for fighting in the initial period of war on the defensive, Soviet planners also failed to perceive the rudiments of Hitler strategy designed to inflict strategically, operationally, and tactically decisive blows in the initial weeks and months of war. However, Hitler equally underestimated Soviet resources and resiliency. Napoleon's experience in Russia shows that attrition strategies can impose a terrible price on the attacker even after the attacker seemingly has dealt a decisive blow to opposed armed forces and captured vital political or economic centers in the enemy's country. Napoleon's "victories" on the way to Moscow destroyed the cream of his army even before his ignominious retreat from Russian territory.

Soviet army counteroffensive operations during World War II demonstrated that forces equal or inferior to the opponent in numbers of personnel and equipment could launch counterattacks from the defensive and obtain objectives of strategic or operational-strategic importance.[37] The preparation of army counteroffensive operations by Soviet planners was characterized by three attributes. First, counteroffensives were organized in parallel with defensive operations. Second, the attacker usually had the initiative and superiority in equipment and personnel. Third, the time available to armies and other formations for transition from defensive to offensive forms of war was very limited.

Table 3.2 summarizes some of the more important army level counter-offensives conducted by the Soviet armed forces during their battles against the Wehrmacht on the Eastern front. The reader should appreciate how far removed these ratios are from the more favorable ratios of Soviet to enemy forces that are preferred for well-prepared offensive operations. From mid-1943 onward, as German forces on the Eastern front lost the initiative and were forced to fight more frequently on the defensive, the ability of the Germans to fight on the operational and tactical defensive improved through bitter experience. Thus, Soviet leaders who planned major offensive campaigns in the third and conclusive period of the Great Patriotic War had to assume that decisive breakthroughs of a prepared defense could be accomplished only by superior numbers of personnel and by fire superiority in the attacked sectors. By early 1944, the state of Soviet force regroupment permitted their commanders to plan for the exploitation of force and fire superiority, as shown in Table 3.3 for selected offensive operations during that final period.

The Russian military is, on the basis of its own and Soviet experience, thoroughly familiar with the defensive as an operational and strategic prelude to a decisive counteroffensive. Certainly, any invasion of Russian territory will call forth not only an effort to expel the attacker but also a riposte that attempts to crush the attacker's armed forces on his own territory. Attrition strategies and other varieties of nonoffensive defense are nonoffensive only to the degree that they forgo reliance on preemptive or overly prompt offensives as decisive moves. Attrition neither precludes a robust counteroffensive nor prohibits the eventual grinding down of opposed forces and the occupation and reconstruction of their governments.

CONCLUSION

Force postures and doctrines of attrition warfare may form part of the military transition toward a deterrent, crisis, and arms race stable repolarization of Europe. Russia's geopolitical and military setting is not inconsistent with a greater emphasis on planning for defensive warfare, and the Gorbachev era emphasis on defensive sufficiency set a small precedent in the right direction. Russia's nuclear arsenal makes her secure against invasion from outside her borders. Greater danger lies in the possible disintegration of the Russian military, accompanied by political anarchy and the repatriation of weapons of mass destruction to republics other than Russia. Assuming Russia escapes both invasion and disintegration, the next chapter considers other aspects of her ability and willingness to take part in a new Eurasian security architecture.

TABLE 3.2
Selected Soviet Army Counteroffensive Operations, World War II: Personnel and Equipment Ratios

Name	Front	Army	Date Begun	Personnel	Tanks and Self-propelled Artillery	Guns and Mortars
Counteroffensive at Rostov	Southern	9th	November 17, 1941	2.4:1	1:2.4	1.6:1
Counteroffensive at Tikhvin	Leningrad	54th	December 3, 1941	1.1:1	1:7	1.2:1
Klin-Solnechnogorsk Offensive	Western	16th	December 7, 1941	1.2:1	1:1.2	1.7:1
Tula Offensive	Western	50th	December 8, 1941	1.2:1	1:1.2	1.3:1
Klin-Solnechnogorsk Offensive	Western	5th	December 11, 1941	1.2:1	1.4:1	1.5:1
Kotelnikovo Offensive	Stalingrad	51st	December 26, 1942	1.5:1	1.1:1	1:1.5
Orel Offensive	Central	13th	July 15, 1943	1.6:1	1.1:1	2.4:1
Front Counteroffensive on Belgorod/Kharkov Axis	Voronezh	6th Gds.	July 20, 1943	2.8:1	1.4:1	13:1
Zhitomir/Berdichev Counteroffensive	1st Ukrainian	60th	December 26, 1943	2.1:1	2.6:1	1.5:1
East Pomeranian Offensive	1st Belorussian	61st	March 1, 1945	2.5:1	1:1.2	10:1
Vienna Offensive	3rd Ukrainian	26th	March 20, 1945	1.6:1	2.2:1	2.3:1

Source: Compiled from USSR TsAMO (Central Archives of the Ministry of Defense), in Y. F. Yashin and V. I. Kuznetsov, "Army Counteroffensive Operations: (Historical Experience)," *Voennaya mysl'*, No. 1 (January 1992): 26–34, JPRS-92-UMT-006-L, p. 16.

TABLE 3.3
Ratios of Soviet to German Personnel and Equipment: Selected Offensive Operations, 1944–45

Operation	Dates	Men	Artillery	Tanks and Self-propelled Guns	Aircraft
Korsun'-Shevchenkovskiy	January 24–February 17, 1944	1.5:1	2.0:1	2.2:1	0.8:1
Belorussia	June 23–August 29, 1944	2.0:1	3.8:1	5.8:1	3.9:1
L'vov–Sandomir	July 13–August 29, 1944	1.2:1	2.6:1	2.3:1	4.6:1
Iasi-Kishinev	August 20–August 29, 1944	1.4:1	2.1:1	4.6:1	2.7:1
East Prussia	January 13–February 3, 1945	2.1:1	3.1:1*	5.5:1	4.0:1
Visla-Oder	January 12–February 3, 1945	3.9:1/4.2:1†	6.0:1	5.5:1/8.0:1†	8.0:1
Berlin	April 16–May 8, 1945	2.5:1	4.0:1	4.2:1	2.0:1

*Excludes rocket launchers and antiaircraft guns
†The higher figures are German estimates; the lower, Russian.

Source: C. J. Dick, *The Operational Employment of Soviet Armour in the Great Patriotic War* (Sandhurst: Soviet Studies Research Centre, RMA Sandhurst, 1988), p. 38; see also B. V. Panov, V. N. Kiselev, I. I. Kartavtsev, et al., *Istoriya voennogo iskusstva* (Moscow: Voenizdat, 1984), JPRS-UMA-85-009-L, March 21, 1985, p. 308 on Visla-Oder and p. 323 on Berlin operations; on East Prussian operations, see also V. A. Matsulenko, *Operatsii i boi na okruzhenie* (Moscow: Voenizdat, 1983), JPRS-UMA-84-019-L, September 28, 1984, pp. 166–67.

NOTES

1. David R. Jones, "The Napoleonic Paradigm: The Myth of the Offensive in Soviet and Western Military Thought," in *Military History and the Military Profession*, eds. David A. Charters, Marc Milner, and J. Brent Wilson (Westport, Conn.: Praeger Publishers, 1992), pp. 211–28, provides ample documentation on this point.

2. See, for example, V. E. Savkin, *Osnovnye printsipy operativnogo iskusstva i taktiki* (Fundamental Principles of Operational Art and Tactics), translated by U.S. Air Force, (Moscow: Voenizdat, 1972), p. 41; a useful U.S. study is Nathan Leites, *Soviet Style in War* (Santa Monica, Calif.: RAND, 1982), esp. pp. 205–8.

3. See, for example, Horst Afheldt, "New Policies, New Fears," *Bulletin of the Atomic Scientists* (September 1988): 24–28; John Grin and Lutz Unterseher, "The Spiderweb Defense," *Bulletin of the Atomic Scientists* (September 1988): 28–30. According to Stephen J. Flanagan, there are four basic types of nonoffensive defense concepts: area defense, wide area covering defenses, the fire barrier, and integrated and interactive forward defense. See Stephen J. Flanagan, *NATO's Conventional Defenses* (Cambridge, Mass.: Ballinger, 1988), esp. pp. 110–20; Andreas Von Bulow, "Defensive Entanglement: An Alternative Strategy for NATO," in *The Conventional Defense of Europe: New Technologies and New Strategies*, ed. Andrew J. Pierre (New York: Council on Foreign Relations, 1986), pp. 112–52; Andreas Von Bulow, "O nesposobnosti k napadeniyu" (On the Impossibility of Attack), *Kommunist* 7 (May 1989): 122–25.

4. A critique of conventional deterrence strategies, including territorial self-defense schemes, in the context of their viability in a NATO-Warsaw Pact war scenario is provided in Josef Joffe, *The Limited Partnership: Europe, the United States and the Burdens of Alliance* (Cambridge, Mass.: Ballinger, 1987), pp. 148–65.

5. Robert Jervis, "Cooperation under the Security Dilemma," *World Politics* (January 1978): 167–86, in *International Politics: Anarchy, Force, Political Economy and Decision Making*, eds. Robert J. Art and Robert Jervis (New York: Harper Collins, 1985), pp. 86–101, esp. p. 88.

6. Soviet intelligence appreciation failures in this regard are noted in John Erickson, "Threat Identification and Strategic Appraisal by the Soviet Union, 1930–1941," in *Knowing One's Enemies: Intelligence Assessment before the Two World Wars*, ed. Ernest R. May (Princeton, N.J.: Princeton University Press, 1984), pp. 375–423.

7. Douglas Porch, "Arms and Alliances: French Grand Strategy and Policy in 1914 and 1940," in *Grand Strategies in War and Peace*, ed. Paul Kennedy (New Haven, Conn.: Yale University Press, 1991), pp. 125–44; Eliot A. Cohen and John Gooch, *Military Misfortunes: The Anatomy of Failure in War* (New York: The Free Press, 1990), pp. 197–230.

8. The definitive study of the Schlieffen plan is Gerhard Ritter, *The Schlieffen Plan: Critique of a Myth* (London: Oswald, Wolff, 1958), pp. 134–47, which includes the text of Schlieffen's great memorandum of December 1905. See also A.J.P. Taylor, *War by Time-Table: How the First World War Began* (New York: American Heritage, 1969), pp. 25–28; Holger H. Herwig, "The Dynamics of Necessity: German Military Planning during the First World War," in *Military Effectiveness, Vol. I: The First World War*, eds. Allan R. Millett and Williamson Murray (Boston, Mass.: Unwin Hyman, 1988), pp. 80–115.

9. Ritter, *The Schlieffen Plan*, p. 21.

10. Aleksandr A. Svechin, *Strategiia* (Strategy), translated and edited by Kent D. Lee (Minneapolis, Minn.: East View, 1991), p. 241.

11. Ibid., p. 247. Of course, there can be campaigns of annihilation within a general war of attrition, as discussed in the text further on. Soviet military historical

studies of the Manchurian campaign against Japan in 1945 emphasized the point.

12.   For which views Svechin was roundly chastised by Red commanders. See M. Tukhachevskii, "Protiv reaktsionnykh teorii na voenno-nauchnom fronte (kritika strategicheskikh i voenno-istoricheskikh vzgliadov prof. Svechina)" (Against Reactionary Theories on the Military-Scientific Front: A Critique of the Strategic and Military-Historical Views of Professor Svechin), *Problemy marksizma* 8–9 (1931): 187–209. Recent scholarship on Svechin has been more flattering, especially during the Gorbachev era and subsequent to renewed interest in Russian research institutes in strategic defense. See, for example, A. A. Kokoshin, "A. A. Svechin: O voine i politike" (A. A. Svechin: On War and Politics), *Mezhdunarodnaia zhizn'* 10 (October 1988): 133–42.

13.   P. H. Vigor, *Soviet Blitzkrieg Theory* (New York: St. Martin's, 1983), p. 147 and *passim*.

14.   S. P. Ivanov, *Nachal'nyi period voiny* (The Initial Period of War) (Moscow: Voyenizdat, 1974); A. I. Yevseev, "O nekotorykh tendentsiyakh izmenii soderzhaniia i kharaktera nachal'nogo perioda voiny" (On Certain Tendencies in the Changing Content and Character of the Initial Period of War), *Voenno-istoricheskii zhurnal* 11 (November 1985): 10–20; M. M. Kir'yan, "Nachal'nyi period Velikoi Otechestvennoi Voiny" (The Initial Period of the Great Patriotic War), *Voenno-istoricheskii zhurnal* 6 (June 1988): 11–17; M. Cherednichenko, "O nachal'nom periode Velikoi Otechestvennoi voiny" (On the Initial Period of the Great Patriotic War), *Voenno-istoricheskii zhurnal* 4 (1961): 28–35. Recent literature is well-traced in Richard H. Phillips, *Soviet Military Debate on the Initial Period of War: Characteristics and Implications* (Cambridge, Mass.: MIT, Center for International Studies, 1989). For historical perspective see Jacob W. Kipp, *Barbarossa, Soviet Covering Forces and the Initial Period of War: Military History and AirLand Battle* (Ft. Leavenworth, Kan.: Soviet Army Studies Office, undated).

15.   Andrei Kokoshin and Valentin Larionov, "Kurskaia bitva v svete sovremennoe oboronitel'noe doktriny" (The Battle of Kursk in View of Contemporary Defensive Doctrine), *Mirovaia ekonomika i mezhdunarodnye otnosheniia* 8 (1987): 32–40. Excerpts from debates among Soviet historians about the responsibility for failures attendant to Barbarossa are included in A. M. Nekrich, "June 22 1941," in *June 22 1941: Soviet Historians and the German Invasion*, translated and ed. Vladimir Petrov (Columbia: University of South Carolina Press, 1968).

16.   For a discussion of reasonable sufficiency, See L. Semeiko, "Razumnaya dostatochnost' — put' k nadezhnomy miru" (Reasonable Sufficiency — Path to Reliable Peace), *Kommunist* 7 (May 1989): 112–21. The concept of reasonable sufficiency was first promulgated at the Twenty-seventh Party Congress of the Communist Party of the Soviet Union. Variable approaches to stability with different mixes of offensive and defensive conventional force postures are outlined very schematically in Andrei Kokoshin and Valentin Larionov, "Protivostoianiia sil obshchego naznacheniia v kontekste obespecheniia strategicheskoe stabil'nosti" (The Counterpositioning of Conventional Forces in the Context of Guaranteeing Strategic Stability), *Mirovaia ekonomika i mezhdunarodnye otnosheniya* 6 (1988): 23–31. Examination of the Kokoshin-Larionov and other past and possible future approaches to Soviet or Russian defensivism is provided in David M. Glantz, *Soviet Military Strategy after CFE: Historical Models and Future Prospects* (Ft. Leavenworth, Kan.: Soviet Army Studies Office, 1990).

17.   For perspective and additional information on this issue, see Stephen R. Bowers, "Ethnic Conflict in the 'Soviet' Commonwealth," *Low Intensity Conflict and Law Enforcement* (Summer 1992): 42–56.

18.   John J. Mearsheimer, *Conventional Deterrence* (Ithaca, N.Y.: Cornell University Press, 1983), Chap. 2.

19.   Dennis E. Showalter, "Total War for Limited Objectives: An Interpretation of German Grand Strategy," in *Grand Strategies in War and Peace*, ed. Paul Kennedy (New Haven, Conn.: Yale University Press, 1991), pp. 105–24.

20.   Michael Howard, "Europe on the Eve of the First World War," in *The Lessons of History*, ed. Michael Howard (New Haven, Conn.: Yale University Press, 1991), pp. 113–26; see also Michael Howard, "British Grand Strategy in World War I," in *Grand Strategies in War and Peace*, ed. Paul Kennedy (New Haven, Conn.: Yale University Press, 1991), pp. 31–42.

21.   On the interwar doctrine and planning of French armed forces, see Robert A. Doughty, "The French Armed Forces, 1918–40," in *Military Effectiveness: Vol. II*, eds. Allan R. Millet and Williamson Murray (London: Unwin Hyman, 1988), pp. 39–69; on the reasons for French failure in 1940, see Eliot Cohen and John Gooch, eds., *Military Misfortunes: The Anatomy of Failure in War* (New York: The Free Press, 1990), pp. 197–230.

22.   Yuri Danilov, *La Russie dans la Guerre Mondiale (1914–1917)* (Paris: Payot, 1927), expresses the exasperation of general staff war planners over the fortresses issue.

23.   I. I. Rostunov, ed., *Istoriya pervoi mirovoi voiny*, Vol. I (Moscow: "Nauka," 1975), pp. 196–97; Danilov, *La Russie dans la Guerre Mondiale*.

24.   Rostunov, *Istoriya pervoi mirovoi voiny*, Vol. I, pp. 196–97.

25.   T. N. Dupuy, *Numbers, Predictions and War: Using History to Evaluate Combat Factors and Predict the Outcome of Battles* (Indianapolis, Ind.: Bobbs-Merrill, 1979), pp. 12–15.

26.   Svechin warned in the second edition of *Strategy* that "a strategy of attrition in no way renounces in principle the destruction of enemy personnel as a goal of an operation. But in this it sees only a part of the mission of the armed front rather than the entire mission" (p. 26).

27.   Brian Caven, *The Punic Wars* (London: Wiedenfeld and Nicolson, 1980), p. 127.

28.   For these distinctions, see Paul Kecskemeti, *Strategic Surrender: The Politics of Victory and Defeat* (Stanford, Calif.: Stanford University Press, 1958), p. 11; he notes that a series of tactical surrenders may lead to strategic surrender. Strategic surrender concerns "not merely the belligerent role of military units" but the "maintenance of belligerency itself."

29.   I. I. Rostunov, *Russkii front pervoi mirovoi voiny* (Moscow: "Nauka," 1976), esp. pp. 64–66; see also Rostunov, *Istoriya pervoi mirovoi voiny*, Vol. I, pp. 176–84 on Russian military doctrine from the Franco-Prussian War until World War I. On the implications of Russian pre–World War I manpower policy for its military strategy, see N. N. Golovin, *The Russian Army in the World War* (New Haven, Conn.: Yale University Press, 1931) (reissued by Archon Books, 1969).

30.   Rostunov, *Istoriya pervoi mirovoi voiny*, Vol. I, pp. 176–84, notes that Russian military theory in the latter nineteenth and early twentieth centuries acknowledged the likelihood that future war could involve coalitions of states, be protracted, and depend as much on the economic and social resources of the country as on the fighting power of combat forces. Nevertheless, Russian tactical and operational art during this period had a decidedly offensive cast, emphasizing wide ranging maneuver battles and the advantages of taking the initiative.

31.   One could argue that the Reagan modernization was record setting even for strategic nuclear forces, in addition to the obvious precedent-setting pace for general purpose forces. Although the McNamara years represented a period of active force posture growth in numbers of missile launchers and in the configuration of the basic strategic nuclear triad, McNamara retired many bomber and air defense forces and cancelled other proposed strategic offensive forces, including the B-70 bomber, the

Snark cruise missile, and the Skybolt air-launched ballistic missile. During the Reagan years, the United States supported modernization programs for two intercontinental ballistic missiles and two bombers, and the modernized systems were more expensive per unit (and presumably more capable) than their predecessors. For relevant cost estimates, see Kevin N. Lewis, *Historical U.S. Force Structure Trends: A Primer* (Santa Monica, Calif.: RAND, 1989), pp. 46–49.

32.   These typologies are explained in David M. Glantz, "Future Directions in Soviet Military Strategy," in *The Lost Empire: Perceptions of Soviet Policy Shifts in the 1990s*, ed. John Hemsley (New York: Brassey's, 1991), pp. 123–44, esp. p. 137.

33.   A point eventually acknowledged by Soviet military theorists in the Brezhnev years, most emphatically during the latter 1970s and early 1980s. Ironically, this was at the very time that some critics of U.S. strategy argued that it was deficient for lack of counterforce competency and war fighting and war survival capability, allegedly hallmarks of Soviet military doctrine and strategy. For comments on these variations as applied to the 1920s and 1930s, see Glantz, "Future Directions in Soviet Military Strategy," p. 137.

34.   Glantz, *Soviet Military Strategy after CFE.*

35.   Glantz, "Future Directions in Soviet Military Strategy," p. 127.

36.   Ibid., p. 128.

37.   V. F. Yashin and V. I. Kuznetsov, "Army Counteroffensive Operations: Historical Experience," *Voennaya mysl'* 1 (January 1992): 26–34, JPRS-92-UMT-006-L, May 14, 1992, pp. 15–20.

4

Russian Peacekeeping Potential in Political and Military Context

Military peace operations have moved to center stage with the end of the Cold War and the demise of the Soviet Union. The United Nations finds itself sponsoring more peace operations of various kinds, by multinational forces under its political and military command or by individual state actions that have received tacit or explicit UN blessing. The future success of international peacekeeping depends upon the acquiescence, if not the active participation, of the United States and Russia.[1] The United States' global military preeminence and Russia's political and military centrality in Eurasia make both states vital supporters and potential participants in military peace operations.

In this chapter, I consider the political and military context of Russia's continued support for, and potential involvement in, post–Cold War multinational or unilateral peace operations. Russia inherits from the former Soviet Union a UN Security Council veto to protect itself against international peace operations deemed hostile to Moscow's interests. The more interesting question is whether Russia will take upon itself a participatory role in peacekeeping, either within its own geographical neighborhood or more broadly. Several obstacles to a more prominent profile for Russia in peace operations are noted in this chapter. They include the uncertain future of Russian civil-military relations and the rundown of Russia's conventional military capabilities that leaves Russia with an unhealthy nuclear dependency.

THE MULTIPLE PEACE MISSIONS

The official UN terminology distinguishes among peacekeeping, peacemaking, peacebuilding, and peace enforcement as follows:

peacekeeping — deployment of UN forces in the field with the consent of all parties concerned, usually including military or police and frequently civilians;

peacemaking — action taken by the UN to bring hostile parties to agreement, using peaceful means such as those foreseen in Chapter VI of the UN Charter;

peacebuilding — action to prevent a relapse into conflict by creating support structures for peaceful settlement;

peace enforcement — action taken by UN armed forces under Chapter VII to restore peace (often termed "collective security").[2]

What military missions follow from these definitional constructs? If we take the four generic missions identified by the United Nations (peacekeeping, peacemaking, peacebuilding, and peace enforcement), possibly derivative military missions are summarized in Table 4.1.

Most of the commentary about UN activities has focused on peace-keeping and peacemaking. Article 42 authorizes the UN Security Council to take collective actions to restore peace in the face of aggression. The United Nations has never acted under Article 42, however, the Korean and Desert Storm operations were authorized under Article 52, dealing with collective self-defense.[3] Peacemaking, thus, comes about under UN responsibility only when peacekeeping or other operations evolve into peacemaking, not by means of the designed "collective security" route.

UN peacekeeping operations, on the other hand, have been its big business. More than 30 peacekeeping operations have been authorized by the UN Security Council and administered through the office of the UN Secretary-General. Approximately 1,000 UN personnel have been killed during peacekeeping operations over the organization's lifetime, including more than 200 in the past two years (1992–94). About $10 billion has been spent on all peacekeeping operations since the origin of the United Nations, but about half of that total has been accumulated within the past two years (1992–94).[4]

RUSSIA AFTER THE COLD WAR: PEACEKEEPING AND POLITICIZATION

Between 1988 and 1994, the shrinkage in the size of the Soviet or Russian empire in Eurasia was dramatic. Soviet armed forces, including border guards, totalled about 5.5 million in 1988; as of October 1994, the post-Soviet Russian military numbered about 1.5 million active duty forces.[5] The dismantling of Moscow's contiguous empire in Eastern Europe and the breakup of the Soviet Union in 1991 remade the security map of Eurasia. U.S. and allied North Atlantic Treaty Organization (NATO) priorities shifted from deterring Soviet military attack to incorporating Russia within an enlarged Eurasian security community. Russia found itself eager to be included as a peaceful partner in new Eurasian security structures. Yet, Russia also found herself besieged by instabilities on her borders and within the federation itself that called

TABLE 4.1
UN Military Missions Derived from Peace Support Functions

Peacemaking	Peacebuilding	Peacekeeping	Peace Enforcement
Assessments	Assessments	Assessments	Assessments
Monitoring	Monitoring	Monitoring	Show of force
	Counterterrorism	Counterterrorism	Counterterrorism
	Observers	Observers	Free passage
	Law and order	Law and order	Blockade
	Humanitarian assistance	Humanitarian assistance	Air/naval campaign
	Disarm/demobilize	Hostage rescue	Hostage rescue
	Organize/train	PW protection	Limited major regional conflict
	Counterdrug	Noncombatant evacuation	Major regional conflict
	Protect elections	Preventive diplomacy	
	Reconstruction	Buffer force	
	Environmental protection		

Source: Martha Bills, et al., *Options for U.S. Military Support to the United Nations* (Washington, D.C.: Center for Strategic and International Studies, 1992), p. 3. The study includes definitions for each term in the matrix.

for peacekeeping and other highly politicized post–Cold War military missions. As Russia completed its withdrawal of more than 300,000 troops from Germany by the deadline of August 31, 1994, and its removals of forces from the formerly occupied Baltic states of Estonia, Latvia, and Lithuania by the same date, Russia's security dilemma shifted to the east and south.

Because nuclear weapons acted as a stabilizing force during the Cold War, the post–Cold War Soviet collapse and the U.S.-Russian agreements on nuclear force reductions were not necessarily contributory to peace and stability. Much would depend on how Russia fitted into the new world order, both in Europe and in global terms.[6] Russia's post-Soviet defense perimeter was now shrunken to exclude from Russian military control the former Warsaw Pact states of Eastern Europe, the Baltics, and the former Soviet republics now contiguous to the Russian federation. These republics in the Russian "near abroad" included Ukraine, Belarus, and Kazakhstan, vital for the defense of Russia's extended security west and south and also holding in each case former Soviet strategic nuclear weapons supposedly under continuing Russian and Commonwealth of Independent States control.

This was an extremely vulnerable defense perimeter except for Russia's remaining nuclear weapons. The status of the Russian armed forces by 1992 was one of great political turbulence and economic neglect.[7] The defense-industrial complex that the Soviet system had built to sustain its military buildup was flying apart. Desertions from draft calls were out of control, and military leaders acknowledged that Russia would eventually have to move toward armed forces based at least partly on voluntary enlisted recruitment. Officers sold military equipment on the black market, including portions of the Black Sea fleet contested for ownership between Russia and Ukraine until 1993. Political turbulence on Russia's borders in Georgia, Tajikistan, Azerbaijan, and territories contiguous to former Soviet republics (Moldova, Armenia) argued for continued military vigilance, but Russia's conventional military forces were being downsized to comply with the Conventional Forces in Europe agreement (signed in 1990) and, in any case, were being split apart by divided political loyalties and economic distress.

The capability of Russia's armed forces for the repelling of external aggression was only one imponderable facing President Boris Yeltsin and his newly constituted Russian defense establishment. Another was the reliability of Russian armed forces in case of internal insurrection and civil war. There is danger in drawing inferences about the relative power of "military" compared with "civil" institutions in Russia from the coups-manque of 1991 or 1993. Two false images easily present themselves to outsiders: first, of a monolithic military-security bloc of former Communists and fellow travelers awaiting the restoration of the Brezhnev era or, second, of an adventurist politician like Zhirinovskiy backed by the Russian military winning electoral office and launching post-Soviet Russia on a new imperialism.[8]

Politics in Russia both inside and outside the military are too fluid for either of these undesirable end states to be realistic alternatives. The military in Russia is now a divided political house and will remain so for the foreseeable future. There is no expectant unified military coalition for a putsch. The military in Russia is politicized about a variety of issues, but it is not aspiring to hold political office.[9] To do so would be to partake of the unpopularity and distrust Russians historically and presently accord to all their political institutions. A majority of Russians, according to University of Strathclyde's New Russia Barometer survey research project, distrust political parties, President Yeltsin, parliament, the police, the KGB, the courts, and local government.[10] Table 4.2 shows the results of a 1994 survey of 3,535 Russians reporting the levels of trust for political objects.

TABLE 4.2
Percentages of Russians Trusting Political Institutions

Trust political parties	6
Trust Parliament	12
Trust the president	18
Identify with a party	23
Believe the constitution guarantees	
Territorial unity of Russia	15
A lawful, democratic state	17
Think the shelling of Parliament could recur	60

Source: University of Strathclyde, New Russia Barometer III surveys, reported in Richard Rose, "Getting By Without Government: Everyday Life in Russia," Daedalus (Summer 1994): 53.

The most interesting thing about the October revolt of 1993 was how long it took for the armed forces to coalesce behind Yeltsin. Thirteen days of parliamentary maneuvering and defiance of the president went unanswered, and even the storming of the television station by Rutskoi's sympathizers found Russian armed forces still uncertain as to their ultimate loyalties. Western pressure, Yeltsin's steadfastness, and the power of the paycheck in the hands of the Russian government finally caused the military to throw in unreservedly with the government. Yeltsin's victory opened the door for further consolidation of his executive power as against that of the legislative institutions, including Parliament. It raised the potential for the military, having received credit for keeping Yeltsin's regime afloat, to enhance its prestige and political veto over the drift of defense and security affairs in Russia.[11]

In November 1993, a new Russian military doctrine was approved by the Russian security council and President Yeltsin, and concessions to the defense establishment led by Pavel Grachev were suspected.[12] In some ways, the new doctrine was unsurprising: it echoed most of the geopolitical emphases expressed in the draft doctrine of May 1992, but many expert Western observers had dismissed the 1992 draft doctrine as of marginal importance. The 1993 reaffirmation of Russian military doctrine disavowed any intention to commit military aggression against other states. However, it departed from the final version of Soviet strategy in several respects. First, the new Russian doctrine did not renounce first use of nuclear weapons as the last Soviet version had done. Second, the former Soviet doctrine, under Gorbachev's guidance, had taken an explicitly defensive orientation: if attacked, Soviet armed forces would seek to expel the invader from their territory but not to carry the war into the attacker's own territory. This "defensive defense" was not reaffirmed by the 1993 doctrine; the latter averred that, if Russia is attacked by a foreign power, the war initially would be fought by Russia on the defensive. Eventually, Russia would go over to the offensive, and the offensive would not be confined to expelling of the invader from the territory of Russia.

Russia's 1993 version repeated the emphasis laid down in the draft doctrine of 1992 on Russian responsibilities for their nationals living in former Soviet republics other than Russia. Although avoiding any statement of declaratory imperialist objectives with regard to its near abroad, Russia's military leadership asserts an interest in protecting Russian nationals in other states from political discrimination and oppression. This sort of ethnic extended deterrence is complemented by entrepreneurial armed forces, formerly Soviet and nominally Russian, that have taken up regional causes for or against established governments. In Georgia, for example, Russian troops provided security for railways on behalf of the Shevardnadze government in autumn 1993 against rebels favoring the former regime of Gamsakhurdia. In Moldova, both trans-Dniester liberationists and Lieutenant General Alexander Lebed's Fourteenth Army, an elite former Soviet unit now more or less privatized by its commander, challenged state authorities. By all accounts, the Fourteenth Army was answerable not to the commander-in-chief of Russian ground forces in Moscow or even to Boris Yeltsin but to its local and regional leaders.[13]

In November 1994, Yeltsin threatened a Russian crackdown on the Caucasian republic of Chechnya, which declared itself independent of the Russian federation in 1991. Chechnya President and former Soviet General Dzhokhar Dudayev blamed Russia for arming and leading opposition forces against his government, including attacks on the airport of the Chechen capital, Grozny, by Russian airplanes and helicopters. Yeltsin demanded the release of Russian prisoners held by Chechnya and the disbanding of forces on both sides within 48 hours on

November 29 and said Russia would otherwise declare and impose a state of emergency. Chechen military and political leaders remained defiant.[14] Subsequently, Yeltsin authorized a military incursion into Chechnya by troops of the Russian interior ministry.

Yeltsin's dilemma, with regard to attempted pacification of the mostly Muslim breakaway republic, was acute. Chechen criminal gangs infiltrated business and law enforcement throughout Russia, and Dudayev's thus-far-successful defiance of Moscow created a disturbing precedent. On the other hand, Russia's massive and acknowledged military intervention to suppress independent Chechnya might set off another Muslim holy war against Russian imperialism, reminiscent of Afghanistan in the 1980s. Terrorist reprisals by Chechens inside Russia were another possibility. U.S. official reactions to the Russian incursion against Chechnya were cautious, treating the matter as an internal Russian issue. Yeltsin risked not only a protracted military struggle but also alienation of his political support base in Parliament and among members of his own government.

Russia's borders will be the occasions for multiple security dilemmas, and the diversification and modernization of Russia's border troops has already begun. Russian troops guarding Tajik frontiers or serving elsewhere in Central Asia have regular confrontations with narcotraffickers, illegal arms traffickers, and insurgents. An objective of General Andrei Nikolaev, current commander of the border troops, is to upgrade their quality and performance. Accordingly, Nikolaev, formerly a Russian Armed Forces general staff officer, has brought general staff colleagues into the border troops high command. Additions will be made to a border troops force structure that already includes border post units, maneuver groups, and some air assault elements. In addition, Nikolaev plans to create a specialized counterterrorist force. The force would be composed of at least five groups of 15–20 personnel located near border areas.[15]

Among the missions anticipated for this counterterrorist force is hostage rescue. This mission is expected to include hostage rescue in the territory of states other than Russia. Personnel for this force and mission will be carefully selected, emphasizing experienced service personnel and excluding conscripts. Training of the hostage rescue-counterterrorist force probably will be conducted by Russia's widely known "Alfa" counterterrorist unit.[16] It is also rumored that airborne and navy personnel will be transferred to the border troops to improve the troops' capabilities for mobile warfare. However, enhancement and mission enlargement of the border troops presupposes that troops of the appropriate quality can be recruited and maintained. Problems of discipline that have affected other Russian military units are not unknown in the border troops. The ethnic and national diversity of the former Soviet Union ensures that the border troops, augmented as above, will find plenty to do.

The ethnic diversity of the former Soviet Union and the growing proportion of nationalities other than Slavs, especially Central Asians, ensures that ethnonationalistic conflicts on the Russian rimland will provide additional opportunities for peacekeeping. The distribution of nationalities in the former Soviet union from 1959 through 1989 is noted in Table 4.3.

RUSSIA FACES THE WORLD:
POST–COLD WAR ALTERNATIVES

Russia's credibility as a pacifier outside the borders of the former Soviet Union depends in part on its ability to maintain the image of a global military power. Unfortunately, Russia remains in the big league of military powers, for the short term, only if Russia is able to maintain something approaching nuclear equivalence with the United States, or, at least, Russia must maintain a position in nuclear weapons capability that is second in rank, not yielding to equivalency with France, Britain, China, or other nuclear armed states. Russia's nuclear weapons remained as an ironical Cold War legacy, given that it was the West that feared Russia's overwhelming manpower and tanks and, therefore, insisted that only a nuclear centered defense strategy would suffice for deterrence. Post-Soviet Russia now was gripping its nuclear hostages with the tenacity of a reformed alcoholic, while its conventional forces were being decimated in a budgetary no man's land. A Russia dependent on nuclear weapons for deterrence and for self-defense in the initial period of a major war would be, at best, an equivocal force for the stabilization of post–Cold War Europe.

Would Russia in NATO augment or complicate the alliance's shift from a traditional deterrence-defense mission to one of peacekeeping or peacemaking? Boris Yeltsin has more than once indicated that he would like to join NATO, but the attitudes of the Russian armed forces, especially in view of the declared doctrine of November 1993, are less certain. NATO also can expect to receive membership petitions from Hungary, the Czech Republic, and Slovakia; Poland has already indicated a strong desire for formal affiliation.

Taking on the former Warsaw Pact East Central European states as NATO members, to say nothing of former Soviet republics and Russia itself, adds cognitive complexity to military planning in a time of enormous transition in NATO's definition of its most probable missions. NATO preferred to proceed with caution. The Atlantic alliance extended diplomatic overtures for military cooperation via the North Atlantic Cooperation Council (NACC), formed in December 1991 and including, in addition to NATO members, states of Eastern and Central Europe and former Soviet republics. The Clinton administration subsequently proposed a Partnership for Peace (PFP) under which newly independent states of the former Soviet Union and Eastern Europe would affiliate

TABLE 4.3
Nationalities (Union Republic Status) as Shares of
Total U.S.S.R. Population, Selected Years
(figures are percent of total population)

	1959	1970	1979	1989
Slavs				
Russians	54.6	53.4	52.4	50.99
Ukrainians	17.8	16.9	16.2	15.45
Belorussians	3.8	3.7	3.6	3.51
Subtotal	76.2	74.0	72.2	69.95
Central Asians				
Uzbeks	2.88	3.8	4.75	5.84
Kazakhs	1.73	2.19	2.50	2.85
Tadzhiks	0.67	0.88	1.11	1.48
Turkmen	0.48	0.63	0.77	0.95
Kirgiz	0.46	0.60	0.73	0.89
Subtotal	6.22	8.10	9.86	12.01
Groups of Transcaucasia				
Azeris	1.41	1.81	2.09	2.38
Armenians	1.33	1.47	1.58	1.62
Georgians	1.29	1.34	1.36	1.39
Subtotal	4.03	4.62	5.03	5.39
Baltic Groups				
Lithuanians	1.11	1.10	1.09	1.07
Latvians	0.67	0.59	0.55	0.51
Estonians	0.47	0.42	0.39	0.36
Subtotal	2.25	2.11	2.03	1.94
Other				
Moldavians	1.06	1.12	1.13	1.17

Notes: Numerous other national groups without Union Republic status inhabited the former Soviet Union. Those with more than 1 million population in 1989 included Tatars, Germans, Chuvash, Bashkir, Jews, Mordvinians, and Poles. Tatars were granted the status of an autonomous republic instead of union republic (the former a lower-level administrative entity), because Tatars are concentrated in the Russian republic. Tatars, Bashkirs, and other groups demanded union republic status in 1990 and 1991.

Sources: Ann Sheehy, "The National Composition of the Population of the USSR According to the Census of 1979," *Radio Liberty Research Bulletin*, No. 123/80 (March 27, 1980), p. 14 for 1959, 1970, and 1979 data; 1989 data calculated from Goskomstat, *Natsional'nyi sostav naseleniya* (Moscow: Information-Publication Center, 1989), in Joan DeBardeleben, *Soviet Politics in Transition* (Lexington, Mass.: D. C. Heath, 1992), p. 154.

with NATO on a consultative basis. PFP grew from experience gained
in cooperative exchanges under NACC. PFP moves from the NACC
level of general common activities to specific bilateral programs of
cooperation worked out between individual PFP affiliates and the
alliance. The scope of PFP objectives includes transparency in defense
planning and budgeting, democratic control of defense forces, and joint
planning, training, and exercises in support of peacekeeping, humanitarian operations, or other suitable missions.[17] The first exercises held
in 1994 under the PFP umbrella focused on training and doctrine for
peacekeeping, as summarized in Table 4.4.

Russia held back from commitment to PFP in the hope that her
great power reputation would entitle Russia to a special relationship
with NATO and an actual voice in NATO military decision making. In
this regard, Russia was to be disappointed. Russia's inclusion in PFP
would avoid the embarrassment that leaving Russia out would otherwise create: a potential dividing line between the security zones of
NATO and Moscow.[18] In early December 1994, Russian Foreign
Minister Kozyrev disappointed Clinton administration and allied NATO
governments by rejecting immediate partner status for Russia, and
President Yeltsin publicly warned against extending NATO membership to former members of the Warsaw Pact.

Still, Russian expectations for special treatment among former
Soviet states are not unrealistic, with or without Russian partnership
with NATO. Russia expects, according to its approved military doctrine
of December 1993, to assume special responsibilities for pacifying its
near abroad of contiguous former Soviet states. Russia also defines as
an aggressive act any significant and averse change in the military
correlation of forces between Moscow and its neighbors, and equally
construed as aggressive are states bordering Russia that open their
frontiers to anti-Russian military presence.[19] In 1994, Russia still
deployed troops in all other 14 former Soviet republics; some were there
on peacekeeping missions, so described, and others as the result of
various basing agreements. The most significant Russian troop
deployments outside the Russian federation as of mid-1994, including
self-described peacekeeping forces, are summarized in Table 4.5.

Meanwhile, NATO reserves the right to reconstitute traditional
deterrence and defense capabilities should a newer version of the older
Soviet threat, in the form of Russian imperialism, rear its head. The
reservation is logical insofar as only NATO could take collective action
against such a contingency. The likelihood of this development fortunately is not very high.[20] Russia's armed forces will have all that they
can do in the next half decade to meet basic training and personnel
recruitment and retention objectives. The possibility of a renewed
Russian march on Prague, Warsaw, or Budapest can be dismissed as a
serious NATO and U.S. military planning contingency unless and until
two things, at least, transpire. First, U.S.-Russian relations would have

TABLE 4.4
Partnership for Peace Training Exercises, 1994

Name, Date of Exercise	Purpose	Participants
Cooperative Bridge 94 (September 12–16, 1994)	Company- and platoon-size units training on individual and unit peacekeeping tasks; develop common understanding of operational procedures and improve ability of NATO and PFP to work together in peace operations	Bulgaria, Czech Republic, Denmark, Germany, Italy, Lithuania, Poland, Romania, Slovakia, the Netherlands, Ukraine, United Kingdom, and United States (about 600 soldiers)
Cooperative Venture 94 (September 28–October 7, 1994)	Train maritime forces in command and control tactics and basic maritime procedures; train to conduct peacekeeping, humanitarian, and search and rescue maritime operations (exercises held in Skagerrak area of North Sea and in Norwegian Sea)	Belgium, Canada, Denmark, Germany, Italy, Lithuania, the Netherlands, Norway, Poland, Russia, Spain, Sweden, United Kingdom, United States (10 NATO participants and 4 cooperation PFP states, 15 ships)
Cooperative Spirit (October 21–28, 1994)	First joint training exercise held on Allied NATO territory under PFP (in Netherlands); platoon- and company-size units training in peacekeeping operations	Canada, Czech Republic, Estonia, Germany, Lithuania, the Netherlands, Poland, Slovakia, Sweden, Ukraine, United Kingdom, United States (approximately 1,000 personnel)

Source: NATO Review, October 1994, p. 24.

TABLE 4.5
Russian Troop Deployments in the Near Abroad as of Summer 1994

Armenia	9,000 troops on Turkish and Iranian borders
Azerbaijan	500 military guards at oil installations
Belarus	25,000–30,000 troops
Georgia	5,000 troops at five bases and three ports; about 18,000 temporary peacekeepers sent in 1994
Kazakhstan	1,000 troops guarding nuclear missiles and Baikonur space center
Kyrgyzstan	3,500 troops
Moldova	5,000 peacekeeping troops sent in 1994
Tajikstan	24,000 troops on Afghan border in support of government in Dushanbe (includes 6,000 troops designated by Moscow in 1994 as peacekeeping forces)
Turkmenistan	15,000 troops on Afghan and Iranian borders
Ukraine	15,000 sailors in Black Sea fleet; 2,000 guards from 43rd Missile Army
Uzbekistan	5,000 troops

Source: Arms Control Today, Factfile, October 1994, p. 25.

to turn as sour as they were during the height of the Cold War tension. Second, constitutional government in Russia would have to be subverted by a military-nationalist junta that seeks to cure Russia's domestic turbulence by administering shock treatment in the form of foreign aggression.

Whatever the fate of constitutional government in future Russia, a turn of U.S.-Russian relations toward Cold War hostility is improbable, for reasons apart from their geopolitical stakes in Europe. There is no ideological propeller driving communism and capitalism against one another with the assumption that one economic system must eventually subside. Future relations between even ultranationalist Russians and Americans will be obstructed, if they are obstructed, by more concrete and less philosophical matters: U.S. aid to Russia for economic and disarmament support, U.S. reactions to any Russian use of force to contain aggression originating in its near abroad, and U.S. willingness to include Russia in NATO or in some Eurasian security framework in which confidence-building measures and arms control proceed in a businesslike manner, despite the inevitable diplomatic disputes. In short, Russia will expect to be treated as China is now treated; without prejudgment as to her domestic institutions and crises, and only on the basis of her reliability as a trading and negotiating partner in foreign policy.

CONCLUSION

Russia's peacekeeping potential is considerable if her economic, political, and military organizational acts can be gotten together.

Russia's geographical location offers numerous opportunities for involvement in multinational or unilateral peacekeeping, including opportunities in the former Soviet republics adjacent to Russia's borders and now teeming with civil strife or irredentism. Some of Russia's peace operations in the near abroad may be self-serving, and some may entail the risk of further entrapment in low-intensity conflict for wary military professionals burned by the memory of Afghanistan.

NOTES

1. For one scenario of joint U.S.-Russian peacekeeping, see A. V. Demurenko, V. K. Kolpanov, and Timothy L. Thomas, "Peacekeeping: A Joint Russian-US Operational Scenario," *Journal of Slavic Military Studies* 6 (September 1994): 522–37.

2. Boutros Boutros-Ghali, *An Agenda for Peace: Preventive Diplomacy, Peacemaking and Peace-keeping* (New York: United Nations, 1992), defines the first three functions. Peace enforcement is defined in other studies; see Martha Bills et al., *Options for U.S. Military Support to the United Nations* (Washington, D.C.: Center for Strategic and International Studies, 1992), p. 3. Other sources use the terms "peacemaking" and "peace enforcement" synonymously to refer to Chapter VII type operations. U.S. Army doctrine divides types of peace operations into support to diplomacy (peacemaking, peacebuilding, and preventive diplomacy), peacekeeping, and peace enforcement (Headquarters, Department of the Army, *FM 100-23, Peace Operations*, Version #7 [draft] [Washington, D.C.: Department of the Army, 1994], p. ii).

3. Bills et al., *Options for U.S. Military Support to the United Nations*, p. 9.

4. Figures in this section are from Congress of the U.S. Congressional Budget Office, *Enhancing U.S. Security through Foreign Aid* (Washington, D.C.: Congressional Budget Office, 1994), pp. 31–32.

5. *Arms Control Today*, Factfile, October 1994, p. 25.

6. For U.S. foreign policy options in postcommunist Russia, see Mark Medish, "Russia: Lost and Found," *Daedalus* (Summer 1994): 63–90, esp. pp. 86–87.

7. Stephen M. Meyer, "The Military," in *After the Soviet Union: From Empire to Nations*, eds. Timothy J. Colton and Robert Legvold (New York: W. W. Norton, 1992), pp. 113–46.

8. An assessment of the Zhirinovskiy phenomenon is provided in Jacob W. Kipp, "The Russian Elections and the Future of Military-to-Military Contacts: The Specter of Zhirinovsky," in *Does Russian Democracy Have a Future?*, eds. Stephen J. Blank and Earl H. Tilfor, Jr. (Carlisle, Pa.: U.S. Army War College, Strategic Studies Institute, 1994), pp. 43–82.

9. For diverse perspectives on civil-military relations in the Soviet era, see Roman Kolkowicz, *The Soviet Military and the Communist Party* (Princeton, N.J.: Princeton University Press, 1967); Timothy Colton, *Commissars, Commanders and Civilian Authority: The Structure of Soviet Military Politics* (Cambridge, Mass.: Harvard University Press, 1979); Harriet Fast Scott and William F. Scott, *Soviet Military Doctrine: Continuity, Formulation, and Dissemination* (Boulder, Colo.: Westview Press, 1988); Thomas M. Nichols, *The Sacred Cause: Civil-Military Conflict over Soviet National Security, 1917–1992* (Ithaca, N.Y.: Cornell University Press, 1993).

10. Richard Rose, "Getting By Without Government: Everyday Life in Russia," *Daedalus* (Summer 1994): 41–62, esp. p. 53.

11. For analysis and assessment of post-1993 Russian military influence, see Brian D. Taylor, "Russian Civil-Military Relations After the October Uprising,"

Survival (Spring 1994): 3–29; Thomas M. Nichols, "The Impact of the Russian Elections on Civil-Military Relations," in *Does Russian Democracy Have a Future?*, eds. Stephen J. Blank and Earl H. Tilford, Jr. (Carlisle Barracks, Pa.: U.S. Army War College, 1994), pp. 83–110. Taylor contends that the Russian military would prefer depoliticization and that one reason for their support of Yeltsin in the 1993 crisis was the ineptness with which Khasbulatov and Rutskoi tried to involve elements of the military on their side. Nichols argues that the influence of the Russian military in politics is waxing and that many officers favor a renewed Russian imperial state.

12.   Fred Hiatt, "Russia Toughens Military Doctrine," *Washington Post* news service in *Philadelphia Inquirer*, November 4, 1943, p. A1. In fact, the military-security organs in Russia have been politicized, off and on, since the time of Peter the Great, if by politicization we mean a sense of institutional or corporate professionalism apart from loyalty to the regime, a willingness or ability to block political initiatives deemed adversarial to military institutional growth and development, and a doctrinal theory of war that was not necessarily consistent with the political proclivities of the leadership. See Hugh Seton-Watson, *The Decline of Imperial Russia, 1855–1914* (New York: Frederick A. Praeger, 1966), and Nichols, *The Sacred Cause, passim.*

13.   "Russia's Armed Forces: The Threat That Was," *The Economist*, August 28, 1993, pp. 17–19.

14.   *Philadelphia Inquirer*, November 30, 1994, p. A14.

15.   For information on Border troops, I am grateful to Graham H. Turbiville, Jr., Foreign Military Studies Office, Ft. Leavenworth, Kansas, e-mail communication, November 23, 1994.

16.   Ibid.

17.   Gebhardt von Moltke, "Building a Partnership for Peace," *NATO Review* 42 (June 1994): 3–6.

18.   "NATO Pact: Historic Step for Europe," *The Moscow Times*, June 26, 1994, p. 25.

19.   James F. Holcomb, "The Implications of Russia's Military Doctrine," in *Russia's New Doctrine: Two Views*, James F. Holcomb and Michael M. Boll, eds. (Carlisle Barracks, Pa.: U.S. Army War College, Strategic Studies Institute, 1994), pp. 1–11.

20.   Richard H. Ullman, *Securing Europe* (Princeton, N.J.: Princeton University Press, 1991), p. 42 and *passim.*

5

Doing Away with Nukes: Can Russia Get a Fair Deal?

During the Cold War years, the U.S. and Soviet strategic nuclear arsenals were of such size and diversity that more than enough weapons existed to fulfill the requirements for any mission assigned by policy makers. The large and diverse arsenals eventually simplified theory, too. The early years of the nuclear age did challenge theorists to think through anew some important problems of strategy and defense, including the very concept of deterrence.[1] By the mid-1960s, original thinking on the subject of nuclear deterrence strategy had largely played out in the academic and the policy arenas.[2] Successor generations nibbled at the edges of seminal works by Bernard Brodie, Thomas Schelling, Albert Wohlstetter, and other giants of the first half of the Cold War.[3]

The end of Cold War and the improved relations between the United States and Russia/Commonwealth of Independent States (CIS) have opened the door to strategic nuclear force reductions even more drastic than those agreed to under the Strategic Arms Reduction Treaty (START). Presidents Bush and Yeltsin have signed the START II Agreement, involving a commitment to reduce the U.S. and Russian force loadings to a range of 3,500–3,000 strategic nuclear warheads for each side. Expert testimony and various studies have suggested that future U.S. and Russian forces might be reduced in the near term to 3,000 warheads and ultimately to 1,000, assuming favorable political conditions

I am grateful to Michael Mazaar and David Tarr for stimulating my thinking on this topic and to Kosta Tsipis for sharing MIT research reports on topics of mutual interest. They bear no responsibility for arguments herein. Portions of this chapter draw upon Stephen J. Cimbala, "From Deterrence to Denuclearization: U.S. and Russian Nuclear Force Reduction Options," *The Journal of Slavic Military Studies* 7 (September 1994): 421–42 and Stephen J. Cimbala, "Deterrence Stability with Smaller Forces: Prospects and Problems," *Journal of Peace Research* 32 (February 1995), 65–78, with permission.

continue between Moscow and Washington and provided that other major nuclear powers follow suit with proportional reductions.[4]

Getting from the Cold War condition of mandated deterrence to a security community in which deterrence is no longer necessary involves a way station through phased nuclear force reductions and minimum deterrence. Can this way station be managed successfully? This chapter compares the nuclear deterrence stability of notional START I, prospective START II, and various hypothetical U.S. and Russian post–Cold War deployments, down to 1,000 warheads for each side. I discuss the viability of these deterrents for different missions, and I offer conclusions about the implications of these findings for future nuclear forces planning. The findings also have implications for the potential control of nuclear weapons spread.

APPROACH

This study uses notional forces for the United States and Russia/CIS (assumed to have inherited provisionally the strategic nuclear forces of the former USSR, although I make no further assumption about permanent political durability) at five different levels in order to develop indicators of strategic force viability under various scenarios. The five force levels discussed here are

the U.S. and Russian/CIS strategic nuclear forces adjusted for compatibility with the START I guidelines and according to the Bush modernization plan for the United States;
both sides limited to 6,000 actual RVs (re-entry vehicles)
both sides limited to 3,000;
both sides limited to 2,000;
both sides limited to 1,000.

The force structures used for the 6,000, the 3,000, and the 1,000 thresholds were adapted from those developed by the Congressional Budget Office (CBO) for its analysis of future U.S. strategic and arms control options.[5] In addition, a second 1,000 level notional force described by Ted Corbin, Arsen Hajian, and Kosta Tsipis was used for comparison with the 1,000 CBO case, because that case represents the smallest force sizes examined here.[6] These forces have the attractive properties for this analysis that they were designed to provide roughly symmetrical, survivable, and flexible force deployments for each side, maintaining land, sea, and air based components of their strategic nuclear forces as multiple hedges against nuclear strategic surprise. I generated a 2,000 RV case of my own, also emphasizing survivable and roughly symmetrical deployments. Finally, a sixth case is provided by the START II forces likely to be deployed by each side if that agreement is fully carried out. Those forces are tested here under conditions similar to the other, and mostly hypothetical, forces.[7]

To determine whether these or other forces would provide for stable deterrence, it is necessary to subject the forces to dynamic exchange modeling. Dynamic exchange models allow the user to approximate the kinds of targeting decisions and war strategies that military planners could be tasked to develop by their political leaderships. Leaders would lack confidence in their deterrents if, for example, their general staffs reported that their forces were first strike vulnerable. However, vulnerability is a matter of degree, and assessments of vulnerability, such as the debate over the U.S. intercontinental ballistic missile (ICBM) "window of vulnerability" during the latter 1970s and early 1980s, do not always take into account the diverse operational environments of U.S. or Russian forces. In addition, missions for which forces are tasked help to determine the extent to which force survivability is important and the kinds of forces that need to survive.

Analysts have generally supposed that the side striking first in a nuclear war would launch primarily counterforce attacks in order to destroy the other side's strategic retaliatory forces. It is less consensual or obvious what the retaliator, however war has begun, is supposed to do in response. Some have argued that proportional nuclear response to the scale and character of the attack is the preferred course of action. Others have said that only massive nuclear response against a wide variety of target sets is appropriate. Students of U.S. nuclear strategic planning have noted that until the 1970s, the U.S. Single Integrated Operations Plan (SIOP) provided few, if any, options short of massive retaliatory response. Beginning with the "Schlesinger doctrine" promulgated in 1974, U.S. declaratory policy acknowledged a need for more selective nuclear strategic options well below the level of massive response, including limited counterforce options. Although academic communities and arms control advocates expressed considerable skepticism about limited strategic options, U.S. Department of Defense planning guidance from Nixon through Reagan called for an expanded menu of selective nuclear options using U.S. and allied North Atlantic Treaty Organization (NATO) strategic and theater nuclear forces.[8]

Despite considerable interest during those years in selective nuclear options, no U.S. administration departed from the bedrock of assured retaliation or assured destruction as the most important mission for retaliatory forces. The arguments subsequent to McNamara were, for the most part, about what else forces and their associated command and control systems might be expected to do.[9] However, every administration since Eisenhower's maintained that second strike capability based on the ability to inflict unacceptable retaliatory damage against Soviet society was the bedrock of stable deterrence. This policy consensus on the bottom line of mutual deterrence at the declaratory level did not resolve disputes about the operational definitions for assured destruction or unacceptable damage. Subsequent analysis will provide measurements for those criteria to assist in the estimation of viability for various force levels and configurations.

ASSURED DESTRUCTION AND ASSURED RETALIATION

Assured destruction as defined by McNamara equated to 200 equivalent megatons (EMT) inflicted on Soviet value targets even after U.S. forces had absorbed a surprise attack. McNamara's estimates were that 200 EMT delivered by 400 warheads would result in either prompt fatalities among 25 to 33 percent of the Soviet population and the destruction of about two-thirds of its industrial capacity or prompt fatalities of 20 to 25 percent of the Soviet population and the destruction of 50 to 75 percent of its industrial capacity.[10] Assured destruction was not necessarily the same as unacceptable retaliation. What was acceptable to the first striker might not be known by the retaliator, and vice versa. U.S. analysts admitted that U.S. knowledge of Soviet leaders' definitions for unacceptable damage was subject to uncertainty. Although models of U.S. abilities to destroy various classes of targets could be developed, Cold War Politburo leaders' scale of values for those target classes was not available except by guesswork.[11] During the Carter administration, a major policy review concluded that Soviet leaders valued most of their military forces and leadership survival. Both Carter and Reagan defense policy makers, therefore, argued that these target sets should receive high priority, although not necessarily greatest time urgency, in U.S. nuclear strategic target planning. These assumptions about Soviet valuation of objectives would not necessarily carry over into a democratic Russia or CIS, and the profound transformation in the former Soviet military, subsequent to the demise of the USSR, makes the relationship between leaders and followers in Moscow very different from Cold War contexts.

The difference between assured destruction as defined by McNamara and assured retaliation are at least two-sided. First, assured destruction attempted to establish a metric for defining the optimal delivery of weapons on urban and industrial target classes. Weapons and destruction above the threshold suggested by this metric were superfluous. Assured retaliation prescribes no particular metric.[12] The assured retaliation criterion has been used by Pentagon planners, independent analysts, and critics of U.S. nuclear deterrence strategy. A second difference between assured destruction and assured retaliation is that the latter concept begs the question of how much retaliatory damage is unacceptable to a first striker. Theorists have attempted to get at this by defining "unacceptable damage" at various thresholds. One definition, widely cited in the literature and used here, was provided by McGeorge Bundy. Bundy's guideline was that ten one-megaton equivalent warheads directed at ten cities would constitute a "disaster beyond history."[13] Bundy's definition for unacceptable damage and McNamara's for assured destruction are used in this chapter, as explained below.

Lower levels of U.S. and Russian forces disarmed of most of their START-accountable prompt, hard target counterforce still could be tasked for countermilitary missions by military planners in the early stages of any conflict. Forces remaining after countermilitary and counterforce exchanges had been concluded would be the available assured destruction or unacceptable retaliation forces. In Kosta Tsipis' terminology, planners have wanted forces that were "stratolytic," capable of carrying out missions against opposed forces and other military targets, in addition to forces that were "econolytic," or capable of destroying social and economic value.[14] One should not be deluded that counterforce attacks can be "surgical" and somehow avoid creating unprecedented, and unacceptable except for lunatic leaders, levels of destruction. Thus, there is some merit to the admonition by von Hippel, Levi, Postol, and Daugherty that "it is the very reliance on counterforce strategies that blocks stabilizing nuclear-force reductions beyond those currently being considered in START negotiations."[15] It is equally valid to recognize, on the other hand, the purposeful distinction between preserving flexible counterforce capabilities for deterrence and engaging in a counterforce potlatch, of the kind supported in some Cold War U.S. policy pronouncements, in order to establish "escalation dominance" or military victory if deterrence fails.[16]

The problem of preserving forces capable of assured retaliation defined as assured destruction, unaccept-able damage, or in some other fashion seemed trivial in the days of U.S. and Soviet Cold War forces that exceeded 12,000 and 10,000 strategic nuclear warheads, respectively. Although specialists understandably were concerned about targeting decisions, at such force levels, great redundancy almost guaranteed a wide variety of targeting options for responsive forces under any conditions.[17] As force levels are reduced from their Cold War levels and even well below START-accountable peaks, the problem of maintaining an assured retaliatory capability after absorbing a nuclear first strike cannot be taken as automatically solved. Smaller but equal forces do reduce the level of destruction attendant to any war actually fought by those forces, compared with larger forces. This is a welcome by-product of nuclear force reductions, but with nuclear weapons, the result matters only if the smaller forces serve as viable deterrents. Smaller forces that are less survivable than the forces deployed by the other side, even under benign political conditions, are less reliable guarantors of stable deterrence than forces that are symmetrically survivable.

The ability of the United States and Russia to guarantee survivable forces and assured retaliation at lower U.S. and Russian levels of warheads and equivalent megatonnage is also related to the two countries' efforts to prevent nuclear proliferation. On one hand, each side's Cold War forces dwarfed those of any competitors by comparison, and the Soviet and U.S. forces established a nuclear condominium between Washington and Moscow in favor of a bipolar strategic nuclear world. On the other hand, those larger arsenals were cited by potential proliferators as evidence that the Cold War nuclear superpowers were not willing to abstain from nuclear use in the same sense that Moscow and Washington were demanding of current nonnuclear states. This issue of U.S. and Russian examples for others to follow has already been cited as an agenda item when the nonproliferation treaty comes up for renewal in 1995. It is thought by some experts on the problem of nuclear proliferation that further reductions in U.S. and Russian arsenals would encourage both nuclear supplies and potential proliferators to pay greater attention to the nonproliferation regime established by the treaty.[18]

Arms control and disarmament perspectives on the best ways to reduce U.S. and Russian strategic nuclear forces may follow different prescribed paths. I emphasize central tendencies among disparate views here: there are important perspectives on nuclear force reductions that draw insight from both traditions. Disarmament advocates assume that the smaller the number of weapons, the more stable is the relationship between the two states. An ideal condition for proponents of disarmament would be the elimination of nuclear weapons entirely from the arsenals of the United States, Russia, and other states.

Arms control advocates focus more on the near term management of deterrence stability than on the longer run objective of general and complete disarmament. Arms control proposals emphasize stable deterrence as a worthwhile end in itself and one that is highly dependent on the circumstances of force attributes and military strategy. Disarmers have little or no faith in deterrence even at drastically reduced levels of nuclear weapons, and some can draw on the arms control literature to support the argument that deterrence failure is more likely with smaller forces than between states with larger forces. Arms control emphasizes the elimination of weapons that are militarily superfluous for deterrence and supports the argument that the ability of forces to carry out their essential missions is necessary for deterrence stability. Disarmers consider almost all nuclear weapons politically and militarily superfluous, and a disarmament oriented perspective on minimum or finite deterrence would not be satisfied with freezing forces at low, but still significant, numbers of warheads and delivery vehicles.

This study clearly favors the arms controller's perspective to the disarmer's. Nevertheless, it concedes to the disarmer the recognition that arms control is a partial approach to stability that relies on the management of nuclear deterrent relationships, not on the abolition of nuclear weapons or nuclear crisis management. The dependency of stable nuclear deterrence on weapons that have survivable retaliatory capabilities is not the only dependency on which the avoidance of war in the nuclear age has rested. Equally important have been the abilities of the U.S. and Soviet Cold War leaderships to avoid or manage nuclear crises. The dynamics of Cold War nuclear crisis management have suggested to some that it was a very fragile enterprise that might easily have spilled over into war.[19] Arms control literature can draw on Cold War experience of the nuclear superpowers to argue that nuclear crisis management was successful, avoiding any actual outbreak of war between Moscow and Washington or between their respective allies in NATO and in the Warsaw Pact. Skeptics can point to the gory details of nuclear crisis management, including episodes from the Cuban missile crisis, to illustrate that even great force redundancy and assured survivability for U.S. forces did not alleviate policy makers' concerns about inadvertent escalation and nuclear war.[20]

The disarmer's pessimism and the arms controller's optimism about nuclear crisis management are pertinent here in order to remind us that prominent military strategists as well as lay people will never accept nuclear deterrence as anything but a way station to a nuclear disarmed world. Arguments against continued dependency on nuclear deterrence for the avoidance of war, implying the irrelevancy of criteria for measuring the adequacy of nuclear retaliatory forces, have been forcefully presented in a number of academic and policy studies.[21] Getting to "nuclear zero" will have to be accomplished by means of a gradual rather than an immediate and drastic elimination of U.S. and Russian forces, barring political developments even more turbulent than those of the past few years. On that assumption that gradualism is the preferred approach to nuclear arms reductions, even leaders who favor stable deterrence as an interim condition only must grapple with force structure and targeting decisions during that interim.

It can be expected that, as the normalization of political relations between the United States and Russia and the absorption of Russia into a pan-European security community take place, the operation of U.S. and Russian nuclear forces will be based less on the worst case of nuclear strategic surprise. Future U.S. nuclear forces will, like general purpose forces if present political trends continue, be planned around contingency operations of uncertain locale and duration. The already apparent changes in the European political landscape allow us to foresee the time when rapid and massive response to nuclear strategic surprise will no longer drive U.S. force structure or war plans. The more benign political environment makes it less imperative to operate large numbers of forces in a peacetime condition of quick reaction. Warning and assessment can be more fault tolerant, and response patterns need not be frozen into a simple menu of preselected options but can be varied for specific, if unforeseeable, scenarios of crisis management and deterrence stability.

In the simulations that are summarized below, certain levels of alert are assigned to U.S. and Russian forces based on 1991 published estimates of system reliability and vulnerability. These estimates from public sources obviously are subject to great uncertainty. Nevertheless, the essence of the difference between generated and day to day alert can be modeled with acceptable accuracy. The issue is whether survivability to inflict unacceptable damage or assured retaliation or survivability for the other missions nuclear forces might be assigned is affected by the alert statuses of otherwise symmetrical and basically survivable forces.

DATA

In order to obtain a clearer fix on the extent to which meaningful differences in survivable systems exist, we calculated a measure of Relative Force Advantage (RFA) for those cases in which the forces of both sides or those of the attacker only were on generated alert. In other words, the cases of two-sided day to day alerts were excluded. This left 24 cases: 12 with both sides' forces posed for first strike or prompt retaliation and 12 with the attacker at high readiness and the defender on day to day alert. For each case, the RFA is calculated as a ratio of the U.S. surviving forces to the Russian surviving forces. A ratio of unity means that the United States and Russia have equal remaining forces, a ratio greater than unity favors the United States by the stated number, and a ratio less than unity favors the Russians.

Each RFA is calculated by adding the square root of the surviving EMT to the number of remaining warheads for each side. Then the Russian EMT-warhead figure is divided into the U.S. EMT-warhead figure to produce the measure of RFA, stated as the U.S. percent of Russian forces. For example, an RFA of 5.0 means that the RFA of surviving U.S. forces compared with Russian forces is 500 percent, or five times as large. The square root of the EMT was chosen because EMT numbers get large very quickly even at relatively small force levels. The results of this calculation for all cases involving one- or two-sided generated alerts are summarized in Tables 5.1 and 5.2.

If stability at significantly lower than START II levels is conceivable, as tables 5.1 and 5.2 suggest, then the START II agreement offers considerable insurance against first strike vulnerability even under the most pessimistic assumptions about force and command operations. Corroboration of this is provided by an analysis performed by James J. Tritten, in the Department of National Security Studies at the U.S. Naval Postgraduate School. Tritten compared the postattack outcomes for 1992 U.S. and Russian forces with the outcomes following exchanges with fully treaty compliant START II forces in the year 2003. Table 5.3 summarizes his results.

TABLE 5.1
Both Sides on Generated Alert: Relative Force Advantage
        (as ratio of U.S. to Russian surviving forces)

Forces	First Striker	Relative Force Advantage	Advantage
START I	Russia	3.78	United States
START I	United States	1.08	United States
6,000	Russia	2.82	United States
6,000	United States	1.07	United States
3,000	Russia	0.81	Russia
3,000	United States	0.70	Russia
2,000	Russia	3.12	United States
2,000	United States	0.22	Russia
1,000 (CBO)	Russia	0.94	Russia
1,000 (CBO)	United States	0.35	Russia
1,000 (Corbin et al.)	Russia	1.52	United States
1,000 (Corbin et al.)	United States	0.46	Russia
START II	Russia	5.56	United States
START II	United States	1.26	United States

Source: Compiled by author.

TABLE 5.2
Attackers on Generated Alert: Relative Force Advantage
        (as ratio of U.S. to Russian surviving forces)

Forces	First Striker	Relative Force Advantage	Advantage
START I	Russia	2.79	United States
START I	United States	65.11	United States
6,000	Russia	1.76	United States
6,000	United States	24.30	United States
3,000	Russia	0.53	Russia
3,000	United States	6.38	United States
2,000	Russia	1.40	United States
2,000	United States	15.43	United States
1,000 (CBO)	Russia	0.55	Russia
1,000 (CBO)	United States	16.20	United States
1,000 (Corbin et al.)	Russia	1.11	United States*
1,000 (Corbin et al.)	United States	6.19	United States
START II	Russia	2.65	United States
START II	United States	13.84	United States

*Corbin et al. 1,000 force with Russian first strike results in survivable warheads favoring United States and survivable EMT favoring Russians as a result of the kinds of forces deployed. My composite measure gives more credit for warheads than for EMT, perhaps overstating the U.S. advantage when the difference is so close as to appear nonexistent.

Source: Compiled by author.

TABLE 5.3
Postattack Outcomes of U.S.-Russian Exchanges: 1992 and START II Forces

Summary Item	1992 Outcomes	START II Outcomes
Total Russian deliverable warheads	1,401	844
Total Russian deliverable EMT	618	405
Deliverable Russian reserve warheads	668	361
Deliverable Russian reserve EMT	272	158
Percent deliverable Russian reserve warheads	0.48	0.43
Percent deliverable Russian reserve EMT	0.44	0.39
Total U.S. deliverable warheads	2,222	1,060
Total U.S. deliverable EMT	618	350
Deliverable U.S. reserve warheads	1,087	441
Deliverable U.S. reserve EMT	277	138
Percent deliverable U.S. reserve warheads	0.49	0.41
Percent deliverable Russian reserve EMT	0.45	0.39
Correlation of deliverable warheads	1.59–1*	1.26–1*
Correlation of deliverable EMT	1–1**	1.15–1†
Correlation of reserve warheads	1.63–1*	1.22–1*
Correlation of reserve EMT	1.02–1*	1.02–1†

*United States
†Russia
**Even

Source: James J. Tritten, U.S. Naval Postgraduate School, unpublished data used in classroom exercises. I am grateful to Tritten for permission to cite this material. He is not responsible for any use made of it here.

This analysis and my own presume that operating tempos for forces and command and control viability remain about the same for U.S. and Russian forces throughout the remainder of the 1990s as they were for 1991–92 U.S. and Soviet forces. Given reasonably favorable prognoses for force survivability on both sides, it requires only a fraction of the peak Cold War forces to establish credible deterrence. The situation with regard to extended deterrence, of attack on allies, is not explored here. Clearly, however, the two sides in the START II agreement have made a commitment to reduce arsenal redundancy and the risks of accidental/inadvertent war at the price of some targeting flexibility and redundancy for extended deterrence missions. Russian extended deterrence is, in all likelihood, going to be restricted to the use of conventional forces for controlling the effects of outbreaks of ethnic and national separatism within Russia and, perhaps, states bordering Russia. Opportunities may present themselves in the Abkhazia region of Georgia, in the Nagorno-Karabakh disputed region of Azerbaijan, in the trans-Dniester part of Moldova, and elsewhere.

CONCLUSIONS

The present study makes plausible but modestly favorable assumptions about the future performance attributes of U.S. and Russian strategic nuclear forces based on present force attributes. It then asks whether smaller forces remain survivable, after a minimum number of counterforce attacks, in order to guarantee either assured destruction or unacceptable retaliation. The results suggest that even if U.S. and Russian strategic nuclear forces undergo major, symmetrical reductions in size, the impact on the true survivability of their deterrents will be asymmetrical. At very low force sizes, Russia will be quite vulnerable to strategic attack without warning if there is no future force modernization and operational rethinking of the kind that Russia may be unwilling or unable to undertake. In some political environments, U.S-Russian nuclear deterrence may no longer matter, but in other environments, the sensitivity of strategic stability to Russian military stasis could threaten progress toward a stable world of no, or few, nuclear weapons.

The evidence presented here shows that projected nuclear forces, even those reduced in size drastically, have the survivable countervalue and flexible countermilitary power to maintain stable deterrence provided that reduced force components perform about as well as their 1990 predecessors would have. In the U.S. case, the assumption seems safe; for Russia, it is less certain, given domestic political and economic uncertainties. Alert rates and operational procedures of the various force components become progressively more important as force levels are reduced from 6,000 down to 1,000. As a study for Lawrence Livermore Laboratory and the Brookings Institution noted, at levels below 6,000 RV, "the survivability and alert rates of the forces become more and more important if a disarming first strike is to remain an impossibility and if there are to be enough residual forces to carry out the specified military missions and maintain reserves."[22] Russian reductions to 6,000 START-accountable warheads and 1,600 delivery vehicles over a seven-year period was most advisable; however, additional reductions to 4,500 or 4,700 warheads were not acceptable until the START treaty was fully implemented over a seven-year period.

It is apparent from these simulations that Russia faces a significant challenge if it wishes to retain a highly survivable and operationally flexible strategic nuclear deterrent force over the next several decades. START and post-START reductions will tilt the balance of nuclear strategic deterrent capability toward weapons systems operated with far greater survivability and lethality during the Cold War years by the United States than by the Soviet Union. Russia inherits from the Soviet Union a tradition of bomber forces entirely subject to destruction and submarines almost entirely vulnerable in port under conditions of normal peacetime readiness. Of course, Russian design bureaus and general staffs of the future are not necessarily fated to follow past Soviet practice. Investments can be withdrawn from ICBM modernization and devoted to bomber and submarine improvements, including improvements in the survivability of both types of forces.

To get the United States and Russia much below 3,000 warheads, one must take into account the modernization plans of Britain, France, and China.[23] This is not an issue of proliferation in the traditional sense, that is, horizontal proliferation from the nuclear haves to the have-nots; these states already deploy nuclear weapons of intercontinental range. The British and French systems together will provide, as a high estimate, some 640 survivable RVs by the mid-1990s if present modernization plans in both countries are played out.[24] Possible economies of scale and joint operations might be considered by London and Paris, with the aims of restraining both expenditures for military procurement and arms races. However, the future modernization plans of China are uncertain, and China has indicated no interest in coordinating modernization plans with those of other nuclear powers. Because limited ballistic missile defense (BMD) systems deployed by the United States or Russia (alone or jointly) would be intended for the mission of protection against accidental or deliberate small attacks, other nuclear armed states may conclude that BMD deployments are intended to restrain their deterrents while leaving those of Washington and Moscow in a position of international primacy.

The Gulf War of 1991 left no doubt in the minds of many analysts that conventional high technology weapons could displace nuclear weapons for many assignments and with obviously less collateral damage.[25] Precision guided munitions and improvements in sensing and information processing now make possible the destruction of strategic targets to the depth of an opponent's defenses. Russian reflections on the outcome of Desert Storm draw exactly this conclusion about possible future competency of strategic conventional offensives.[26] It is also the case that the total withdrawal of Russian forces from Eastern Europe and the transformation of NATO into a more political than military organization could open the door to a pan-European security structure in which nonexistent threats of aggression are buttressed by commitments to nonoffensive defenses. In such an environment, extended nuclear deterrence of the kind provided by U.S. and Soviet forces during the Cold War years would be unnecessary. U.S. nuclear weapons could serve only as forces of last resort in cases of nuclear attack on the U.S. homeland.

The argument here, that diminishing deterrence is a discernible stage during which force posture stability is significant, also implies something about the proliferation of nuclear weapons. Some U.S. analysts have contended that well-managed or -contained nuclear proliferation, even in Europe, could be more stable than a regional or global power setting with fewer or no nuclear forces.[27] This variant of 'neorealism" mistakes the stability of nuclear deterrence for the rules of the game operative in conventional deterrence.[28] In conventional deterrence, according to John J. Mearsheimer, attackers are loath to strike if they anticipate that a protracted and costly military stalemate will result.[29] This rational/utility-maximizing view of leaders' decision making in conventional deterrence situations works because there is some potentially meaningful relationship, based on historical precedent, between prewar estimates and postwar outcomes of military conflict. No comparable experience exists for nuclear weapons.

The second unrealistic expectation of proliferation-permissive neorealists is the expectation that future nuclear armed adversaries will behave as responsibly as U.S. and Soviet leaders eventually learned to. Optimism about nuclear learning spillover from the Cold War into a more proliferation-permissive environment is unjustified: issues of command and control, nuclear weapons custody, and force operations management are cultural as well as technical, and they cannot be transferred across states and regimes as easily as equipment can.[30] A third reason for lack of transferability for Cold War nuclear stasis into the new world order is that Cold War stability was overdetermined: bipolarity and memories of the costs of World War II supported fears of nuclear catastrophe to restrain leaders and military planners.[31]

The "good news" is that, regardless of relative performance characteristics, neither the United States nor Russia can circumvent the prospect of unprecedented and unacceptable societal damage, even after striking first, with the actual START II or with other hypothetical forces shown here. There is still no fightable or winnable nuclear war. On the positive side, minimum deterrent forces do away with strategic largesse that might invite attack on itself or raise policy makers' misplaced faith in nuclear flexibility. On the negative side, minimum deterrent forces rapidly deteriorate into city busting and other strictly countervalue forces, which might inhibit leaders from making credible threats based on limited first use. As the text already suggests, minimum deterrence is on balance the right way to go, but it raises important policy-planning issues that until now have been smothered under the weight of force ponderosity and doctrinal complacency.

APPENDIX

Forces in the Analysis[32]

START I Forces
> U.S. Forces
>> ICBMs
>>> A. 500 Small ICBMs (SICBMs) (1 RV)
>>> B. 316 MM III (1 RV)

  C. 50 MX (10 RV)

  D. 35 MM IIIa (3 RV)

 SLBMs

  A. 18 Trident submarines with 24 Trident D-5 missiles (8 RV)

 Bombers — Bombers carry air launched cruise missiles, gravity bombs, and short range attack missiles in different combinations. The above sources were used to estimate appropriate loadings for each platform. No short range attack missiles were assigned to Russian bombers.

  A. 75 B-2 (Stealth)

  B. 95 B-52H air-launched cruise missiles (ALCMs)

  C. 97 B-1B

Russian/CIS Forces

 ICBMs

  A. 60 SS-24 (10 RV)

 SLBMs

  A. 10 Delta IV SSBN with 16 SSN23/boat (4 RV)

  B. 6 Delta III SSBN with 16 SSN18/boat (3 RV)

  C. 6 Typhoon SSBN with 20 SSN20/boat (6 RV)

 Bombers

  A. 70 Blackjack

  B. 130 Bear ALCM

 Mobile Land-Based Missiles (MICBM)

  A. 36 SS-24M (10 RV)

  B. 715 SS-25 (1 RV)

6,000 RV

 U.S. Forces

  ICBMs

   A. 200 SICBM (1 RV)

   B. 50 MX (10 RV)

   C. 86 MM III (1 RV)

  SLBMs

   A. 8 Trident submarines with 24 Trident C4 missiles (8 RV)

   B. 10 Trident submarines with 24 Trident D5 missiles (8 RV)

  Bombers

   A. 87 B-1B

   B. 30 B-2 (Stealth)

 Russian Forces

  ICBMs

   A. 115 SS-24 (10 RV)

  SLBMs

   A. 6 Typhoon submarines with 20 SSN20/boat (6 RV)

   B. 10 Delta IV submarines with 16 SSN23/boat (4 RV)

   C. 6 Delta III submarines with 16 SSN18/boat (3 RV)

Bombers
    A. 50 Blackjack
    B. 130 Bear-H
MICBMs
    A. 600 SS-25 (1 RV)
    B. 36 SS-24M (10 RV)

3,000 RV

U.S. Forces
    ICBMs
        A. 208 MM III (3 RV)
    SLBMs
        A. 8 Trident submarines with 24 Trident C4/boat (3 RV)
        B. 10 Trident submarines with 24 Trident D5/boat (3 RV)
    Bombers
        A. 90 B-1B
Russian Forces
    ICBMs
        A. 50 SS-24 (10 RV)
    SLBMs
        A. 6 Typhoon submarines with 20 SSN20/boat (3 RV)
        B. 10 Delta IV submarines with 16 SSN23/boat (3 RV)
    Bombers
        A. 100 Bear-H
    MICBMs
        A. 500 SS-25 (1 RV)
        B. 36 SS-24M (10 RV)

2,000 RV

U.S. Forces
    ICBMs
        A. 300 MM III (1 RV)
    SLBMs
        A. 10 Trident submarines with 24 Trident C4/boat (1 RV)
        B. 15 Trident submarines with 24 Trident D5/boat (1 RV)
    Bombers
        A. 90 B-1B
Russian Forces
    ICBMs
        A. None
    SLBMs
        A. 5 Typhoon submarines with 20 SSN20/boat (3 RV)
        B. 5 Delta IV submarines with 16 SSN23/boat (3 RV)
    Bombers
        A. 100 Bear-H

MICBMs
    A. 500 SS-25 (1 RV)
    B. 50 SS-24M (10 RV)

1,000 RV (CBO)
  U.S. Forces
    ICBMs
      A. 200 MM III (1 RV)
    SLBMs
      A. 8 Trident submarines with 24 Trident C4/boat (1 RV)
      B. 10 Trident submarines with 24 Trident D5/boat (1 RV)
    Bombers
      A. 90 B-1B
  Russian Forces
    ICBMs
      A. None
    SLBMs
      A. 10 Delta IV submarines with 16 SSN23/boat (1 RV)
    Bombers
      A. 85 Bear-H
    MICBMs
      A. 500 SS-25

1,000 RV (Corbin et al.)
  U.S. Forces
    ICBMs
      A. 300 SICBM (1 RV)
    SLBMs
      A. 30 Trident submarines with 24 Trident D5/boat (1 RV)
    Bombers
      A. 100 B-1B ALCMs
  Russian Forces
    ICBMs
      A. None
    SLBMs
      A. 30 Delta IV submarines with 16 SSN23/boat (1 RV)
    Bombers
      A. 100 Bear-H
    MICBMs
      A. 300 SS-25 (1 RV)

START II Agreement
  U.S. Forces
    ICBMs
      A. 500 MM III (1 RV)

SLBMs
  A. 8 Trident submarines with 24 Trident C4/boat (4 RV)
  B. 10 Trident submarines with 24 Trident D5/boat (4 RV)

Bombers
  A. 106 B-1 (Approximately 1,270 warheads will be carried on bombers under the Bush-Yeltsin agreements of 1993. The actual configuration of weapons platforms depends upon modernization and procurement decisions taken by Congress subsequent to Start II. I have used a notional force of B-1 each loaded with 12 accountable warheads. According to Jerome Weisner, Philip Morison, and Kosta Tsipis, a 3,500 warhead U.S. START II force would probably include 20 B-2s and 100 B-52Hs [*Beyond the Looking Glass: The United States Military in 2000 and Later* (Cambridge, Mass.: MIT, Program in Science and Technology for International Security, 1993)].)

Russian Forces

ICBMs
  A. None

SLBMs
  A. 6 Typhoon submarines with 20 SSN20/boat (6 RV)
  B. 7 Delta IV submarines with 16 SSN23/boat (4 RV)
  C. 12 Delta III submarines with 16 SSN18/boat (3 RV)

Bombers
  A. 20 Blackjack
  B. 34 Bear-H

MICBMs
  A. 504 SS-25 (1 RV)

Simulations and Calculations

Simulations were performed using the formulas provided by Salman, Sullivan, and Van Evera.[33]

The SIOP computerized nuclear exchange model requires that the user allocate warheads against seven classes of targets: submarine bases; mobile ICBM bases; bomber bases; command, control, and communications facilities; air defense interceptor bases and other air defense facilities; other military targets; and value targets. The model calculates an optimum allocation against ICBM silos and command centers after the user has specified allocations against other targets.

Countersilo attacks allocate the attacker's most lethal warheads against the retaliator's most important targets: SIOP ranks the ICBMs of the retaliator according to the net value destroyed by using the attacker's best weapons against them. Net value is calculated by multiplying the value of each missile (calculated as the number of warheads it carries, the EMT of its payload, or the lethality of its payload, according to user choice) multiplied by (1) the expected probability that the missile has not yet been destroyed or fired; (2) the reliability and availability of the missile; (3) the kill probability (Pk) that the attacker's best warhead could achieve against it. The formula for calculating warhead lethality is:

$$R \times Y^{2/3} / CEP^2$$

where: R = warhead reliability
         Y = yield
         CEP = estimated accuracy or circular error probable in nautical miles

Users can choose among four formulas for calculating the single shot kill probability (SSKP) of a reliable warhead: the full General Electric (GE) formula, simplified GE formula, full RAND formula, or simplified RAND formula. All are explained in Davis and Schilling[34] and also discussed in Salman, Sullivan, and Van Evera.[35] Only the full GE formula can be applied to silos with hardnesses above 1,000 pounds per square inch. All of these formulas may underestimate the lethality of countersilo attacks by omitting the effects of electromagnetic pulse, ground shock waves, and cratering. However, they may overestimate the same effects by ignoring fratricide effects among attacking warheads, bias in aiming, gravitational anomalies, and other factors. All of the formulas for SSKP follow the same general rule:

$$SSKP = 1 - .5^{(LR/CEP)2}$$

but they differ in the manner in which they calculate lethal radius.

An additional nuance of countersilo attacks is that they are constrained by the "footprint" of attacking warheads delivered by a multiple, independently-targetable re-entry vehicle launcher.[36] Warheads released on different trajectories against different targets cannot be arbitrarily distant from one another. Trajectories are limited by the amount of fuel carried by the "bus" that contains the re-entry vehicles and by the range of the missile. Tsipis also addresses classes of errors in ballistic missile flight,[37] and calculations and uncertainties pertinent to countersilo attacks.[38]

Alert rates and reliability assumptions for various U.S. and Russian force components on generated and day to day alert follow generally accepted and publicly available estimates. In most instances, SIOP users can employ the alert rates and reliability assumptions given for 1990 U.S. and Soviet force structures, but some caution is useful with regard to mobile missiles. May, Bing, and Steinbruner address variable estimates of these parameters at different force sizes.[39]

NOTES

1. An important landmark study was Glenn H. Snyder, *Deterrence and Defense: Toward a Theory of National Security* (Princeton, N.J.: Princeton University Press, 1961). Deterrence prior to the nuclear age is discussed in George H. Quester, *Deterrence before Hiroshima: The Airpower Background of Modern Strategy* (New Brunswick, N.J.: Transaction Books, 1986). Bernard Brodie's singular contributions to the study of U.S. nuclear deterrence strategy, especially during the early years, are noted in Barry H. Steiner, *Bernard Brodie and the Foundations of Nuclear Strategy* (Lawrence, Kan.: University Press of Kansas, 1991).

2. See Lawrence Freedman, *The Evolution of Nuclear Strategy* (New York: St. Martin's Press, 1981); Colin S. Gray, *Strategic Studies: A Critical Assessment* (Westport, Conn.: Greenwood, 1982); Robert Jervis, *The Meaning of the Nuclear Revolution: Statecraft and the Prospect of Armageddon* (Ithaca, N.Y.: Cornell University Press, 1989) on the development and assessment of U.S. nuclear strategy.

3. For example, Thomas C. Schelling, *The Strategy of Conflict* (Cambridge, Mass.: Harvard University Press, 1960); Albert Wohlstetter, "The Delicate Balance of Terror," *Foreign Affairs* 37 (January 1959): 212–34. Brodie's contributions are covered extensively in Steiner, *Bernard Brodie, passim*. Brodie revisits much of his important strategic thinking in Bernard Brodie, *War and Politics* (New York: Macmillan, 1973). See also Bernard Brodie, *Strategy in the Nuclear Age* (Princeton, N.J.: Princeton University Press, 1959); John Baylis, Ken Booth, John Garett, and Phil Williams, *Contemporary Strategy, I: Theories and Concepts* (London: Holmes and Meier, 1987), pp. 113–39. The early contributions of seminal nuclear strategists are considered in Marc Trachtenberg, *History and Strategy* (Princeton, N.J.: Princeton University Press, 1991), pp. 3–46.

4. Richard L. Garwin, "Post-START: What Do We Want? What Can We Achieve?" testimony published in U.S. Congress, Senate Committee on Foreign Relations, *Hearings*, 102nd Congress, 2nd sess., pp. 130–47. See also National Academy of Sciences, Committee on International Security and Arms Control, *The Future of the U.S.-Soviet Relationship* (Washington, D.C.: National Academy Press, 1991).

5. David Mosher and Michael O'Hanlon, *The START Treaty and Beyond* (Washington, D.C.: Congressional Budget Office, 1991). For other analyses of 6,000 and 3,000 RV cases, see Michael M. May, George F. Bing, and John D. Steinbruner, *Strategic Arms Reductions* (Washington, D.C.: Brookings Institution, 1988), pp. 42–59.

6. Ted Corbin, Arsen Hajian, and Kosta Tsipis, *Nuclear Arsenals for the 21st Century* (Cambridge, Mass.: MIT, Program in Science and Technology for International Security, 1991), p. 69. For post-START U.S. forces lower than 1,000 warheads, see Jerome Weisner, Philip Morison, and Kosta Tsipis, *Beyond the Looking Glass: The United States Military in 2000 and Later* (Cambridge, Mass.: MIT, Program in Science and Technology for International Security, 1993), esp. pp. 10–11, 34.

7. The distinction between actual and hypothetical or notional forces has in recent years been blurred as a result of dramatic and rapid changes in the former Soviet Union and its military. For example, even though there was a START I agreement assented to by the U.S. and Soviet leaderships, the Soviet Union ceased to exist before the agreement was fully implemented. Meanwhile, negotiations were already under way for START II. Therefore, no actual START I force ever existed, but the START I agreement helped to bridge the arms control negotiations from the Soviet to the post-Soviet era. We have used here plausible force structures that would have been START I compliant for both sides, and START II forces projected on the basis of agreements signed by Russian President Boris Yeltsin and U.S. President George Bush shortly before the expiration of Bush's term in office. For additional detail on the

START agreements, see Thomas Bernauer, Michele Flournoy, Steven E. Miller, and Lee Minichiello, "Strategic Arms Control and the NPT: Status and Implementation," in *Cooperative Denuclearization: From Pledges to Deeds*, eds. Graham Allison, Ashton B. Carter, Steven E. Miller, and Philip Zelikow (Cambridge, Mass.: Harvard University, Center for Science and International Affairs, John F. Kennedy School of Government, 1993), pp. 26–86.

8.   Desmond Ball, "U.S. Strategic Forces: How Would They Be Used?" *International Security* (Winter 1982–83): 31–60.

9.   For an account, see Scott D. Sagan, *Moving Targets: Nuclear Strategy and National Security* (Princeton, N.J.: Princeton University Press, 1989), pp. 10–57.

10.   The first estimates by McNamara were provided in 1965, the second in 1967. See Alain C. Enthoven, and K. Wayne Smith, *How Much is Enough? Shaping the Defense Program, 1961–69* (New York: Harper & Row, 1971), pp. 207–10. Alternative criteria for assured destruction are presented in Michael Salman, Kevin J. Sullivan, and Stephen Van Evera, "Analysis or Propaganda? Measuring American Strategic Nuclear Capability, 1969–1988," in *Nuclear Arguments: Understanding the Strategic Nuclear Arms Debate*, eds. Lynn Eden and Steven E. Miller (Ithaca. N.Y.: Cornell University Press, 1989), esp. pp. 209–11; see also Gary John Schaub, Jr., *Strategic Nuclear Exchanges: An Assessment of the Literature*, unpublished paper, p. 21. I am grateful to Joseph Coffey for this last reference.

11.   For estimates of assured destruction for attacks on the Soviet Union, see Barbara G. Levi, Frank N. Von Hippel, and William Daugherty, "Civilian Casualties from 'Limited' Nuclear Attacks on the Soviet Union," *International Security* 12 (Winter 1987–88): 168–89. Estimates for the assured destruction criterion for attacks on the United States appear in William Daugherty, Barbara Levi, and Frank Von Hippel, "The Consequences of 'Limited' Nuclear Attacks on the United States," *International Security* 10 (Spring 1986): 3–45. For other estimates, see U.S. Office of Technology Assessment, *The Effects of Nuclear War* (Montclair, N.J.: Allanheld, Osmun, 1980).

12.   As part of the effort to develop operational definitions for assured retaliation, Carter defense planners examined whether U.S.-Soviet strategic equivalence was meaningful, how equivalence in counterforce systems ought to be measured, and what kinds of hard target capability U.S. forces really needed. The issue of second strike counterforce targeting was also considered at great length by internal Carter studies, and spirited debates took place within the government over the relative importance of slow compared with prompt retaliatory counterforce (maturing of cruise missile technology in the 1970s made this a very live issue). I am grateful to Paul Davis and Leon Sloss for background on this issue, although they bear no responsibility for the interpretations presented here. See also Walter Slocombe, "The Countervailing Strategy," in *Strategy and Nuclear Deterrence*, ed. Steven E. Miller (Princeton, N.J.: Princeton University Press, 1984), pp. 245–54.

13.   McGeorge Bundy, "To Cap the Volcano," *Foreign Affairs* 48 (October 1969): 9–10.

14.   Kosta Tsipis, "The Future of Nuclear Deterrence," in *World Security: Trends and Challenges at Century's End*, eds. Michael T. Klare and Daniel C. Thomas (New York: St. Martin's Press, 1991), pp. 45–67.

15.   Frank N. Von Hippel, Barbara G. Levi, Theodore A. Postol, and William Daugherty, "Civilian Casualties from Counterforce Attacks," *Scientific American* (September 1988): 42. According to May, Bing, and Steinbruner, the von Hippel and others estimates are at the high end of the range of prompt fatalities from counterforce attacks: their estimates are provided in Michael M. May, George F. Bing, and John D. Steinbruner, *Strategic Arms Reductions* (Washington, D.C.: Brookings Institution, 1988), pp. 60–69. The different estimates may be explained by some differences in

scenario-targeting assumptions as well as differences in methodology. What is more important for our purposes is that both of these studies confirm the large damage that can be accomplished against countervalue targets, especially urban targets, with numbers of warheads much smaller than those posited in exchange models requiring massive counterforce strikes.

16.   This case is argued in Sagan, *Moving Targets*, pp. 58–97.

17.   Background on the development of U.S. targeting doctrine is provided in Desmond Ball, *The Evolution of United States Strategic Policy since 1945: Doctrine, Military Technical Innovation and Force Structure* (Canberra: Australian National University, Strategic and Defence Studies Centre, 1989); Desmond Ball, "The Development of the SIOP, 1960–1983," in *Strategic Nuclear Targeting*, eds. Desmond Ball and Jeffrey Richelson (Ithaca, N.Y.: Cornell University Press, 1986), pp. 57–83. On Soviet nuclear targeting and command and control, see Desmond Ball, *Soviet Strategic Planning and the Control of Nuclear War* (Canberra: Strategic and Defence Studies Centre, Reference Paper No. 109, 1983); Stephen M. Meyer, "Soviet Nuclear Operations," in *Managing Nuclear Operations*, eds. Ashton B. Carter, John D. Steinbruner, and Charles A. Zraket (Washington, D.C.: Brookings Institution, 1987), pp. 470–534. How much of this transfers over to the post-Soviet military planning mind set is unknown.

18.   For background, see Leonard S. Spector and Jacqueline R. Smith, *Nuclear Ambitions: The Spread of Nuclear Weapons 1989–1990* (Boulder, Colo.: Westview, 1990); Janne E. Nolan, *Trappings of Power: Ballistic Missiles in the Third World* (Washington, D.C.: Brookings Institution, 1991).

19.   Richard Ned Lebow, *Nuclear Crisis Management: A Dangerous Illusion* (Ithaca, N.Y.: Cornell University Press, 1987). James G. Blight argues that the experience of crisis management fragility may have improved the quality of official decision making during the Cuban missile crisis of 1962. See James G. Blight, *The Shattered Crystal Ball: Fear and Learning in the Cuban Missile Crisis* (Savage, Md.: Rowman and Littlefield, 1990).

20.   See James G. Blight and David A. Welch, *On the Brink: Americans and Soviets Reexamine the Cuban Missile Crisis* (New York: Hill and Wang, 1989), for insights into the perspectives of crisis participants. For background on Cuban crisis decision making in Moscow and in Washington, see Raymond L. Garthoff, *Reflections on the Cuban Missile Crisis* (Washington, D.C.: Brookings Institution, 1989).

21.   The best of these in my judgment is Freeman Dyson, *Weapons and Hope* (New York: Harper Colophon, 1984), esp. pp. 272–85.

22.   May, Bing, and Steinbruner, *Strategic Arms Reductions*, p. 71. It is worth noting that reserve levels withheld in the simulations done for this study are smaller than those posited for the May, Bing, and Steinbruner study, generally 10 percent of the force in the latter case.

23.   On the relationship between nuclear multipolarity and minimum deterrence, see David W. Tarr, *Nuclear Deterrence and International Security: Alternative Nuclear Regimes* (London: Longmans, 1991), p. 138. On the subject of minimum deterrence generally, see Michael J. Mazarr, "Nuclear Weapons after the Cold War," *The Washington Quarterly* (Summer 1992): 185–201; and Michael E. Brown, *The "End" of Nuclear Arms Control*, PRAC Paper No. 1 (College Park, Md.: University of Maryland, Center for International Security Studies, 1993), esp. pp. 12–15.

24.   This assumes the following: France decides to maintain two ballistic missile submarines (SSBNs) at sea at all times, and Britain keeps at least one and possibly two SSBNs at sea at all times. If the French replace the M-4 submarine-launched ballistic missiles (SLBMs) with the M-5 and if all M-5s are equipped with a maximum of 12 warheads, then France would deploy 384 assuredly survivable warheads on SSBNs (2 x 16 x 12). The M-5 is not expected to begin deployment until 2005, and the

French mobile intermediate-range ballistic missile program has been canceled. France probably would continue to deploy strategic or prestrategic nuclear weapons in other basing modes, including fixed silo intermediate-range ballistic missiles on the Albion plateau, short range ballistic missiles, and air delivered munitions. If Trident D-5 SLBMs replace all British Polaris A-3 and if the D-5s all carry the maximum eight warheads, then Britain with two boats would have a total of 256 assuredly survivable warheads (2 x 16 x 8). Actual total deployed may be lower than these because the British government has stated its intention not to deploy the maximum number of warheads on the D-5, and France is judged by expert analysts as unlikely to deploy 12 warheads on each M-5. Approximately 300–400 assuredly survivable warheads would be a more conservative figure for estimating combined British and French survivable RVs in the first decade of the twenty-first century. I am grateful to Michael Brown, Senior Fellow, International Institute for Strategic Studies, London, for correcting earlier figures and for providing helpful additional information. He bears no responsibility for interpretations here.

25.   The reduced utility of nuclear compared with conventional weapons for tactical missions was argued effectively by Richard L. Garwin, "Reducing Dependence on Nuclear Weapons: A Second Nuclear Regime," in *Nuclear Weapons and World Politics*, eds. David C. Gompert, Michael Mandelbaum, Richard L. Garwin, and John H. Barton (New York: McGraw-Hill, 1977), pp. 83–147, esp. p. 108. On the substitution of conventional for nuclear weapons in strategic missions, see Carl H. Builder, *Strategic Conflict Without Nuclear Weapons* (Santa Monica, Calif.: RAND Corporation, 1983).

26.   For interesting statements to this effect, see the draft Russian military doctrine appearing in the special edition of *Voennaya mysl'* (Military Thought), May 1992, esp. pp. 3–9.

27.   John J. Mearsheimer, "The Case for a Ukrainian Nuclear Deterrent," *Foreign Affairs* (Summer 1993): 50–67. See also Kenneth N. Waltz, *The Spread of Nuclear Weapons: More May Be Better*, Adelphi Papers No. 171 (London: International Institute for Strategic Studies, 1981).

28.   Neorealism is distinguished from traditional realism in that neorealism emphasizes systemic and structural roots for conflict more than traditional realism did, the latter having placed greater emphasis upon sources of conflict rooted in human nature. For a paradigm neorealist argument, see Kenneth N. Waltz, *Theory of International Politics* (Reading, Mass.: Addison-Wesley, 1979).

29.   John J. Mearsheimer, *Conventional Deterrence* (Ithaca, N.Y.: Cornell University Press, 1983), esp. Chap. 2.

30.   See Peter Douglas Feaver, *Guarding the Guardians: Civilian Control of Nuclear Weapons in the United States* (Ithaca, N.Y.: Cornell University Press, 1992).

31.   John Lewis Gaddis, *The United States and the End of the Cold War: Implications, Reconsiderations, Provocations* (New York: Oxford University Press, 1992), pp. 106–8; see also John Mueller, *Retreat from Doomsday: The Obsolescence of Major War* (New York: Basic Books, 1989).

32.   Force characteristics, including operational parameters such as alert rates, are drawn from Michael Salman, Kevin J. Sullivan, and Stephen Van Evera, "Analysis or Propaganda? Measuring American Strategic Nuclear Capability, 1969–88," in *Nuclear Arguments: Understanding the Strategic Nuclear Arms and Arms Control Debates*, eds. Lynn Eden and Steven E. Miller (Ithaca, N.Y.: Cornell University Press, 1989), pp. 172–244; Michael Salman, Kevin J. Sullivan, and Stephen Van Evera, "Appendix: How Our Simulations Were Performed," in *Nuclear Arguments: Understanding the Strategic Nuclear Arms and Arms Control Debates*, eds. Lynn Eden and Steven E. Miller (Ithaca, N.Y.: Cornell University Press, 1989), pp. 245–63, unless otherwise specifically noted. Force structures were derived primarily from these

sources and from David Mosher and Michael O'Hanlon, *The START Treaty and Beyond* (Washington, D.C.: Congressional Budget Office, 1991); Ted Corbin, Arsen Hajian, and Kosta Tsipis, *Nuclear Arsenals for the 21st Century* (Cambridge, Mass.: MIT, Program in Science and Technology for International Security, Report #23, 1991). I also am grateful to Ted Warner, RAND Corporation and office of the secretary of defense, for helpful suggestions and background papers on strategic arms control.

33. Salman, Sullivan, and Van Evera, "Analysis or Propaganda?" pp. 172–263, esp. 245–64.

34. Lynn Etheridge Davis and Warner R. Schilling, "All You Ever Wanted to Know about MIRV and ICBM Calculations but Were Not Cleared to Ask," *Journal of Conflict Resolution* 27 (June 1973): 213–14.

35. Salman, Sullivan, and Van Evera, "Analysis or Propaganda?" p. 249.

36. Kosta Tsipis, *Arsenal: Understanding Weapons in the Nuclear Age* (New York: Touchstone Books, 1983), p. 122.

37. Ibid., pp. 115–16.

38. Ibid., pp. 130–46.

39. May, Bing, and Steinbruner, *Strategic Arms Reductions*, p. 35.

III

COLLECTIVE SECURITY: OBSTACLES AND OPTIONS

6

Collective Security and Escalation

The theory and practice of collective security after the Cold War face a potentially intractable problem of escalation management. Collective security may be powerless in the face of accelerated nuclear proliferation. Even prior to the nuclear age, collective security suffered from the contradiction that it sought to encourage escalation in the short term in order to bring about deescalation later. This deescalation-by-escalation is highly risk acceptant even in the absence of weapons of mass destruction. Post–Cold War nuclear proliferation, even if well-managed, is almost certainly on a collision course with collective security, to the probable detriment of the latter.[1]

The following discussion proceeds in two stages. The first part outlines some general problems in bringing about congruity between the behaviors of states under collective security and the expectations of states in crisis management. In the second part of the discussion, I focus on the particular problem of nuclear proliferation and the incompatibility of even controlled proliferation with collective security.

COLLECTIVE SECURITY AND CRISIS MANAGEMENT

Collective security theory assumes that in most interstate conflict situations, one can determine with reasonable clarity the identity of the aggressor and of the defender.[2] The identity of the aggressor having been established, it follows that the member states of the world community will permit their forces to be used to reestablish international order according to the *status quo ante*. No judgment is required about the correctness of the cause for which any of the combatants may be fighting. The assumption is that a state that disturbs the international status quo by military means has defined itself as an aggressor under international law. The legal obligation of other states is to resist that aggression. Collective security is, therefore, in practice, if not explicitly in theory, a formula that favors the international status quo.

Little is said in the literature on collective security about the problem of crisis management. The assumption is that the overwhelming force of the majority of states arrayed against the possible aggressor will deter the aggressor state from actual resort to violence. The assumption that superior force will deter aggression is one that seems to meet standards of common sense; regretfully, historical evidence does not always support the assumption. States have gone to war against individual states or coalitions with actual or potential power superior to their own. Argentina's attack on the Falkland Islands in 1982 and Hitler's willingness to take on the United States, Britain, and the Soviet Union simultaneously offer recent examples. In neither of these cases did the entire world community attempt to deter the aggressor before the fact, so, neither case really falsifies collective security theory as stated.

The cases in which the entire international community acts in crisis management or war against a potential or actual aggressor are so rare as to defy inference by means of sampling. Usually one or several of the great powers acts as the representative of the world community or of an international organization on behalf of the world community. In those instances, it is not actually the world community that is doing the deterrence or war fighting, but one or more great powers on behalf of the world community. For example, the United Nations authorized a coalition led by the United States to take military action in 1991 to expel Iraq from Kuwait. Approximately 30 states participated in the victorious coalition under the UN umbrella, but U.S. military power was the makeweight of the operation and the basis of Bush's attempts at prewar compellence through diplomacy.

The fact that one or more of the great powers must exercise deterrence or crisis management on behalf of the world community does not necessarily invalidate collective security as an approach to peace, but it does introduce asymmetries into process of conflict termination, either by crisis management or by war. When Saddam Hussein in the autumn of 1991 debated whether to stay in Kuwait or to make a face-saving retreat, his decision was based primarily on what he thought U.S. President George Bush would accept in the way of Iraqi behavior. The acceptability of Iraq's actions to other heads of state was less significant to Saddam, because only U.S. military power could, if necessary, guarantee to drive him out of Kuwait at an acceptable cost to the victors.

The allocation of costs among members of the collective security coalition is an important matter in itself, because it bears on the probability that the coalition will hold together under the duress of later crisis states and war. Heads of state may share the political aim of deterring or compelling an aggressor, but governments and their publics are rarely willing and able to pay equal shares of the cost of deterrence and compellence. The credibility of deterrence, at least by means of conventional forces without any prospect of nuclear escalation, depends very much on the actual war-fighting capability of the states that are attempting to deter. Those with the greater capabilities almost certainly will be expected to take the lead in military operations and to accept higher costs in blood and treasure, compared with those secondary and tertiary members of the coalition.

In a comprehensive study of how wars ended between 1800 and 1980, Paul Pillar classified the possible endings of wars as absorption, extermination or expulsion, withdrawal, international organization or other third party proposed settlement acceptable to combatant sides, capitulation, negotiation before armistice, and negotiation after armistice.[3] Some of these meanings are self-evident, but some are not. In a case of absorption, the immediate conflict of interest is absorbed into a larger war before being terminated, as in the July 1914 conflict between Austria and Serbia. If one side stops fighting without having decided to stop, its opponent has rendered it incapable of continuing to fight, either through extermination or expulsion from the theater of operations. If a war ends as the result of decisions made by both parties, it may occur without any explicit agreement, as in a withdrawal, or by acceptance of an explicit agreement. If the parties reach an explicit agreement by negotiation, the agreement may either precede or follow a cease-fire. If they cannot reach agreement, they may accept a solution offered by a third party, or one side may capitulate, with or without conditions, to the superior strength of the other. Using a three-fold typology of wars developed by J. David Singer and Melvin Small, Pillar classified patterns of war termination for the three types of conflicts fought between 1800 and 1980: interstate wars, extrasystemic wars, and civil wars (Table 6.1).[4] Two immediately striking findings from Table 6.1 have implications for collective security after the Cold War. First, civil wars usually are not terminated by mutual agreement. As many civil wars are ended by one side's capitulation to the other as are terminated by negotiation before or after armistice. In addition, the number of Civil wars ended by extermination or expulsion of one side exceeds the number of conflicts ended by explicit mutual agreement. Second, and related to the first finding, the category "international organization" is marked by a dearth of cell entries: no tabulated extrasystemic wars (colonial or imperial wars during this period) and only a single civil war were terminated as a result of third party or international organization proposals acceptable to both sides. Taken together, the two findings suggest that civil wars are especially hard to terminate and that international organizations through 1980 had not made an impressive track record in terminating any kinds of wars.[5] The findings here also carry implications for efforts by international organizations to engage in deterrence by means of collective security, even if the international organization mounts a credible threat to confront the designated aggressor state with overwhelming force. The case of

TABLE 6.1
Patterns of War Termination, 1800–1980: Interstate,
Extrasystemic, and Civil Wars

| | War Type | | | |
| | | | | Row |
Outcomes	1	2	3	Total
A	1	5	0	6
E	7	12	7	26
W	4	2	1	7
IO	8	0	1	9
C	11	20	6	37
NA	28	9	1	38
NB	10	4	5	19
Column Total	69	52	21	142

Notes:

War types: 1, interstate war; 2, extrasystemic war; 3, civil war.

Outcomes: A, absorption; E, extermination or expulsion; W, withdrawal; IO, international organization; C, capitulation; NA, negotiation after armistice; NB, negotiation before armistice.

Source: Paul R. Pillar, *Negotiating Peace: War Termination as a Bargaining Process* (Princeton, N.J.: Princeton University Press, 1983), p. 22. Pillar recalculates this table for a reduced number of outcome categories (Ibid., p. 25).

collective security deterrence in its compellent form as applied to the Gulf War of 1991 is discussed in a later section of this chapter.

The deterrent aspect of collective security, thus, involves a certain willingness on the part of international organizations and their member states to engage in crisis brinkmanship.[6] States that are committed to defend the status quo must signal that they are prepared to go to war on short notice if the status quo is altered by force without legal sanction. However, brinkmanship is not always facilitated by certainty. Brinkmanship sometimes can be aided by leaving ambiguity in the signals sent to potential attackers about the precise costs of aggression. Making explicit the terms on which a coalition is willing to accept the aggressor's demands may embolden, rather than deter, the aggressor. Chamberlain's experience with Hitler in September 1938 provides one example, and counterpoint is provided by the decision for deliberate ambiguity on the part of the British foreign office about Britain's continental commitment during the July crisis of 1914.

Another theoretical issue is the tenuous relationship between the techniques and approaches thought to be useful for the avoidance of war through crisis management on one hand and the positioning of the state and its armed forces to wage war successfully on the other. Views of political and military leaders are apt to differ on this question, for reasons of position and of world view based on historical experience. Political leaders want the widest possible latitude and the most flexible options for steering themselves and their states through crisis decisions. Military planners want their war machines to be poised for advantage at the outbreak of war and not vulnerable to surprise attack based on political or technical surprise. Military organizations are highly dependent on standard operating procedures and decision repertoires for carrying out their assigned missions. These procedures and organizational routines may reinforce organizational values such as morale and cohesion in addition to their practical value of rehearsing forces and command systems for the main event.

Organizational routines and standard operating procedures can tie the hands of crisis ridden leaders who seek options that cannot be improvised. When Kaiser Wilhelm asked Chief of the German General Staff Helmuth von Moltke (the younger) to reverse the direction of German mobilization prior to the outbreak of World War I (eastward against Russia, instead of westward against France), von Moltke informed the kaiser that this could not be done. The machinery of mobilization, set in motion according to the Schlieffen plan for a first strike westward against France, could not be adjusted at the last minute to launch the main offensive against Russia. Whether this was actually the case, a matter of some dispute among military historians, is less the issue than the perception held by the German general staff in 1914 that they were confined by the dictates of the Schlieffen plan to a single option.[7]

Indeed, the relationship between mobilization and war is itself a significant aspect of crisis management and military preparedness. Under some conditions for some states, mobilization becomes tantamount to war. Mobilization for self-defense cannot easily be distinguished by potential opponents from preparation for surprise attack. When defensive and offensive mobilization are virtually indistinguishable, the probability of inadvertent escalation or accidental war is increased.[8] Germany's and Russia's mobilization planning prior to World War I illustrates some of the trade-offs between mobilization undersigned to avoid "Type I" errors (enemy attacks us and we are not ready) compared with military preparations skewed toward the avoidance of "Type II" errors (we expect imminent attack although the other side is not really intent upon doing so).

Mobilization planning prior to World War I contributed to war wariness and heightened states of alert for military forces on the eve of battle. However, the duration of World War I showed the irrelevancy of quick victory strategies in coalition warfare where military technology favored stalemate and wars of attrition. That coalition wars would be destructive beyond societal endurance was a nineteenth century concern of military strategists, economic thinkers, and political leaders in Europe. In some ways, it would not overstate conditions to argue that leaders planned for a short war because they feared to face the consequences of a longer war.[9] Prewar Britain, Russia, and Germany were all concerned about the domestic economic and political impacts of protracted coalition war. For Russia, regime survival obviously was at stake after the domestic shock waves of Russia's defeat by Japan almost toppled the empire in 1905. In Germany, the aristocratic classes feared the growing political and economic power of the workers and socialism, and the general staff sought to exclude socialist tendencies from the officer corps.

For Britain, the security of its own harbors and the risks of continental commitment in Western Europe were only the most obvious of concerns. The government and economy also might fall on the basis of what happened to the remnants of British imperial rule outside Europe in the aftermath of an extended coalition war.[10] Superficially, it appeared to many immediately upon the conclusion of World War I that Britain had not only maintained, but also expanded, her global empire. In fact, Britain's waning international power was further extended across a broader perimeter that she would be unable to defend from future aggressors without dependency on the United States and other allies. The second extended war of the twentieth century mortally taxed British economic resources and political sufficiency for world power.

The obvious question here is whether the members of the pre–World War I triple alliance or entente would have been better off with a "true" collective security system as opposed to a collective defense system. A collective defense system is pointed at a particular outside threat: the probable sources of aggression have been identified in advance of an outbreak of crisis or war. A collective security system is dispassionate with respect to probable sources of aggression: any state can, in theory, aggress against any other, and the remainder of the international community is obligated to come to the defense of the victim. The powers of the nineteenth century had established a collective security system of sorts by means of the Congress of Vienna and the Concert of Europe. Although given to periodic outbursts of bloc politic and to disagreements about the expectations for great power intervention to suppress nationalist revolutions, the concert functioned reasonably well as a collective security system from the end of the Napoleonic wars to the onset of the Crimean War. Thereafter, until the turn of the century, a more classical balance of power obtained among the five or six major powers (Britain, France, Russia, Germany, Austria-Hungary, and Italy, with Turkey in and out), followed by the hardening of opposed alliances that eventually faced off in August 1914.

Some evidence suggests that the consultative system put into place by the Congress of Vienna was marginally superior to its predecessors in controlling the outbreak of some kinds of wars. For example, in the 99 years following the congress, the incidence of war and armed intervention was lower than the rate of occurrence for the preceding 99 years

(1715–1814). The earlier period was marked by one war every 2.8 years, and the later period by one every 3.3 years.[11] Whether this is a statistically or substantively significant difference is arguable. Nevertheless, it can be argued with some confidence that the incidence of great power wars was smaller in the nineteenth century compared with the eighteenth century and that the congress system of consultative diplomacy had something to do with this.[12] It can also be argued that, when the consultative machinery of the concert system began to break down, the powers turned away from collective security and toward collective deterrence in the form of traditional alliances. The hardening of these alliances into a rigid bipolarity in the early twentieth century contributed to the outbreak of World War I.[13]

The Concert of Europe was not a universal system of collective security, nor was it an especially democratic one. The concert model of collective security, embodied today in the UN Security Council, allocates to the great powers a disproportionate share of the responsibility for the maintenance of international peace and security. The Concert of Europe held together cohesively as long as the threat of French revanchism stirred common fears. The reintegration of France, presumably shorn of aspirations for European hegemony and democratic universalism, into the great power system was envisioned by the other powers as part of the post-Napoleonic balancing mechanism for stability in Europe. However, it also removed the common threat that had bound democratic Britain and autocratic Russia, Prussia, and Austria together. The demise of the French threat to European stability after 1820 had an effect on the concert version of collective security similar to the demise of the Soviet threat and its impact on the North Atlantic Treaty Organization (NATO) collective defense in the 1990s. Both collective security against the French version of international liberation under Napoleon and collective defense by West European democracies against Soviet aggression were missions that became obsolete before their organizational sponsors acknowledged the fact.

If collective security is clearly distinguished from collective defense, can either be distinguished reliably from collective deterrence? The problem is exacerbated by the important distinction between general and immediate deterrence, that is, between the onset of a crisis and the point at which an imminent failure of crisis management makes an outbreak of war highly probable.[14] Day to day international relations may be characterized by some writers as a legal state of nature in which the possibility of war is ever present. This is actually what Thomas Hobbes referred to when he discussed a state of war: the "known disposition" to fighting was sufficient to create what modern writers have called the security dilemma.[15] One state arms itself for motives of self-defense, and other states, fearing the military potential of the first state, arm themselves in response. The sequence of action and reaction can be extended indefinitely. However, the existence of a security dilemma in interstate relations does not make unavoidable the existence of a particular crisis or outbreak of war. The system permits but does not dispose states to threaten and to attack one another.

Because the security dilemma does not necessarily lead directly into crisis or war, deterrence may fail in stages. Strictly speaking, the onset of a crisis is not yet a failure of deterrence but is a failure of diplomacy. Crisis management begins when opposed interests bring states into conflict, although the possibility still exists of avoiding the actual exchange of blows. The next section of this chapter considers the problem of crisis management with more specificity. For now, we observe that crisis is open ended with regard to its resolution by the parties to the dispute: it may lead to war or it may not. Properly speaking, it is a failure of deterrence (immediate deterrence) only if crisis management is unsuccessful in avoiding war.

The preceding observation raises the point of whether crisis management is something that just occurs more or less spontaneously or whether it must be self-consciously adopted by leaders as a political-military strategy. The same question might be asked about the balance of power on which states have depended as an alternative to collective security. Both balance of power and crisis management are discussed by some writers as if they come about more or less automatically and by others as if only the dedicated pursuit of crisis management or balancing objectives can make them happen. To further complicate matters, we are speaking here of crisis management and balance of power as processes, not outcomes of some process. As outcomes, crisis management and balance of power can be the results of various processes; if they are coincidentally the product of processes not self-consciously selected for their crisis management or balancing attributes, they may be favorable results but not pertinent to future cases or to general theory.

COLLECTIVE SECURITY AND NUCLEAR PROLIFERATION

Collective security in Eurasia will have a larger obstacle course to the extent that nuclear proliferation adds to the difficulty of coordinating defense and foreign policies across states.[16] At first blush, it might seem that nuclear proliferation within Europe, as opposed to that outside of Europe, would not necessarily be destabilizing. European nuclear proliferation would take place in democratic states, within which elites would be held accountable by their citizens for decisions on defense spending and military preparedness. In addition, the military-technical aspects of nuclear forces favor defensive over offensive strategies: first strikes do not pay and retaliatory strikes do, as long as forces are survivable. Optimism about the stability of additional nuclear forces in Europe may not be transitive from the experience of U.S. and Soviet nuclear forces, however. There are reasons for being cautious about nuclear proliferation in Europe.[17]

First, additional nuclear weapons deployed in Europe will not be located in the mature and experienced nuclear command and control systems of the United States, former Soviet Union, Britain, and France. Some of thee command and control systems might be no better than those of newly industrialized third world states that aspire to become nuclear powers. A key issue is how the new nuclear powers of Europe would resolve the "always-never" dilemma, balancing the need for peacetime security against accidental or unauthorized nuclear use with the requirement for prompt response to duly authorized crisis and wartime commands.[18] Another issue is force survivability to avoid trigger-happy military forces and provocative alerts. The most survivable forces today are those deployed on submarines, but submarines require bases and ready access to suitable ports. Not all potential proliferators in Europe would have prompt access to oceanic deployment areas, and some might be forced to rely totally on more vulnerable air delivered and land launched weapons.

A second issue for collective security and nuclear weapons, in or outside Europe, is whether any future multistate organization can successfully employ "extended" deterrence. Extended deterrence is the deterrent value of nuclear weapons that are tasked to dissuade attacks not only against their owners but also against other states.[19] The other states may be allied formally with the first state, but not necessarily so. A collective security system for Europe, even without further nuclear proliferation, would require that a multistate entity, such as the hypothetical European concert discussed earlier, acquire its own nuclear arsenal or the power to order into action individual state arsenals. This power might be granted to a new regional concert if fears of nuclear proliferation were sufficiently great. Without that alternative, states would be left to their own devices: nuclear powers could choose to extend deterrence to their nonnuclear allies, or they could use nuclear weapons only for the deterrence of attacks on their territorial homelands.

Cold War history suggests that states would never part with nuclear weapons by transferring them to a multistate entity, nor would they empower a regional organization to command their own nuclear weapons into battle. However, Cold War precedent may not be reliable here. There was little danger of nuclear proliferation outside the ranks of the Soviet Union, Britain, and France during the Cold War. The lock held by U.S. and Soviet forces over European security issues and the sizes of the U.S. and Soviet nuclear arsenals made it difficult for any state to increase its perceived security by acquiring nuclear weapons. Any use of nuclear weapons in Europe almost certainly would have escalated into societal holocausts for West and Central Europeans if not for Soviets and Americans. Because of the political and military reach of the Cold War U.S. and Soviet forces, there was no fightable and controllable war possible anywhere in Europe, begun with or without nuclear weapons.

It is not impossible that the release of the Soviet and U.S. security grips on Europe's future will create no new incentives for nuclear weapons in Europe. Germany needs no nuclear force to emerge as Central Europe's major economic and political power; nuclear weapons, and even massive investment in modernized conventional weapons for theater warfare, could raise the fears of neighbors who already have nuclear forces. A German remilitarization outside NATO, with or without a German nuclear force, would be provocative to Russia and to France. There is no evidence that the latter wants to give up its nuclear force: The French never even talked for declaratory purposes, as Gorbachev did, about the advantages of a nuclear free world. Thus, although from a military-technical standpoint of nuclear force management the Germans might be the most security conscious proliferator in the new Europe, from a practical political standpoint German nuclear weapons constitute a potential European flashpoint and a probable kiss of death for concert based European security systems.

If European nuclear forces seem politically unlikely and nuclear devolution from states to multistate organizations impractical, then the containment of nuclear spread becomes the responsibility of the present nuclear powers in and outside Europe.[20] Nuclear weapons pull military planning and organization in the direction of state autarchy and against multistate control of military adventurism. Perhaps the attribute that *le nucleaire ne se partage pas* can be used in favor of security and stability instead of causing political uncertainty and arms races. Downsizing of U.S. and Russian arsenals, as scheduled in the START II agreement signed by Bush and Yeltsin in 1992, will encourage limitation on the sizes and modernization of other great power nuclear holdings, including those of Britain and France. China is a wild card but with little in the way of influence on future prospects for European nuclear proliferation or containment (Asiatic Russia is another matter). Assuming state and not multistate control over whatever nuclear forces are deployed in future Europe, the characteristics of those forces may lend themselves to eventual management through collective security organizations. Much depends on how the forces are designed, deployed, and commanded.

Forces and command systems that are first strike vulnerable are almost certain to increase the risks of war and to deflect any effort to incorporate controls over nuclear use into the auspices of multistate organizations, including a reconstructed NATO. On the other hand, a completely denuclearized Eurasia is not necessarily the most stable of political communities. The mixture of democratic and nondemocratic states and the variety of nationalisms left over from Soviet disintegration could lead to hypernationalistic aggression and military confrontation, without any policing power provided by the formerly assertive NATO and Soviet military establishments. NATO has an important transitional role to play in this regard, one of reassurance that ill-gotten gains from surprise offensives and irredentist wars will not be permitted to stand permanently. Denuclearization of Europe will obviously, and painfully, place more of a burden on the willingness of status quo powers to employ conventional forces in order to reverse unacceptable breaches of the peace. Some of this responsibility can be transferred from state to regional or global security organs, but by no means all of it, if pre–Cold War European history is suggestive.

Collective security in a post–Cold War, denuclearized Europe would pose the same problem as it did for the victorious powers following World War I. In order to keep the peace, the powers must agree to use military force against designated aggressors for the sake of deterring aggression and regardless of whether the use of force is in the national interest of each state. This degree of altruism in the resistance of aggression was unobtainable in the interwar period of the twentieth century, and it would take boldness to proclaim its imminence now. In the more probable near term future of a Europe with smaller nuclear forces instead of none, the management of proliferation constitutes an unavoidable task. Unable to escape the responsibility, leaders can attempt to freeze the situation in place, to control the slow spread of nuclear weapons in Europe, or to bypass nuclear controls and allow the most dedicated proponents of arms competition to prevail.[21]

The first course of action, freezing in place, may be difficult to accomplish without multistate institutions that are more powerful than those now available. The second alternative, controlling the slow spread of nuclear weapons, could be accomplished by states, but it requires the development and use of interstate consultative mechanisms for confidence building, verification, and reassurance against untoward motives. The third alternative, bypassing attempts to control nuclear spread in post–Cold War Europe, risks a march toward a truly anarchic European security landscape by the year 2020. Without a truly federated Europe, a combination of the first and second approaches is the probable forecast for the next decade or so. Britain, France, and Russia are going to hold onto their strategic nuclear weapons for reasons of prestige and political influence; they will be in no hurry to see other neighbors of theirs obtain nuclear weapons. Consultative machinery does exist for controlling the spread of nuclear weapons in Europe in an evolutionary manner and, perhaps, for lowering the size of existing nuclear forces all the while.

Related to the problem of nuclear weapons spread are the dispersion of other weapons of mass destruction, including chemical and biological weapons, and the technology transfer of missiles and other components of high technology armed forces from the developed to the developing states. Separate set of norms, rules, and procedures for verification of compliance, or "regimes," have been established to deal with the problems of nuclear, chemical, and biological weapons spread and manufacture. In addition to these treaty-based efforts, the Missile Technology Control Regime was created in 1987 to restrict the spread of ballistic missiles to which, it was feared, certain countries might attach nuclear or chemical warheads. The progress of Iraq in this regard prior to the Gulf War of 1991 supported the case that this fear of ballistic missiles mated to weapons of mass destruction was well-founded.[22] In addition to the treaty-based and Missile Technology Control Regimes limiting weapons spread and technology transfer, there is an emerging regime for the limitation of transfers of advanced conventional weapons technology (based on discussions among the five permanent members of the UN Security Council). An additional regime survivor of the Cold War, the Coordinating Committee for Multilateral Export Controls, has an uncertain future in view of its Cold War mission to prevent military and other technology transfer from the West to the Warsaw Pact and China. Aspects of these regimes are summarized in Table 6.2.

A study by Leonard Spector and Virginia Foran has suggested possible means for consolidating or harmonizing aspects of these six regimes, in four ways: by combining or supplementing the treaties, by consolidating inspection agencies or sharing procedures, by integrating the various export control regimes, and by combining sanctions against various offenders, across different regimes, under common auspices, such as the United Nations.[23] There is certainly some precedent for at least the last of these four approaches. The UN Security Council has, in effect, adopted a uniform approach toward sanctions related to nuclear, biological, and chemical weapons. Leaders of the council member states adopted in January 1992 a statement asserting the readiness of the council to consider sanctions against any proliferators of weapons of mass destruction.[24] Two problems with this approach to weapons spread limitation are obvious. First, the ability of nuclear armed states to preach the gospel of nonproliferation is limited by their unwillingness to throw away the makeweights of their own arsenals, although the START II agreement signed by Presidents Bush and Yeltsin in December 1992 helps considerably with this "exemplary" problem. Second, it is not obvious to all nuclear have-nots that regional or global stability is better served through nuclear abstinence.

NATO nuclear weapons support stability in Europe to the extent that such stability is threatened by a revival of Russian imperialism. Without a Russian threat to the stability of Western and East Central Europe, NATO nuclear weapons constitute a deterrent force that has lost its rationale. The status of U.S. nuclear weapons deployed in Europe becomes especially problematical in a post–Cold War world. One cannot have the new world order without new world military forces and military tasking. If Russia is fully integrated within the Eurasian community of states and if a security community excluding resort to force characterizes relations among those states, then NATO's military doctrines and military forces must be adapted to new times. Ultimately, the making permanent of a Eurasian security community calls for an organization very different from NATO, the most successful peacetime military alliance of the twentieth century.

However valuable its contributions to the Cold War order, NATO is not, and was never intended to be, mainly a collective security organization. Had it been so, it would not have fulfilled its Cold War purpose.[25] NATO's nuclear weapons become hostages to the march of history in Europe for the same reason that NATO now passes into transitional relevancy. Nuclear weapons are ideal weapons for deterrence and for extending the protection of the strong to the weak. They are mischievous weapons in a collective security system, predicated as it is on a very different concept of military persuasion compared with nuclear. Nuclear deterrence works by presenting a credible threat of unacceptable punishment to a prospective attacker, regardless of the attacker's capacity to prevail in battle with conventional forces. Conventional deterrence in a balance of power system depends upon the threat to deny attackers the spoils of victory and to defeat their armed forces in battle. Conventional deterrence in a collective security system depends upon the willingness of a majority of states to coalesce against aggression committed against any other state.

These differences in approach among state-dependent conventional deterrence, conventional deterrence by means of collective security, and nuclear deterrence have significant implications for the war terminations envisioned in each approach. Conventional deterrence based on state self-help admits a variety of endings to war, but the central tendency in modern wars is for the continuation of struggle until the forces of one side submit to the other. Conventional deterrence based on collective security assumes that the strength of the larger coalition will rapidly dispose of the armed power of the minority, which has dared to commit aggression against international norms. In both cases, the expected objective of armed forces is to bring about the most rapid and decisive defeat of the opposed armed forces and to obtain the most propitious surrender terms.

The model of nuclear deterrence differs from the other two in its implications for the relationship between war and policy, whether at the beginning or at the end of a war. The use of nuclear weapons on behalf of collective security is almost inconceivable unless an outlaw state first attacked a nonnuclear state with weapons of mass destruction. The international community would be loath to approve nuclear use except in the case of retaliation for nuclear first strike. Even then, if the nuclear aggressor's forces could be disarmed by the combined might of the world community's nonnuclear forces, as would happen now, this path would be a preferable means to the restoration of peace. Nuclear

TABLE 6.2
Nonproliferation and Technology Transfer Regimes (Global)

Treaty or Agreement	Countries of Concern	Verification System
Nuclear weapons 1970 Nuclear Nonproliferation Treaty (NPT)	Non-NPT states with nuclear weapons capability: Israel, India, Pakistan NPT parties, future compliance uncertain: Iran, Iraq, Libya, North Korea	International Atomic Energy Agency
Biological weapons 1972 Biological and Toxin Weapons Convention Geneva Protocol of 1925 (prohibits use)	Biological weapons programs publicly identified by United States: China, Iran Libya, North Korea, Russia, Syria, Taiwan	None (member states may request investigation by UN Security Council)
Chemical weapons Chemical Weapons Convention (open for signing in 1993) Geneva Protocol of 1925 (prohibits use)	Chemical weapons programs publicly identified by the United States: China, Egypt, France, India, Iran, Iraq, Israel, Libya, Myanmar, North Korea, Pakistan, Russia, South Korea, Syria, Taiwan, United States, Vietnam	Organization for the Prohibition of Chemical Weapons

Missiles		
Missile Technology Control Regime (no treaty — a set of restricted export controls by suppliers)	MTCR-range missiles or space launchers or development programs: Argentina, Brazil, China, Egypt, European Space Agency, France, India, Indonesia, Iran, Iraq, Israel, Japan, Libya, North Korea, Pakistan, Russia, Saudi Arabia, South Africa, South Korea, Syria, Taiwan, United Kingdom, United States, Yemen	Supplier enforced restrictions on end use and reexport
Conventional weapons		
No global treaty: Conventional Forces in Europe Treaty limits numbers and deployments of major classes of conventional weapons	Former Soviet republics engaged in regional wars or threatened with civil strife; newly democratic states of East Central Europe	Supplier enforced restrictions on end use and reexport

Source: Condensed and adapted from Leonard S. Spector and Virginia Foran, *Preventing Weapons Proliferation* (Warrenton, Va.: Stanley Foundation, 1992), pp. 32–33.

punishment, even for nuclear aggression, is an all or nothing affair and necessary only when all other options have failed to bring about desired war aims. For example, had Saddam Hussein's Iraq succeeded in acquiring deliverable nuclear weapons by the time of the Gulf War of 1991 and had he used some of them against Saudi Arabia, it is not obvious that the UN coalition should have dealt with this by nuclear retaliation.

In general, collective security is incompatible with nuclear spread. Beyond traditional measures to prevent nonnuclear states from going nuclear, the nuclear powers of the UN Security Council should cooperate to ensure that those cases of proliferation that cannot be avoided are well-managed. Those new nuclear arsenals that are added to the world's inventory in the next decade or two should be, to the extent possible, not first strike vulnerable and not based on preemption prone command, control, and communications systems. Given the dependency of modern military systems on satellite communications and other aspects of high technology, the scientific and technical means available to the great powers for inducing aspiring nuclear states to cooperate in military-technical stability and restraint should be considerable.

COLLECTIVE SECURITY AND DEMOCRATIC CHANGE

The argument so far has sought to demonstrate that collective security and nuclear proliferation are antithetical even under the assumption that proliferation occurs no faster in the next few decades than it did in the past few, nor need one assume that future states acquiring nuclear arsenals will be less responsible, with regard to self-protection against accidental or inadvertent launch, than those already in possession of nuclear charges. Even slow proliferation minimizes the opportunities for collective security, because nuclear weapons are force multipliers above and beyond the multiplication of force made possible by coalition politics. For example, a rogue state capable of delivering 20 or so weapons against an outside power that sought to prevent its regional hegemony would be in an intimidating position, regardless of the alliance support available to that outside power from friendly states. Even if the outsider and allies had nuclear weapons of their own, they would still expect to absorb significant, and, perhaps, politically unacceptable, military casualties and other losses at the hands of the instigator's nuclear forces. Consider what Iraq armed with 20 to 30 nuclear weapons for its Scud missiles in January 1991 might have done to the forces of the U.S.-led coalition or to Israel's cities. More to the point, consider the deterrent effect a known Iraqi capability of this type might have had on planning for Desert Storm.

Because no one can guarantee against nuclear or other weapons of mass destruction spreading to aspiring hegemonies, reconstruction of the international system by aligning stronger defenders against weaker aggressors leaves plenty of room for international mischief. Some have argued, for this and other reasons, that tinkering with alliance and coalition relationships among states will not suffice for a durable post–Cold War international order. In addition, according to these voices among scholars and heads of state, the character of political regimes must be transformed. The kinds of states in the system, whether autocratic or democratic, help to determine the likelihood of wars and the kinds of wars that are fought.

For those who see a strong connection between the kinds of regimes that predominate in any system and the probability of war within that system, the path toward the eradication of interstate conflict lies in the homogenization of the kinds of states and regimes distributed throughout the international system. If only all states were democracies, for example, then wars based on the hatred of democracies for autocracies and vice versa would end. Further, it is sometimes posited, in what has become a new tradition in Western political science, that democracies do not fight against one another. Creating democratic states where authoritarian polities once stood is, according to the maxim of democratic pacifism, the most durable means to ensure international tranquility.[26] Authoritarian and totalitarian states have their own preferred means for homogenizing the interstate system, of course, by conquest or by subversion of governments based on other principles. In principle, a state of legal anarchy permits states based on different organizing principles to live together without feeling in peril of their regime survival. In practice, the coexistence of different political forms based on ideological diversity often is followed by the assumption that a bad example next door must be stamped out, lest its contagion spread to others.

Ideological diversity, thus, tends toward a domino effect or toward the assumption by leaders of a domino effect, which impedes the stabilization of foreign relations based only on self-interest and power politics.[27] What is wrong with the balance of power and national interest model of interstate relations developed by Morgenthau and others is not that it is too pessimistic but that it is too optimistic about the influence of values issues on politics.[28] Balance of power models assume rational actors who value power aggrandizement for its own sake and who are prepared to sacrifice almost any other values for the opportunity to increase state power. Power is both an end and a means. These rational actors of a balance of power system will be willing to assume short-term losses for long-term gains, as long as the system stays in equilibrium and precludes the development by any single actor of hegemonial claims.

Ideological diversity militates against a willingness to value stability or equilibrium for its own sake. One reason for this is that conflicting ideologies involve states in wars for principle instead of wars for position. Wars for principle tend to be longer in duration and more intense in the commitment of participants to the fighting. The revolutionary nationalism of Napoleonic France brought a level of intensity to warfare not previously known. Ideological diversity also contributes to the difficulty in terminating coalition wars. Victorious coalitions characterized by ideological diversity find it difficult to agree on peace terms or on the responsibilities of the victors for regulating the postwar world. The aftermaths of the Congress of Vienna and World Wars I and II provide abundant evidence to support the argument that ideologically heterogeneous victorious coalitions have more difficulty arranging peace than homogeneous coalitions do.

The assumption that democracies and autocracies behave differently in foreign and security policy combines arguments about regime type and ideological diversity. As Melvin Small and J. David Singer have noted, there is no consensus among scholars on an exhaustive list of regime types, and scholarly disagreement also exists on the assignment of particular states to regime types.[29] Small and Singer defined a category of "bourgeois democracies," including those states that met, between 1816 and 1965, the following criteria: periodic elections were held with competitive parties; at least 10 percent of the adult population was enfranchised to vote for a parliament or legislature; and the legislature in question either controlled or shared equal power with the executive.[30] Using these criteria, Small and Singer than investigated whether bourgeois democratic states were involved in proportionately more interstate wars between 1816 and 1965 than nondemocratic states were. They also asked whether democracies initiated more or fewer wars than nondemocracies did and if wars involving democracies were longer or bloodier than wars that did not. Small and Singer also investigated the propensity of democracies to fight other democracies.[31]

Data on the duration and severity of interstate wars (excluding extrasystemic wars fought mostly by great powers against minor powers outside Europe) between 1816 and 1965 revealed the patterns summarized in Table 6.3.

It turns out that wars involving democracies were longer than wars not involving democracies if the world wars of the twentieth century are included. If the world wars are treated as exceptional and excluded, then the wars involving democracies are not longer than those not involving democracies. The pattern for severity of wars involving, or excluding, democracies shows that wars including democracies, on the average, had fewer average battle deaths per nation than those excluding democracies. It would appear from these data that wars involving democracies, compared with those that do not involve democracies, are longer but less bloody. However, the less bloody character of wars involving democracies is not consistent with the results of the two world wars, which were as costly as any in European history.

TABLE 6.3
Average Duration and Severity of Interstate Wars, 1816–1965, by
Type of Regime (Democratic versus Nondemocratic)

Type and Participation	Number of Wars	Average Duration (Months)	Number of Nations	Average Battle Deaths per Nation
Democratic participation	19	15.8	47	91,000
Nondemocratic participation	31	11.8	144	167,000
Democratic participation (world wars excluded)	17	10.5	30	5,100
Nondemocratic participation (world wars excluded)	31	11.8	118	38,400

Source: Melvin Small and J. David Singer, "The War-Proneness of Democratic Regimes, 1816–1965," *Jerusalem Journal of International Relations* (Summer 1976): 63. I have excluded the extrasystemic wars originally included in this table.

The issue of whether some kinds of regimes are more likely to initiate aggression than other types is also important as part of the relationship between ideology or regime type and the likelihood of stability. More than one peace proposal has been based on the assumption that authoritarian systems are more war prone than democratic systems. However, bourgeois democracies between 1816 and 1965 participated in 19 interstate wars, and they initiated the war or were on the side of the initiator in 11 of them (58 percent).[32] There is no apparent difference between the willingness of democracies and that of other states to initiate interstate wars.[33] There is some evidence that democracies are less willing to fight with other democracies and that democracies seek one another as allies, as noted previously.

The lesser frequency of wars among democracies, compared with wars involving democracies with other types of political systems, is partly an artifact of the smaller number of democracies compared with authoritarian systems for much of European history. Of the 30 interstate wars between 1871 and 1965, 15 (50 percent) included one or more democratic participants. Of the 129 states that participated in those wars, 42 (32 percent) were democracies. In contrast, the period from 1816 to 1870 witnessed 20 interstate wars; four of those wars included one or more democracies (230 percent), and democracies at war in this period constituted 6 states of a total of 62 (less than 10 percent).[34] The argument that democracies are less likely to go to war against other democratic states, compared with their propensity to fight against nondemocratic states, finds partial but incomplete support in the data on nineteenth- and twentieth-century interstate wars, including major coalition wars.

A system in which regimes were more hesitant to fight against constitutional colleagues could be less or more war prone than a diverse system, but the historical data suggest a tendency toward less war proneness, that is, states that look alike and think alike might coexist more peacefully than those that do not. On the other hand, the relations among the great powers on the eve of World War I offer evidence that similarity of constitutions or regime types does not stand in the way of interstate war if other variables push leaders toward war. Among these other variables are leaders' perceptions of their security dilemmas. Of particular interest is how vulnerable they feel to surprise attack. Leaders perceiving a high degree of vulnerability will care less about the compatibility of values between their regimes and those of potential adversaries. Those who perceive that vulnerability is low have more latitude to overlook regime differences and to exploit regime similarities.

Perceived vulnerability to surprise attack makes leaders feel that alliances are more necessary for their survival, regardless of whether those alliances are with states having similar or different regimes. Hitler and Stalin were willing to join together to create a temporary community of interest in 1939, in order to minimize the size of potentially opposed coalitions against Germany and the Soviet Union on other issues. Similarity of regime type can lead two or more states to reduce their perceived probability of attack from one another, provided other variables can be favorably manipulated. Those other variables include available war technology and military doctrine. If technology and doctrine are conducive to the offensive, then perceived vulnerability will grow, independently of similarity among regime types. If technology and doctrine favor the defense, then the scope for regime like-mindedness to push leaders toward cooperation and peace is greater. The issue of the perceived security dilemma of leaders is important for many reasons, but for our immediate purposes, the significance of the security dilemma is that it is a fruitful concept for linking systemic and actor levels of analysis.[35]

CONCLUSIONS

Collective security as crisis management aims to reduce the likelihood of war by convincing potential aggressors of the inevitability of their overwhelming defeat. A problem with this approach, even before the nuclear age, was the risk that it would frighten the state being deterred into launching preemptive attack at one or more members of the security coalition. As an approach to war termination, collective security recommends the threat of war widening as a means of intrawar deterrence and conflict resolution. The approach calls for leaders who are willing to make believable threats of escalation now in order to achieve deescalation later. An international system with significantly greater proliferation of weapons of mass destruction and of long range delivery systems involves high risks for collective security as an approach to deterrence and to crisis management.

NOTES

1.   For an approach to analysis of the post–Cold War world based on the comparison of integrating and disintegrating forces, see John Lewis Gaddis, *The United States and the End of the Cold War: Implications, Reconsiderations, Provocations* (New York: Oxford University Press, 1992), pp. 193–216.

2.   On the theory of collective security, see Inis L. Claude, Jr., *Swords Into Plowshares: The Problems and Progress of International Organization* (New York: Random House, 1964), pp. 223–60.

3.   Paul R. Pillar, *Negotiating Peace: War Termination as a Bargaining Process* (Princeton, N.J.: Princeton University Press, 1983).

4.   J. David Singer and Melvin Small, *The Wages of War 1816–1965* (New York: John Wiley and Sons, 1972). Interstate wars are those wars in which a member of the state system fights on each side. Extrasystemic wars usually are colonial or imperial wars with a member of the state system on one side.

5.   A seminal discussion of the problem of terminating civil wars appears in Roy C. Licklider, "How Civil Wars End: Preliminary Results from a Comparative Project," in *Controlling and Ending Conflict: Issues before and after the Cold War*, eds. Stephen J. Cimbala and Sidney R. Waldman (Westport, Conn.: Greenwood, 1992), pp. 219–38. For case studies of United Nations efforts in war termination, see Sydney D. Bailey, *How Wars End: The United Nations and the Termination of Armed Conflict, 1946–1964*, Vol. II (Oxford: Clarendon Press, 1982).

6.   Brinkmanship is a deliberately chosen risky behavior that may be used in various kinds of crisis. It is also a kind of crisis. See Richard Ned Lebow, *Between Peace and War: The Nature of International Crisis* (Baltimore, Md.: Johns Hopkins University Press, 1981), pp. 7, 57–81.

7.   The definitive study of the Schlieffen plan is Gerhard Ritter, *The Schlieffen Plan, Critique of a Myth* (London: Oswald, Wolff, 1958), in translation. This edition includes the text of Schlieffen's great memorandum of December 1905 (pp. 134–47).

8.   Robert Jervis, "Cooperation Under the Security Dilemma," *World Politics* 30 (January 1978): 167–86; Thomas J. Christensen and Jack Snyder, "Chain Gangs and Passed Bucks: Predicting Alliance Patterns in Multipolarity," *International Organization* (Spring 1990), reprinted in Paul R. Viotti and Mark V. Kauppi, eds., *International Relations Theory: Realism, Pluralism, Globalism* (New York: Macmillan, 1993), pp. 154–86.

9.   Geoffrey Blainey, *The Causes of War* (New York: The Free Press, 1973), pp. 35–56.

10.   J. McDermott, "The Revolution in British Military Thinking from the Boer War to the Moroccan Crisis," in *The War Plans of the Great Powers*, ed. Paul M. Kennedy (London: Allen & Unwin, 1979), pp. 99–118.

11.   Kalevi J. Holsti, *Peace and War: Armed Conflicts and International Order, 1648–1989* (Cambridge: Cambridge University Press, 1991), p. 142.

12.   On the Congress of Vienna, see Sir Charles Webster, *The Congress of Vienna, 1814–1815* (London: Thames and Hudson, 1963). A useful study of post-concert Europe is Arthur J. May, *The Age of Metternich, 1814–1848* (New York: Holt, Rinehart and Winston, 1963).

13.   The mechanism by which alliances contributed to the outbreak of war in 1914 was not that alliances were necessarily bad for peace. Under some conditions within a balance of power system, alliances can contribute to peace by allowing potential defenders to balance the power of potential aggressors. Alliances can

increase the likelihood of war in a multipolar system that depends upon flexibility of alignment to reassure states that surprise attacks cannot succeed. Where the perceived vulnerability of states to surprise attack exceeds the degree of reassurance that they derive from the potential for mobilization of allies, a multipolar system faces an unmanageable security dilemma. The problem of multipolar crisis management is compounded if, in addition to the gap between expected vulnerability and the potential for allied reassurance, military technology is thought to favor the offense instead of the defense. Technology that favors the offense contributes to domino effects: initial gains of attackers multiply, and defense of the status quo without threatening others becomes more difficult. See Robert Jervis, "Domino Beliefs and Strategic Behavior," in *Dominoes and Bandwagons: Strategic Beliefs and Great Power Competition in the Eurasian Rimland*, eds. Robert Jervis and Jack Snyder (New York: Oxford University Press, 1991), pp. 20–50, esp. p. 39.

14.   This distinction is explained in Patrick M. Morgan, *Deterrence: A Conceptual Analysis* (Beverly Hills, Calif.: Sage Publications, 1983).

15.   Thomas Hobbes, *Leviathan* (New York: Washington Square Press, 1964), pp. 84–85. Originally published in 1651.

16.   For an overview of current issues pertinent to proliferation, see Robert D. Blackwill and Albert Carnesale, eds., *New Nuclear Nations: Consequences for U.S. Policy* (New York: Council on Foreign Relations, 1993); Lewis A. Dunn and Sharon A. Squassoni, eds., *Arms Control: What Next?* (Boulder, Colo.: Westview, 1993).

17.   For an argument that well-organized proliferation may be Europe's best available option, see Mearsheimer, "Disorder Restored," in *Rethinking America's Security*, eds. Graham Allison and Gregory F. Treverton (New York: W. W. Norton, 1992), pp. 213–37, esp. p. 230. For an argument that nuclear proliferation may not be dysfunctional for global stability, see Kenneth N. Waltz, *The Spread of Nuclear Weapons: More May Be Better*, Adelphi Papers No. 171 (London: International Institute of Strategic Studies, 1981).

18.   Peter Douglas Feaver, Duke University, suggests this nomenclature in his study on nuclear command and control issues. See Peter Douglas Feaver, *Guarding the Guardians: Civilian Control of Nuclear Weapons in the United States* (Ithaca, N.Y.: Cornell University Press, 1992), pp. 12–21.

19.   Gaddis, *The United States and the End of the Cold War*, p. 117.

20.   For informed assessment of the status of nuclear weapons on European security, see Richard H. Ullman, *Securing Europe* (Princeton, N.J.: Princeton University Press, 1991), pp. 83–106.

21.   Mearsheimer foresees three possible nuclear futures: (1) elimination of nuclear weapons from global arsenals; (2) existing nuclear powers keep their weapons, but no new states acquire nuclear forces; (3) nuclear proliferation, either well managed or poorly managed. According to Mearsheimer, the third possible future is the most likely: poorly managed proliferation spells disaster, but well managed proliferation might be about as stable as the Cold War. Mearsheimer, "Disorder Restored," pp. 230–32.

22.   Leonard S. Spector and Virginia Foran, *Preventing Weapons Proliferation: Should the Regimes Be Combined?* (Report of the Thirty-Third Strategy for Peace, U.S. Foreign Policy Conference, October 22–24, 1992) (Warrenton, Va.: Stanley Foundation, 1992), p. 8.

23.   Ibid., p. 24.

24.   Ibid.

25.   On the other hand, NATO was charged with the objective of detente along with that of defense, thus, opening a window on the post–Cold War world for NATO as a transitional actor and partial contributor to future collective security.

26. A great deal of empirical research has been done on this issue, but the results lend themselves to diverse interpretation. See Melvin Small and J. David Singer, "The War-Proneness of Democratic Regimes, 1816–1965," *Jerusalem Journal of International Relations* (Summer 1976): 50–69; Quincy Wright, *A Study of War* (Chicago, Ill.: University of Chicago Press, 1942), pp. 839–48. Democratic states may be more inclined to ally with other democracies, compared with nondemocratic systems. See Randolph M. Siverson and Juliann Emmons, "Birds of a Feather: Democratic Political Systems and Alliance Choices in the Twentieth Century," *Journal of Conflict Resolution* (June 1991): 285–306, esp. p. 295. Between 1946 and 1965, according to Siverson and Emmons, democracies allied with each other almost 80 percent higher than the rate predicted by chance, but the relationship does not hold for the period between World War I and World War II.

27. Douglas J. Macdonald, "The Truman Administration and Global Responsibilities: The Birth of the Falling Domino Principle," in *Dominoes and Bandwagons: Strategic Beliefs and Great Power Competition in the Eurasian Rimland*, eds., Robert Jervis and Jack Snyder (New York: Oxford University Press, 1991), pp. 112–44.

28. Hans J. Morgenthau and Kenneth W. Thompson, *Politics among Nations: The Struggle for Power and Peace* (New York: Alfred A. Knopf, 1985).

29. Small and Singer, "The War-Proneness of Democratic Regimes," p. 53.

30. Ibid., p. 55.

31. Ibid., pp. 61–68; see also J. David Singer and Melvin Small, *The Wages of War 1816–1965: A Statistical Handbook* (New York: John Wiley and Sons, 1972).

32. Small and Singer, "The War-Proneness of Democratic Regimes," p. 66.

33. In this case, war initiation means being the first to cross a border or firing the first shots in anger.

34. Small and Singer, "The War-Proneness of Democratic Regimes," p. 62.

35. Robert Jervis, "Cooperation Under the Security Dilemma," pp. 167–214.

7

Nuclear Weapons and International Futures: Perspectives on Proliferation

Many are justifiably skeptical that nuclear proliferation is compatible with international political or military stability.[1] However, some experts contend that a controlled process of proliferation would support stability instead of detracting from it.[2] Debates between optimists and pessimists about nuclear weapons spread have sometimes passed one another because of differences in methodology and conceptual focus.[3] There is a particular need to close the gap between two genres of writing about nuclear weapons: discussions of the relationship between nuclear weapons and the long peace of 1945–90 and arguments about whether nuclear weapons spread after the Cold War is likely to contribute to or detract from international stability.

In the discussion that follows, I do not try to revisit all previously published arguments pro and con nuclear proliferation. These are liberally cited in notes. Instead, I review three conceptual perspectives or paradigms through which the nuclear past can be related explicitly and systematically, as is rarely done, to prognosis about nuclear futures. I argue that the inferences from one of these paradigms, nuclear agnosticism, show how uncertainty based deterrence in a bipolar world could be counterproductive under conditions of strategic nuclear multipolarity. Realist or nuclear positivist views cannot be stretched from the uniquely and atypically stable Cold War world into the more complicated and indeterminate post–Cold War universe.

The perspective offered here is different from, although compatible with, criticisms of nuclear optimism (or nuclear positivism, as I call it) offered by other proliferation pessimists, including Bruce Blair, Peter Feaver, and Scott Sagan.[4] These authors and others have pointed to unexplained variation in organizational behavior, including organizational pathologies not accounted for by political realism, pertinent to the risks of nuclear weapons spread. Although valuable, these "organizational" critiques of proliferation positivism are incomplete. Nuclear realism, which, arguably, helped to stabilize a bipolar world, for the same reasons now threatens to destabilize the post–Cold War international environment.[5]

NUCLEAR POSITIVISM

Nuclear positivism based on political realism is of value to the extent that it acknowledges the importance of the nuclear revolution.[6] The nuclear revolution separated the accomplishment of military denial from the infliction of military punishment. The meaning of this for strategists was that military victory, defined prior to the nuclear age as the ability to prevail over opposed forces in battle, now was permissible only well below the level of total war, and less than total wars were risky as never before. Nuclear realists admit that these profound changes have taken place in the relationship between force and policy. They argue, however, that the new relationship between force and policy strengthens, rather than weakens, some perennial principles of international relations theory. Power is still king, but the king is now latent power in the form of risk manipulation and threat of war, instead of power actually displayed on the battlefield.

Other schools can concur with the realists on some of these major points, but implicit in the realist model of deterrence stability are some theoretical (meaning explanatory or predictive) limitations. Each of these limitations or sets of problems with realist explanatory theory limits the inferences that can be drawn from a realist or neorealist perspective, especially from structural realism. The three problem areas are whether the realist view is based on exceptional cases, whether the economic theories on which some neorealist arguments about deterrence stability are based can be transferred from economics to international politics, and whether structural realism can account for both general and immediate deterrence situations.[7]

Exceptional Cases

Realist arguments for the possibility of a stable nuclear multipolar world are based on the Cold War experiences of the United States and the Soviet Union. The supposition is that, just as the U.S. and the Soviet political and military leaderships worked out, over time, rules of the road for crisis management and the avoidance of inadvertent war or escalation, so, too, would aspiring nuclear powers among the current nonnuclear states. However, there are reasons to doubt whether the U.S. and Soviet experiences can be repeated after the Cold War. First, the U.S.-Soviet nuclear relationship between 1945 and 1990 also was supported by bipolarity and by an approximate equality, although an asymmetrical one, in overall U.S. and Soviet military power. Neither bipolarity nor, obviously, U.S.-Russian global military equity is available to support stable relations in the post–Cold War world; in fact, both are irrelevant so long as Russia evolves in a democratic, capitalist direction and prefers cooperative U.S.-Russian foreign relations.

A second reason why the U.S. and Soviet Cold War experiences are unlikely to be repeated by future proliferators is that the relationship between political legitimacy and military control was solid in Moscow and in Washington but was uncertain for many nuclear powers outside Europe. The issue here is not whether democracies are less warlike than are dictatorships. The question is whether the regime can impose either assertive or delegative military control over its armed forces and, if it does, the consequences for its crisis management and normal nuclear operations. Assertive control implies a great deal of civilian intervention in military operations and management; delegative control implies more willingness to let the military have their own way on operational and organizational issues. Assertive control ensures against "never" types of failure in a nuclear command and control system, at the expense of "always" failures (responding promptly to authorized commands). Delegative control has the reverse emphasis.[8]

A third reason why the U.S.-Soviet experience may not be normative for newer nuclear powers is that there were no pieces of territory or other vital interests for which one of the sides was committed to go to war rather than to suffer defeat or stalemate. The two sides were satisfied generally by bloc consolidation and by internal power balancing instead of external adventurism and zero sum competition for territory or resources. The preceding observation does not imply that Cold War crises, such as those that occurred over Berlin and Cuba, were not dangerous. They were dangerous, but the danger was mitigated by the awareness that neither state had to sacrifice a vital piece of its own territory or its own national values (allies were another matter) in order to avoid war. What was at stake in the most dangerous U.S.-Soviet Cold War confrontations was "extended" deterrence, or the credibility of nuclear protection extended to allies, not defense of the homeland per se.

In sum, the first major problem with nuclear realism, based on U.S.-Soviet Cold War experience, is the sampling of exceptional cases. It is as if one were to sample the opinions of the U.S. electorate by taking polls only in Vermont and New Hampshire. The behavior of the United States and the Soviet Union with regard to nuclear weapons was unusual because their vital interests could be defended without nuclear war, because their systems of civil-military relations were proof against military usurpation or command disability in crises, and because other support for stability, especially a widely acknowledged global military bipolarity, reinforced the effects of nuclear weapons.

Microeconomic Analogies

The second major set of theoretical problems with nuclear realism lies in the adaptation of arguments from microeconomic theory to theories of interstate relations. Kenneth N. Waltz explicitly compares the behaviors of states in an international system with the behavior of firms in a market.[9] As the market forces firms into a common mode of rational decision making in order to survive, so, too, does the international system, according to Waltz, dictate similar constraints upon the behavior of states. The analogy, however, is wrong. The international system does not dominate its leading state actors; leading states define the parameters of the system.

International politics is a game of oligopoly, in which the few rule the many. Because this is so, there cannot be any "system" to which the leading oligopolists, unlike the remainder of the states, are subject. The system is determined by the preferred ends and means of its leading members. Structural realists assume that some "system" of interactions exists independently of the states that make it up. This is a useful heuristic for theorists but a very mistaken view of the way in which policy is actually made in international affairs. Because structural realists insist upon reification of the system independently of the principal actors within the system, they miss the subsystemic dominance built into the international order.

An important test of whether meaningful theory can proceed on the basis of the realist, or realpolitik, premise of "system" separateness or whether domestic political forces must also be taken into account by theorists is to test realist and domestic or constrained hypotheses against historical evidence. According to Bruce Bueno de Mesquita and David Lalman, the realist perspective as formalized in their models is not supported by the past two centuries' experience of interstate behavior.[10] The authors deduce an "acquiescence impossibility" theorem that shows that, in a logically developed game structure based on realist assumptions, it is impossible for one state to acquiesce to the demands of another "regardless of the beliefs held by the rivals, regardless of the initial demand made by one of the states, and regardless of initial endowments of capabilities, coalitional support, propensities to take risks, or anything else."[11] None of the deductions derived from the realist or neorealist versions of their international interactions game, according to Bueno de Mesquita and Lalman, were supported in the empirical data set that included 707 dyadic interactions.[12]

One might argue, in defense of structural realists on this point, that the assumption of system determinism is a useful falsehood. It allows for parsimony in expression and in focus on the essential attributes of the international system. However, again, the assumption of "apartness" of the system and its essential state or nonstate actors is only useful, and methodologically defensible, if it leads to insights that are both accurate and not otherwise attainable. Neither exceptional accuracy nor exceptional attainability of insight has been demonstrated by structural realists for the assumption of system and actor "apartness." This is probably one reason why traditional realists, as opposed to neorealists and modern structural realists, do not exclude what Waltz, in another study, refers to as first and second image variables.[13] Realism fails to explain the high degree of international cooperation that takes place despite a legally anarchic international order because of the biased manner in which realism deals with imperfect information. According to Bueno de Mesquita and Lalman:

In the realist world, imperfect information can only encourage violence. Incorrect beliefs about the intentions of rivals can only steer disputes away from negotiation (or the status quo) and toward the blackmail inherent in a capitulation or the tragedy inherent in a war. Incorrect beliefs, secrecy, misperception, misjudgment, and miscalculation are routine features of human intercourse. In that sense, a realist world could be a dangerous world indeed.[14]

In fact, the explanations and predictions made possible by structural realism are successfully carried out only within a closed and very constrained universe. Even within that universe, structural realism works better with conventional weapons than it does with a multitude of nuclear forces. Conventional wars can be fought to rectify an imbalance of power, to challenge the hegemonic rule of imperial states, or to bring about other changes in the international political environment within which states must act. Conventional war and system change can go together.[15] Nuclear weapons, and, in particular, nuclear weapons spread, makes the relationship between war and systems change much more pathological. War as an instrument for the attainment of policy objectives becomes more irrational with nuclear, compared with conventional, weapons. Realists actually count on this fear of a pathological relationship between war and change to preserve peace. Nuclear weapons will freeze the situation in favor of the defenders of the status quo and against those potential aggressors who would disturb the peace.

Structural Realism and Immediate Deterrence

This brings us to the third general set of problems with realist theories and nuclear weapons spread. The structure of the international system is not related to general deterrence in the same way as it is related to immediate deterrence. According to Patrick M. Morgan, the need for general deterrence is inherent in the normal day to day relations of states, based on the distribution of power and states' assumptions about one another's intentions.[16] General deterrence is the latent possibility that many states may opt for war within an anarchic or nonhierarchical international order.[17] Immediate deterrence is a situation in which one side has actually made specific threats against another, the second side perceives itself threatened, and a significant likelihood of war exists in the minds of leaders in at least one of the two states.[18] For example, the onset of a crisis often signifies a failure of general deterrence, but, as yet, immediate deterrence has not failed because states have not yet abandoned diplomacy and crisis management for battle.

It makes sense to assume that there might be a strong correlation between success or failure in general deterrence and system attributes such as distributions of actor capabilities and objectives. However, the relationship between international systems and failures of immediate deterrence is much more indirect. State and substate variables, including the attributes of individuals, groups, and bureaucratic organizations, are among the filters through which any "system" forces must pass before those forces are manifest in state decisions and policies. The distinction between general and immediate deterrence helps to explain why perfectly logical deductions from deterrence theory based on rationality postulates often fly in the face of states' actual behavior.[19]

The significance of the distinction between general and immediate deterrence is illustrated by the Cuban missile crisis. The decision by Khrushchev to put Soviet medium and intermediate range ballistic missiles into Cuba was intended, among other objectives, to diminish the publicly acknowledged (by U.S. government officials) gap between U.S. and Soviet strategic nuclear capabilities. Khrushchev's decision, made in the spring of 1962 after consulting very few key advisors, represented a failure of general deterrence. The Soviet leadership had decided to risk the emplacement of its nuclear weapons outside Soviet territory and in the Western Hemisphere for the first time. However, it was not yet a failure of immediate deterrence. Immediate deterrence was not involved in Khrushchev's clandestine deployment program because the deployments were deliberately kept secret. Had Khrushchev carried through his original plans, he would have completed the missile deployments and then announced their existence.

In that eventuality, the mere existence of Khrushchev's missiles on Cuban soil, however threatening it seemed to U.S. policy makers, would not have created a situation of immediate deterrence. Only the completion of deployments followed by a coercive threat would move the situation from a failure of general deterrence (Soviets make a dangerous move in the arms race) to one of immediate deterrence (for example, Soviets now demand that United States and allies leave West Berlin immediately). The preceding supposition is of the "what if" or counterfactual kind; we may never know the full story of Khrushchev's motives for the missile deployments.[20] The actual shift from a general to an immediate deterrence situation took place on October 22 when President

Kennedy ordered the Soviet missiles removed from Cuba, announced that the United States was imposing a quarantine on Soviet shipments to Cuba, and stated that a nuclear missile launched from Cuba against any target in the Western Hemisphere would call forth a full U.S. retaliatory response against the Soviet Union.

Realist perspectives help to explain the background to general deterrence failure in this instance, but they do little to clarify why the U.S. and Soviet political leaderships chose as they did. If the international power positions of states yield unambiguous deductions about their crisis management strategies, Khrushchev should never have dared to put missiles into Cuba. And the United States, once the missiles had been discovered, need not have hesitated to invade Cuba or to launch an air strike to destroy the missile sites, colocated air defense sites, and other nuclear capable weapons platforms deployed in Cuba by Moscow.[21] Realists would argue, against the preceding statement, that nuclear weapons made the Soviets and the Americans cautious during the Cuban missile crisis. The danger created by nuclear weapons helped to end the crisis without war, following the logic and against my earlier argument.

However, realist arguments will not work in this context. Nuclear weapons did not make the crisis easier to manage, but harder. They added to the risk of escalation, to be sure, and leaders were well aware of these risks. The United States deliberately and, some would say, successfully manipulated the risk of escalation and war in order to force Khrushchev's withdrawal of the missiles. However, the argument for nuclear coercion as to the path to the Cuban crisis settlement will not work, because nuclear weapons, and the Soviet sense of inferiority in the nuclear arms race, were major causes of the crisis.[22] If it is argued that nuclear weapons helped to resolve the crisis, that is true only as a historical tautology: having caused it or helped to cause it and by making it more dangerous, they played a part in ending it.

The Cuban crisis example shows the limitations of realism in explaining even the most set piece, one-against-one confrontation between two relatively mature command and control systems during the Cold War. Structural realism leaves the mold in place and removes the Jello. The essence of Cuban crisis bargaining was about Khrushchev's overestimation of his own risk-taking propensity. His military reach had exceeded his political grasp, and when discovery of the missiles blew his cover, he retreated, not only in the face of U.S. power and determination, but also because he and Kennedy recognized that they had maneuvered themselves very close to an outbreak of inadvertent war, and possible escalation to nuclear war.

The tendency of realism to reification of "systems" may have its methodological uses when systems are posited to do harmless or politically benign things. When systems are charged with the responsibility for maintaining peace and security, then one cannot exclude from the assessment of system stability the decision-making proclivities of states nor the fears and perceptions of their leaders. Realist assumptions can help to explain or to predict failures of general deterrence, as in the case of arms races that get out of control, but what states will choose to do about these systemic processes (actually a series of state decisions, but granting structural realists the benefit of the doubt) remains an open door, a "window of opportunity."

The matter raised here is not simply a level of analysis problem but one of philosophy of analysis. One cannot choose preferred levels of analysis without making some assumption about which level or levels best provide explanations and predictions for those outcomes and processes that matter most. Nuclear positivists who depend upon realism can make interesting statements about the central tendencies of state behaviors within a particular international order, but meaningful theory also must include statements about ranges or variation among values taken on by causal and dependent variables. It is both true and misleading to say, for example, that we had no nuclear wars during the Cold War era; therefore, states in general are risk averse once they have acquired nuclear weapons. The point about states in general remains not proved, and it says nothing at all about what a particular state might do in a specific crisis. Unlike with business firms, with nuclear weapons and nuclear wars, we do want to know the deviant cases and know them intimately: they may drive the entire system into new directions.

NUCLEAR IRRELEVANCY

A second school of thought argues that nuclear weapons were really unnecessary for Cold War stability. One can formulate this argument in harder or softer terms. The harder version is that nuclear weapons were irrelevant subjectively as well as objectively: not only did they have no real impact on the likelihood of major war, but also, leaders paid little regard to the role of nuclear weapons in preserving stable deterrence. The softer form of the argument would contend that leaders did pay attention to nuclear weapons and spend a great deal of time with nuclear planning but that all of this was potlatch, not really necessary for a basically nonmilitary relationship between the United States and the North Atlantic Treaty Organization (NATO), on one side, and the Soviet Union and the Warsaw Pact, on the other.

Representative of the softer form of the argument is John Mueller's *Retreat from Doomsday: The Obsolescence of Major War.*[23] Mueller's book really asserts two very different theses. The first is that large scale, interstate wars already had become obsolete by the turn of the twentieth century. Leaders, having failed to recognize this, plunged foolishly into World War I and paid an unexpectedly drastic price. After World War I, most European political and military leaders, intellectuals, and publics recognized the dysfunctional character of major war. The world was on a linear path toward the absence of great coalition wars, lining up numbers of major powers on each side. This path toward peaceful progress was interrupted by the unexpected dedication of the German and Japanese regimes in the 1930s to achieving their objectives by conquest. After World War II, in a very new international system, the major powers resumed their linear progression toward the obsolescence of war. Like duelling and slavery, war simply was becoming an idea whose time had run out.

This idea that the states of the developed world were on a course toward eventual debellicism was not original with Mueller, of course, and the pre–World War I literature foreseeing the obsolescence of war is discussed (and critiqued extensively) by Geoffrey Blainey in his historical study, *The Causes of War*.[24] Many of Mueller's references are to literary and other sources that support the idea that cultural literati have been gradually turning away from war as an expression of anything purposive or beneficial, but the case that statesmen, generals, and publics even in democratic societies are more opposed to war than formerly requires more evidence than Mueller offers.

The growing obsolescence of major interstate war is only one of Mueller's arguments. It is related to, but distinct from, the second: that nuclear weapons had little to do with Cold War stability. One must dispose of the first argument, about the perceived obsolescence of major war, before addressing the second, about the irrelevance of nuclear weapons during the Cold War. If the first argument by Mueller is largely true, then the second argument can rest in part on a substructure provided by the first: obsolescence of war supports nuclear irrelevancy. The United States, the Soviet Union, and their major allies had had enough of fighting as a result of World War II. The possibility of a World War III fought even without nuclear weapons would have been sufficiently discouraging. Mueller contends that U.S. industrial and economic superiority would have guaranteed victory in a global war waged without nuclear weapons: the United States could have mobilized for victory and overwhelmed any adversary with military production after World War II, as it did between 1941 and 1945. U.S. mobilization potential and economic capacity were the great deterrent against Soviet adventurism, according to Mueller, not nuclear weapons.

Mueller's case for nuclear irrelevancy during the Cold War is supported by Robert S. McNamara, former U.S. secretary of defense. McNamara is something of a paradox. As secretary of defense, he played an essential part in developing U.S. nuclear strategy and force structure that remained influential to the very end of the Cold War.[25] In February 1963, McNamara testified before a congressional committee that Khrushchev was forced to back down: Khrushchev "knew without any question whatsoever that he faced the full military power of the United States, including its nuclear weapons" and that U.S.

officials had faced "the possibility of launching nuclear weapons and Khrushchev knew it, and that is the reason, and the only reason, why he withdrew those weapons."[26] McNamara's reflections out of office, on the other hand, run decidedly against the political or military significance of nuclear weapons. Writing in the 1980s, McNamara argued that nuclear weapons "serve no military purpose whatsoever. They are totally useless — except only to deter one's opponent from using them."[27] Reconsidering the U.S. experience in the Cuban missile crisis in 1987, McNamara reaffirmed that "all those fancy nuclear weapons are militarily useless. You can't *use* them."[28] Note that this position is different from the position taken by some nuclear positivists and agnostics that nuclear superiority is militarily or politically useless. McNamara doubtless would agree about the futility of nuclear superiority, but his position goes beyond that.

Mueller is correct to argue that the Soviet Union and its allies would have been disadvantaged in any global conventional war, compared with the United States and its allies. U.S. economic and industrial strength, especially in the first two decades following the end of World War II, must have seemed very imposing to Soviet leaders. In addition, to the extent that they took seriously their Marxism, Soviet leaders would have believed that military superiority flows from economic potential. Therefore, any war against the capitalist West would make long odds for Moscow.[29] In addition, U.S. maritime superiority throughout the Cold War years would have added to U.S. and allied advantages in any global war of attrition against the Soviet Union and its allies. Moscow's only hope, should war break out against NATO and remain nonnuclear, was to attain its political and military objectives through a blitz campaign. Careful net assessment revealed that the chances that the Soviet Union could have succeeded in a short warning attack against NATO during the 1980s ranged from slight to nonexistent.

However, it does not follow that, if the requirements for deterring the Soviet Union from deliberate attack on NATO could have been met without nuclear weapons, the necessary and sufficient conditions for the prevention of war in Europe were obtained. More than deterrence of the Soviet Union from any deliberate aggression that it might have contemplated was involved in maintaining Cold War European stability. The Soviet Union also had to be persuaded that NATO was "deterred." The very statement that NATO required deterring struck Western military experts as oxymoronic during the Cold War years; it was self-evident to them that the United States and NATO would never launch an unprovoked attack on the Soviet Union, but it was not self-evident to Moscow — what seemed like an unprovoked or unjustified attack to the Soviet leadership might differ from what was defined as an unprovoked attack in Washington, Bonn, or Brussels.

Given the large nuclear and conventional weapons arsenals and numbers of troops deployed in Europe by adverse military blocs poised for war, the major risk was not deliberate but inadvertent war.[30] Incidents growing out of border clashes or other apparently minor skirmishes between NATO and Warsaw Pact forces might have escalated into major confrontations between the Cold War superpowers. Recall that nuclear deterrence theorists touted their logic of manipulation of an unknown, but significant, risk of war as a principal component of deterrence. Testimony to this theory being put into practice by NATO was NATO's forward deployment of U.S. and other short range, or tactical, nuclear forces throughout the European theater of operations. These weapons either would be overrun by enemy forces very early or commanders would demand early release from NATO authorities, raising the likelihood of nuclear first use into a near certainty.

Tactical nuclear weapons were capable of igniting a series of action-reaction sequences over which the combatants would rapidly lose centralized political and military control. Many wars, not one, would be going on at once: a NATO military command and control system cut into pieces of uneven size and complexity would be reacting to a Soviet system similarly disaggregated and confused. Stopping this kind of war would not necessarily be impossible, but it would be about as difficult an undertaking as theorists of war termination had ever imagined. There was very little likelihood that, had war broken out in Europe at any time between the latter 1950s and the mid-1980s, NATO could have used most of its short range nuclear forces in a controlled and purposive way.[31]

The preceding paragraph strengthens Mueller's argument to the extent that it supports the political absurdity of nuclear war fighting doctrines. However, it reminds us that deliberate war was probably not the major risk to stability in post–World War II Europe. The war machines created by the two alliances turned into military museums overstuffed with useless furniture, including superfluous arms and vulnerable command and control systems. These war machines were designed for threatening one another, but, in the event of actual war, they could not have kept the level of violence proportionate to any meaningful political objective. Even throwing away nuclear weapons would have left NATO and the Warsaw Pact with military pterodactyls: forces larger than necessary for any politically acceptable mission, but forces with sufficient size and putative capability to create serious fears on both sides that the other side might launch a surprise attack.

Bernard Brodie's claim about nuclear weapons in 1946, that, from the time of their invention, strategy would be dedicated mainly to the avoidance of major war, was prescient. It also had an ironical destination in Cold War U.S. and Soviet armed forces and military doctrines. The skillful nonuse of military forces turned deterrence into an all-encompassing substitute for military preparedness, for usable war fighting skills, and, especially in the U.S. case, for foreign policy in general. Deterrence became the tapeworm that swallowed the host.

Forces and doctrines justified in the name of deterrence of Moscow often were perceived by the Soviets as strategic compellents. Instead of viewing U.S. forces and doctrines as defensively motivated policies of the status quo, Soviet leaders from the 1960s through the 1980s interpreted U.S. force modernizations and policy pronouncements as U.S. efforts to force Moscow into military and political retreat.[32]

NUCLEAR AGNOSTICISM

Nuclear agnosticism is the position toward which scholars and analysts are driven who reject both the argument of nuclear positivism and that of nuclear irrelevance. Nuclear agnosticism includes a variety of persons and ideas whose views are not easily summarized. The category includes, to use the language given currency by a Harvard nuclear arms control study group, "hawks, doves and owls."[33] Agnosticism shares with nuclear positivism the argument that the nuclear revolution was an important component of Cold War international stability, especially stabilizing for the relationship between the United States and the Soviet Union. At the same time, nuclear agnostics recognize that the problems of inadvertent war and escalation made stability far from a sure thing between 1945 and 1990. For agnostics, it was fortunate that Cold War stability was overdetermined by factors other than fear of nuclear war, including bipolarity. Agnostics doubt that technology fixes or new models of political decision making can change the history of human folly a great deal. Thus, agnostics tend to feel that the problem of accidental or inadvertent nuclear war or escalation calls into question the assumptions made by nuclear positivists, who think that arms control can work indefinitely, and by advocates for nuclear irrelevancy, who argue that the march of history bypasses nuclear weapons.

Historian John Lewis Gaddis, physicist Freeman Dyson, and political scientist Robert Jervis are examples of prominent nuclear agnostics, albeit from very different points of departure. Gaddis has written a great deal about the development of U.S. national security policy during the Cold War.[34] He shares with many historians a sense of frustration with many social scientists' approaches to explaining political causes and effects: "Theorists also expend so much of their energy debating methdology — what with neo-realists clashing with neo-Marxists, empiricists with deductivists, quantifiers with non-quantifiers, and behaviorists with particularists — that one wonders at times if they will ever get around to substance at all."[35] Gaddis suggests that interpreters of the Cold War and of the role of nuclear weapons in international relations during that period should take a consumerist approach toward theory. Arguing for paradigm pluralism in explaining the duration of Cold War stability, he contends that arguments drawn from theories of bipolarity, hegemonic stability, "triumphant" liberalism, and long cycle theory can be used, in addition to the argument for nuclear peace, to explain the Cold War stability.[36]

Although arguing for paradigm pluralism, Gaddis leans more toward the perspective of nuclear positivists than he does toward those who would contend that nuclear weapons were irrelevant during the Cold War. According to Gaddis, nuclear weapons have influenced post–World War II international relations in at least four ways. First, nuclear weapons helped to support an already existing reluctance of the great powers to wage war against one another. Second, states that possessed nuclear weapons became more risk averse. Third, nuclear weapons did not create bipolarity after World War II, but they did prolong its life and so, too, helped to prolong stability. Fourth, nuclear weapons helped to perpetuate the Cold War by saving the United States, the Soviet Union, and their allies military expenditures on conventional forces, expenditures that, if necessary, might have forced rethinking of Cold War assumptions sooner.[37]

All four of these arguments go against the grain of nuclear irrelevancy, but only the first three are necessarily supportive of the case for nuclear stability. The fourth argument acknowledges that political relations between the United States and the Soviet Union remained adversarial longer than necessary, partly because of ingrained habits of military hangover. Nuclear weapons helped to freeze a political glacis that became its own worst enemy until a new Soviet leader in 1985 began to take dramatic steps to melt the ice. To the nuclear positivists' contention that nuclear weapons made war less likely because war became more dangerous, Gaddis' fourth argument for nuclear relevancy points to the downside of that contention. The very weapons of mass destruction that some would contend were instruments of deterrence or peace were also causes of U.S. and Soviet leaders' fears of devastating surprise attack. The capabilities of these weapons were so unprecedented that the very fact of their being targeted at your state made a relationship hostile in military-operational terms even when it had passed into a stage of nonhostility in policy.

Freeman Dyson is less agnostic than Gaddis about the usefulness of nuclear weapons. Dyson would like to be rid of nuclear weapons altogether. He would not agree with nuclear positivists or nuclear agnostics, who advance arguments in favor of nuclear stability in the long run. On the other hand, Dyson also would disagree with the school of nuclear irrelevancy. Nuclear weapons are not superfluous. They have been incorporated into military doctrines and into war plans as war fighting instruments. Therefore, the possibility that they might be used to devastating effect, deliberately or inadvertently, is very strong.[38]

Dyson is a nuclear abolitionist, but he argues that it is very important to adopt a strategy for nuclear abolition that will work successfully within the current and foreseeable world of technology and politics. Thus, he does not advocate immediate global nuclear disarmament, the abolition of state sovereignty, or other nostrums popular among nuclear disarmers since the advent of those weapons. Instead, Dyson argues for a transitional strategy that gets us from our current condition of nuclear plethora to a condition of nuclear anemia. Once states have reduced their arsenals to very small numbers of nuclear weapons, according to Dyson, the last steps toward abolition will become politically and militarily feasible.

According to Dyson, the history of Quaker involvement in the antislavery movement shows that the eradication of evil is best accomplished one step at a time. Quakers saw that the slave trade itself was an especially obnoxious practice and one that was more vulnerable than slavery as a whole. Therefore, Quakers first sought to abolish the slave trade and made a strategic decision to leave to later generations the task of abolishing slavery altogether.[39] By extension, it follows that the abolition of nuclear weapons is a more feasible objective than the abolition of war, and it also follows that to abolish nuclear weapons, one must have another answer to the perennial question of states: whence our security from attack?

Dyson's answer, what he refers to as the "middle way" or "live-and-let-live" is to build gradually and cooperatively nonnuclear defenses while building down nuclear offenses.[40] Dyson is not an advocate of defenses as door openers to a new arms race in nonnuclear weapons. The purpose of defenses is to give states a sense of security while they are disengaging from nuclear dependency. It also is not necessary to build space based or other ballistic missile defenses in order to rid the world of nuclear weapons: this decision Dyson treats as a contingent one. Nonnuclear ballistic missile defenses may be useful in moving from a condition of few offensive nuclear weapons down to zero: "the proper role of ABM [antiballistic missile] defenses in a live-and-let-live strategy is mainly a question of timing."[41]

During the U.S.-Soviet hostility of the early 1980s, the possibility of cooperative nuclear disarmament and mutual reliance on nonnuclear defenses seemed remote, even after President Reagan's "Star Wars" initiative was launched by his speech of March 23, 1983. However, the new U.S.-Russian relationship made possible by the end of the Cold War and the shared interest in Moscow and in Washington in the reduction of nuclear arsenals worldwide makes Dyson's live-and-let-live option more politically feasible. On the other hand, to the extent that states do decide that ballistic missile defenses are a necessary prelude to offensive force reductions, a nonnuclear military balance is not necessarily any more stable than the previous nuclear balance.

For Dyson and for other agnostics who might share his views, a stable balance of power based on nonnuclear defenses is not beyond the realm of possibility in the next century. Technology can work for or against peace. However, the purpose to which nonnuclear defenses are put can be offensive. Space based weapons, although nonnuclear, can be used as means of preemptive attack, for example, on another state's warning, reconnaissance, or communications satellites. A "defensive" satellite based interceptor using speed of light weapons also can be an "offensive" antisatellite weapon capable of blinding the eyes and ears of a military opponent. In fact, the greater dependency of states on the military uses of space for crisis management implies that antisatellite weapons and other space or ground based weapons used against satellites might become preferred tools of crisis coercion.[42]

Among political scientists writing about nuclear strategy and deterrence theory, Robert Jervis has taken the most influential agnostic position. Jervis argues assertively for the uniqueness of the nuclear revolution and against the conventionalization of nuclear forces into war-fighting strategies analogous to prenuclear thinking.[43] Thus, he maintained that the Cold War U.S.-Soviet nuclear relationship was a world of mutual assured destruction (M.A.D.), regardless of clever theories that might be proposed against that view.[44] On the other hand, it could not be taken for granted that a M.A.D. world was an inherently stable world. Jervis' contributions to the study of decision making showed how the psychological attributes of individuals and the behaviors of small groups influenced the outcomes of decisions. Of particular significance were his works on the importance of perceptions, images, and other aspects of leaders' cognitive or motivational mind sets pertinent to their normal or crisis behavior.[45]

Jervis qualifies as an agnostic because he accepts mutual deterrence through assured retaliation as a basic frame of reference for nuclear stability but recognizes that deterrence is neither automatic nor risk avoidant. In that recognition he is not alone among those nuclear strategists who favor assured retaliation to counterforce damage-limiting strategies.[46] However, one of Jervis' special contributions, his insight into the two-sided character of escalation, results from his agnostic appreciation of the role of nuclear weapons. Escalation is neither impossible nor certain.[47] If escalation were impossible, then war could be waged safely below the nuclear threshold. If escalation were certain, then no one would start a conventional war involving one or more nuclear powers. The indeterminacy of escalation is what makes it work; the same indeterminacy makes it dangerous. It "works" because leaders who engage in a process of competitive risk taking knowingly enter a sequence of events over which they may ultimately lose control.[48] Like nuclear agnostics, some proponents of nuclear irrelevancy count on an important role for fear of escalation in dampening crises and in avoiding wars, but not necessarily, and not preferably, nuclear escalation.[49]

Jervis' insight, that deterrence worked by making escalation neither impossible nor certain, helps to arbitrate between the claims of nuclear optimists who favor post–Cold War proliferation and nuclear pessimists who warn against the potential dangers of nuclear weapons spread. In a world of nuclear certainty in which deterrence could be derived directly from nuclear balances, nuclear weapons spread would create more situations of military stalemate in which aggressors were inhibited and defenders made more secure. However, if nuclear deterrence works primarily by manipulation of risk or by uncertainty, then the widespread dispersal of nuclear weapons increases the insecurity of defenders and motivates them to adopt hair-trigger deterrents.

Other contributions from nuclear agnostics provide grounds for skepticism about a positive association between nuclear weapons spread and international stability, based on case studies of nuclear crisis management and force operations or on the operations of nuclear command and control systems generally. Studies of nuclear crisis management by Richard K. Betts, Alexander L. George, Richard Ned Lebow, and Scott D. Sagan, among others, have called into question many of the assumptions about decision making on which rational deterrence theory is based.[50] These studies were supported by extensive analyses of the U.S. and Soviet nuclear command and control systems, including detailed information about their operational biases and military-doctrinal proclivities, by Bruce Blair, Desmond Ball, Paul Bracken, and others.[51] These "crisis management/force operations" and "command and control" literatures jointly call into question the assumption made by proliferation optimists that new nuclear states will automatically learn the stabilizing crisis management behaviors and develop command/control systems that minimize risks of accidental or inadvertent war.

Contributors to nuclear crisis management and command and control studies have shown that there is often significant tension between the requirements for crisis management and those for protecting forces against vulnerability; political leaders are frequently ill-informed about the capabilities and operations of their own military forces, including nuclear forces; leaders' crisis behavior is marked by very constrained perceptions, expectations, and frames of reference that filter incoming stimuli from the external environment, including deterrent threats from other states; and military organizations enter a crisis with an already established repertoire of standard operating procedures and institutional ethos that cannot be suddenly disposed of without harming organizational performance.

Peter D. Feaver has explained that nuclear command and control organizations must optimize between the "always" requirement, for responsiveness to authorized commands in order to avoid vulnerability, and the "never" requirement, to prevent accidental or unauthorized nuclear use.[52] He notes that one cannot infer the behavior of nuclear command systems without taking into account those environments or domains that might influence nuclear use decisions. These environments are the strategic weapons systems and force structures, the strategic environments in which a state's policy is located, and, most significant in the present context, the strategic culture of a state, including its patterns of civil-military relations and whether that pattern emphasizes "delegative" or "assertive" control by civilians over military operations.[53]

The work of Blair, Sagan, Feaver, and others who are attempting to develop testable hypotheses about nuclear organizational behavior is important for another reason. Testable propositions about leaders' decision-making and command system performances will help to settle some past disputes about how behaviorally correct deterrence theory really is.[54] Deterrence always has been promoted as a species of rational decision theory: it depends upon arguments about cost-benefit ratios and calculations of expected gains and losses.[55] For many of its critics, however, U.S. versions of nuclear deterrence theory suffered from vacuous arguments and insufficient validation in comparative case studies.[56] Much of the deterrence literature, like a great deal of the Marxist literature, served as a scholastic rallying point for polemicist argument instead of a source of disinterested scientific research or policy studies.

Whether deterrence, as related to proliferation or as discussed *sui generis*, was really a behavioral science was not only a philosophical or methodological issue. The U.S. government approach to Cold War decision making, including its uses of coercive diplomacy and threats, was influenced by deterrence theory. Deterrence theory, if some nuclear positivists can be believed, provided for U.S. policy makers an applied behavioral science that supported containment policy and made more predictable relations with the Soviet Union on arms control and other topics. From the standpoint of nuclear irrelevants and agnostics, on the other hand, deterrence appeared to the Soviet military and to Soviet defense intellectuals as a confrontational, coercive strategy designed to manipulate the arms race against Moscow's interests.[57] Seen as the essence of behavioral realism by its proponents, deterrence was a conceptual void and a policy anachronism to its detractors.

Agnostics also are not of one mind about whether the stability of the Cold War was overdetermined or multidetermined. One does not necessarily imply the other. An overdetermined period of peace implies that, even with nuclear weapons out of the picture altogether, a great power peace would have obtained after 1945. A multidetermined peace is one caused by nuclear deterrence, among other factors, including bipolarity, absence of issues sufficiently grave to propel the great powers into war, and so forth.[58] Gaddis, for example, argues for multi-determination: nuclear weapons had at least a supportive role to play in Cold War stability, and without nuclear weapons, the U.S.-Soviet rivalry might have been more likely to erupt into war.[59] On the other hand, advocates of nuclear irrelevancy, like Mueller, contend that nuclear weapons were unnecessary, and, therefore, gratuitously dangerous, to stable Cold War international politics.[60]

Some advocates of nuclear positivism would contend that the nuclear irrelevants and nuclear agnostics have benign intentions about moderating the arms race, but, in the view of positivists, irrelevants and agnostics confuse the desirable with the necessary. The balance of terror is simply a modernized and more dangerous version of the balance of power. Failure to acknowledge this results in weaker deterrence and enhanced, not reduced, risks of war. States frequently have sought to escape the "perpetual quadrille of the Balance of Power," as A.J.P. Taylor has noted, but they have rarely succeeded in doing so.[61] One does not have to endorse the realist paradigm for explanation and prediction of a majority of international phenomena in order to acknowledge that a realist perspective quickly enters into the council chambers and war rooms of crisis bound leaders. Few nuclear positivists would try to argue that the outcomes of nuclear war are acceptable or desirable. However, and in contrast to nuclear agnostics and to advocates of nuclear irrelevancy, positivists do assert with more confidence that deterrence is an acceptable and even desirable modernized form of the balance of power. In fact, some positivists draw heavily upon the argument that nuclear deterrence is a more reliable guarantor of peace than conventional deterrence, on the evidence of an admittedly one-sided historical record.[62]

CONCLUSIONS

The views of those who argue for Cold War nuclear positivism, irrelevancy, or agnosticism are not merely a catalogue of scholarly opinions. As grouped in the preceding discussion, they suggest some points about the transferability of Cold War experience into the new world order. Scott Sagan, for example, outlines three requirements within a rational deterrence framework for nuclear stability and then tests whether nuclear armed states would be likely to meet those requirements: absence of preventive war motives, availability of second strike forces on both sides for potential opponents, and no nuclear arsenals prone to accidental or unauthorized use.[63] Sagan's studies make a strong case for bringing the organizational level of analysis into the study of nuclear proliferation.

However, neorealists who argue that nuclear weapons spread is consistent with international stability are not entirely refuted by showing that accidental, inadvertent, or preventive wars could happen in a new world order. Proliferation positivists can play back the organizational card: U.S., Soviet, and other Cold War organizations learned how to reduce the risks of accidental or inadvertent war to acceptable levels and to eliminate, for all practical purposes, the risks of politically usurped deterrents. Forced to the wall, proliferation positivists can and will leap the fence of rational deterrence theory and forage into other levels of analysis.

A fundamental weakness of realist arguments for proliferation is theoretical or conceptual, in addition to empirical problems with the theory. Realism works by simplifying the reality of political decision makers, and, although nuclear weapons seem to simplify the choices of political and military leaders, it is more probable that pandemic nuclearization would introduce unacceptable levels of international systemic complexity. The interaction dynamics of multilateral nuclear crisis management would be many times as complicated as those of the bilateral U.S.-Soviet Cold War experiences. Imagine a future world even with "second strike capable" Ukrainian, Pakistani, Iranian, and North Korean nuclear forces, and you have arrived at the "realism" to which proliferation positivism leads us.

NOTES

1.   Lewis A. Dunn, *Controlling the Bomb: Nuclear Proliferation in the 1980s* (New Haven, Conn.: Yale University Press, 1982). For more recent assessments, see Leonard S. Spector and Virginia Foran, *Preventing Weapons Proliferation: Should the Regimes Be Combined?* (Warrenton, Va.: Stanley Foundation, 1992); George H. Quester, *The Multilateral Management of International Security: The Nuclear Proliferation Model* (College Park, Md.: University of Maryland, Center for International and Security Studies, 1993); John Hawes, *Nuclear Proliferation: Down to the Hard Cases* (College Park, Md.: University of Maryland, Center for International and Security Studies, 1993); Andrew J. Goodpaster, *Tighter Limits on Nuclear Arms: Issues and Opportunities for a New Era* (Washington, D.C.: Atlantic Council of the United States, 1992) all provide analysis suggestive of proliferation pessimism.

2.   Kenneth N. Waltz, *The Spread of Nuclear Weapons: More May Be Better*, Adelphi Paper No. 171 (London: International Institute for Strategic Studies, 1981). See also Kenneth N. Waltz, "Nuclear Myths and Political Realities," *American Political Science Review* (September 1990): 731–45; John J. Mearsheimer, "The Case for a Ukrainian Nuclear Deterrent," *Foreign Affairs* (Summer 1993): 50–66; Martin Van Creveld, *Nuclear Proliferation and the Future of Conflict* (New York: The Free Press, 1993) are among the more widely cited optimists. An argument for making a distinction between stabilizing and destabilizing cases of proliferation and for emphasizing safety and security of force operations in stabilizing cases is presented in William C. Martel and William T. Pendley, *Nuclear Coexistence: Rethinking U.S. Policy to Promote Stability in an Era of Proliferation*, Studies in the National Security No. 1 (Montgomery, Ala.: U.S. Air War College, 1994). The urgency of denuclearization of existing arsenals, especially those in former Soviet republics other than Russia, is emphasized in Graham T. Allison, Ashton B. Carter, Steven E. Miller, and Philip Zelikow, "Cooperative Denuclearization: An International Agenda," in *Cooperative Denuclearization: From Pledges to Deeds*, eds. Graham T. Allison, Ashton B. Carter, Steven E. Miller, and Philip Zelikow (Cambridge, Mass.: Harvard University, Center for Science and International Affairs, 1993), pp. 1–25. For an assessment of this literature and a critique of rational deterrence theory as applied to proliferation, see Peter D. Feaver, "Proliferation Optimism and Theories of Nuclear Operations," *Security Studies* (Spring/Summer 1993): 159–91.

3.   For recent assessments, see Robert D. Blackwill and Albert Carnesale, eds., *New Nuclear Nations: Consequences for U.S. Policy* (New York: Council on Foreign Relations, 1993); Jacqueline R. Smith, "Nuclear Non-Proliferation Policy in a New

Strategic Environment," in *Arms Control: What Next?* eds. Lewis A. Dunn and Sharon A. Squassoni (Boulder, Colo.: Westview Press, 1993), pp. 58–78.

4.   See the references to these writers in notes 50 and 51 in this chapter.

5.   Additional support for the notion that realism has very different implications for the post–Cold War world, compared with its 1945–90 predecessor, is found in McGeorge Bundy, William J. Crowe, Jr., and Sidney Drell, *Reducing Nuclear Danger: The Road Away from the Brink* (New York: Council on Foreign Relations, 1993), p. 86 and *passim*.

6.   Realists contend that power is based on tangible resources such as population, economic capacity, and territory, and the most influential among them also believe that power is both a means and an end in international politics. See Hans J. Morgenthau, *Politics among Nations: The Struggle for Power and Peace* (New York: Alfred A. Knopf, 1948). Neorealists hold, as do realists, that the structure of the international system, especially system polarity, is the most important determinant of the context for state decision making. Neorealists, in contrast to realists, are more likely to acknowledge sources of power other than tangible ones and to treat power as a means but not an end in itself. For a summary and critique of neorealist views, see Robert O. Keohane, "Theory of World Politics: Structural Realism and Beyond," in *Political Science: The State of the Discipline*, ed. Ada W. Finifter (Washington, D.C.: American Political Science Association, 1983, reprinted in Paul R. Viotti and Mark V. Kauppi, *International Relations Theory: Realism, Pluralism, Globalism* (New York: Macmillan, 1993), pp. 186–227. See also Kalevi J. Holsti, *Peace and War: Armed Conflicts and International Order* (Cambridge: Cambridge University Press, 1991), pp. 328–30.

7.   For the distinction between general and immediate deterrence, See Patrick M. Morgan, *Deterrence: A Conceptual Analysis* (Beverly Hills, Calif.: Sage Publications, 1983).

8.   The distinctions are explained in Peter Douglas Feaver, *Guarding the Guardians: Civilian Control of Nuclear Weapons in the United States* (Ithaca, N.Y.: Cornell University Press, 1992), pp. 3–28 and *passim*.

9.   Kenneth N. Waltz, *Theory of International Politics* (Reading, Mass.: Addison-Wesley, 1979).

10.   Bruce Bueno de Mesquita and David Lalman, *War and Reason: Domestic and International Imperatives* (New Haven, Conn.: Yale University Press, 1992).

11.   Ibid., p. 267.

12.   Ibid., pp. 267–68. The findings of Bueno de Mesquita pertinent to the limitations of realism are important in the context of debates about proliferation, because his work is cited by proliferation pessimists as representative of nuclear realist positivism. See, for example, Scott D. Sagan, "The Perils of Proliferation: Organization Theory, Deterrence Theory, and the Spread of Nuclear Weapons," *International Security* (Spring 1994): 66–108, esp. 66. Sagan cites Bruce Bueno de Mesquita and William H. Riker, "An Assessment of the Merits of Selective Nuclear Proliferation," *Journal of Conflict Resolution* (June 1982): 283.

13.   Kenneth N. Waltz, *Man, the State and War* (New York: Columbia University Press, 1959). The first image includes human nature and individual psychological attributes pertinent to decision making. The second image refers to state level decisions and behaviors. An interesting anomaly is that Waltz's 1959 book offers a much more subtle appreciation of the complexity of international political interaction than does his 1979 book; yet, the latter has proved to be far more influential in spawning "bandwagoning" and balancing responses in the literature. The 1959 Waltz is actually far more convincing than the 1979 Waltz, although the latter book is written in a style perhaps appealing to the new wave of scholastically inclined theorists.

14.   Bueno de Mesquita and Lalman, *War and Reason*, p. 269. The authors acknowledge that, under conditions of imperfect information, states might mistakenly stumble into war as a result of misjudgments based on inaccurate information. However, in a domestically constrained, as opposed to a realist, model of strategic rationality, leaders may also "mistakenly" avoid war and "stumble into negotiation or other peaceful solutions to their differences (p. 269). Waltz argues that the complexity of a multipolar nuclear world will induce risk averse, instead of risk acceptant, behavior on the part of leaders (Waltz, *The Spread of Nuclear Weapons*, p. 30).

15.   On the historical relationship between war and systems change, see Robert Gilpin, *War and Change in World Politics* (Cambridge: Cambridge University Press, 1981).

16.   Patrick M. Morgan, *Deterrence: A Conceptual Analysis*, 2d ed. (Beverly Hills, Calif.: Sage, 1983), pp. 27ff.

17.   Or, as Hobbes explained it, it is a precept or general rule of reason that "every man, ought to endeavour Peace, as farre as he has hope of obtaining it; and when he cannot obtain it, that he may seek, and use, all helps, and advantages of Warre." Thomas Hobbes, *Leviathan* (New York: Washington Square Press, 1964), p. 88. See also Hedley Bull, *The Anarchical Society: A Study of Order in World Politics* (New York: Columbia University Press, 1977).

18.   For a more complete definition of immediate deterrence, see Morgan, *Deterrence: A Conceptual Analysis*.

19.   As Robert Jervis explains, rationality assumptions are not necessarily falsified by cases in which leaders have chosen poorly, but in many other instances, "the beliefs and policies are so removed from what a careful and disinterested analysis of the situation reveals that the failure is hard to fit into the framework generated by rationality." Robert Jervis, "Introduction," in *Psychology and Deterrence*, eds. Robert Jervis, Richard Ned Lebow, and Janice Gross Stein (Baltimore, Md.: Johns Hopkins University Press, 1985), p. 6. In addition, leaders' beliefs about deterrence and credibility are interactive with the probability that particular strategies will succeed or fail. As Jervis acknowledges, "There is no objective answer to the question of which nuclear postures and doctrines are destabilizing, apart from the highly subjective beliefs that decision makers hold about this question. . . . Not only do each side's beliefs constitute an important part of the reality with which the other has to contend, but also states can collude or contend on the constructions of reality that frame these judgments. Robert Jervis, *The Meaning of the Nuclear Revolution* (Ithaca, N.Y.: Cornell University Press, 1989), p. 183.

20.   See Raymond L. Garthoff, *Reflections on the Cuban Missile Crisis* (Washington, D.C.: Brookings Institution, 1989), pp. 6–42.

21.   U.S. officials at the time of the Cuban missile crisis underestimated significantly the size of the Soviets' conventional forces deployed on that island (actually some 40,000), nor did they realize that, in addition to warheads for medium and intermediate range missiles deployed in Cuba, the Soviets also deployed nuclear warheads for tactical weapons launchers. At the time of the crisis, U.S. leaders were uncertain whether any Soviet warheads actually arrived in Cuba. Raymond L. Garthoff, "The Havana Conference on the Cuban Missile Crisis," *Cold War International History Project Bulletin* (Spring 1992): pp. 1–4. According to Bruce Blair, actual orders to the senior Soviet commander in Cuba specifically precluded the use of any nuclear weapons without prior approval from Moscow (Bruce G. Blair, *The Logic of Accidental Nuclear War* [Washington, D.C.: Brookings Institution, 1993], p. 109).

22.   U.S. leaders were not well-informed about the actual Soviet nuclear force deployments in Cuba in October 1962. With regard to nuclear force loadings, Soviet tactical nuclear weapons (in addition to those intended for SS-4 and SS-5 launchers) numbered between 98 and 104: 80 for two regiments of front cruise missiles; 12 for

Luna surface to surface, short range missiles; 6 for gravity bombs for IL-28 bombers; and possible additional charges for nuclear armed naval mines. The approximate maximum range for the cruise missiles, fired from Cuban shore points nearest to U.S. territory, was 90 miles; warheads for these cruise missiles were in the 5-12 kiloton range. The 60 warheads deployed for SS-4 and SS-5 launchers in Cuba (the latter never actually reached Cuba, having been turned back by the U.S. quarantine) were in addition to these tactical weapons; all but the SS-5 warheads apparently reached Cuba in a single shipment on October 4. The existence of a Soviet tactical nuclear force of this size, unknown to U.S. invasion planners, indicates that, for Moscow, the psychological investment in defense of Cuba was apparently much higher than Americans, then and subsequently during the Cold War, believed. The potential for inadvertent escalation was obviously much greater than crisis participants could have known. I am very grateful to Raymond Garthoff, Brookings institution, for updated information on Cuba, based on his extensive discussions with Russian defense experts and many years of study devoted to this issue.

23. John Mueller, *Retreat from Doomsday: The Obsolescence of Major War* (New York: Basic Books, 1989).

24. Geoffrey Blainey, *The Causes of War* (New York: The Free Press, 1988), esp. pp. 35–56.

25. Alain C. Enthoven and K. Wayne Smith, *How Much Is Enough? Shaping the Defense Program, 1961–1969* (New York: Harper & Row, 1971), pp. 165–96.

26. McNamara testimony, U.S. Congress, House of Representatives, Committee on Appropriations, "Department of Defense Appropriations for 1964," February 6, 1963, p. 31, cited in Marc Trachtenberg, "The Influence of Nuclear Weapons in the Cuban Missile Crisis," *International Security* (Summer 1985), reprinted in Sean M. Lynn-Jones, Steven E. Miller, and Stephen Van Evera, eds., *Nuclear Diplomacy and Crisis Management* (Princeton, N.J.: Princeton University Press, 1990), p. 260.

27. Robert S. McNamara, "The Military Role of Nuclear Weapons: Perceptions and Misperceptions," *Foreign Affairs* (Fall 1983): 79, cited in Trachtenberg, "The Influence of Nuclear Weapons in the Cuban Missile Crisis," p. 258.

28. James G. Blight and David A. Welch, *On The Brink: Americans and Soviets Reexamine the Cuban Missile Crisis* (New York: Hill and Wang, 1989), p. 188.

29. On this point see P. H. Vigor, *Soviet Blitzkrieg Theory* (New York: St. Martin's Press, 1983), Chap. 1.

30. Mueller addresses the problem of rationality in crisis and wartime decision and the importance of uncertainty (*Retreat from Doomsday*, pp. 227–31), arguing that major war, although highly improbable, could still occur "if decision makers become confused or demented and act irrationally or if they undergo a change in values and perspectives so that war once again becomes a seemingly sensible procedure" (p. 227). However, these are two very different kinds of issues, and neither says a great deal about the problem of accidental or inadvertent war. Interestingly, Mueller does allow for an important role played by fear of escalation, although not necessarily nuclear escalation.

31. See Paul Bracken, *The Command and Control of Nuclear Forces* (New Haven, Conn.: Yale University Press, 1983), pp. 129–78.

32. For this point, see Raymond L. Garthoff, *Deterrence and the Revolution in Soviet Military Doctrine* (Washington, D.C.: Brookings Institution, 1990), pp. 6–15.

32. Graham T. Allison, Albert Carnesale, and Joseph S. Nye, Jr., eds., *Hawks, Doves and Owls: An Agenda for Avoiding Nuclear War* (New York: W. W. Norton, 1985), esp. pp. 206–22.

34. See, for example, John Lewis Gaddis, *Strategies of Containment: A Critical Appraisal of Postwar American National Security Policy* (New York: Oxford University Press, 1982).

35.   John Lewis Gaddis, *The United States and the End of the Cold War* (New York: Oxford University Press, 1992), p. 169.

36.   Ibid., pp. 171–90.

37.   Ibid., pp. 105–32.

38.   Freeman Dyson, *Weapons and Hope* (New York: Harper Colophon, 1985).

39.   Ibid., p. 202.

40.   Ibid., pp. 272–85.

41.   Ibid., p. 280.

42.   The author's opinion — the matter is not discussed by Dyson.

43.   Jervis, *The Meaning of the Nuclear Revolution*, esp. pp. 1–45.

44.   Ibid., pp. 74–106. See also Robert Jervis, "Why Nuclear Superiority Doesn't Matter," *Political Science Quarterly* (Winter 1979–80): 617–66; Robert Jervis, *The Illogic of American Nuclear Strategy* (Ithaca, N.Y.: Cornell University Press, 1984).

45.   Robert Jervis, *The Logic of Images in International Relations* (Princeton, N.J.: Princeton University Press, 1970); Robert Jervis, *Perception and Misperception in International Politics* (Princeton, N.J.: Princeton University Press, 1976). See also Irving Janis and Leon Mann, *Decision Making* (New York: Free Press, 1977); Patrick M. Morgan, "Saving Face for the Sake of Deterrence," in *Psychology and Deterrence*, eds. Robert Jervis, Richard Ned Lebow, and Janice Gross Stein (Baltimore, Md.: Johns Hopkins University Press, 1985), pp. 125–52; Robert Jervis, "Perceiving and Coping with Threat," in *Psychology and Deterrence*, eds. Robert Jervis, Richard Ned Lebow, and Janice Gross Stein (Baltimore, Md.: Johns Hopkins University Press, 1985), pp. 13–33.

46.   See, for example, Lawrence Freedman, *The Evolution of Nuclear Strategy* (New York: St. Martin's Press, 1981), especially the concluding chapter. For a classification of U.S. deterrence theory into damage limitation, punitive retaliation, and military denial schools, see Charles Glaser, "Why Do Strategists Disagree about the Requirements of Strategic Nuclear Deterrence?" in *Nuclear Arguments*, eds. Lynn Eden and Steven E. Miller (Ithaca, N.Y.: Cornell University Press, 1989), pp. 109–71. I have no particular objection to this framework, although it serves a purpose different from my own: schools of thought are defined primarily on the basis of their targeting strategy. Moreover, leading deterrence theorists views were not necessarily static. Jervis, for example, most recently argued in favor of "M.A.D.-4," or a version of M.A.D. with flexible targeting; see Jervis, *The Meaning of the Nuclear Revolution*, Chap. 3, esp. pp. 79–81.

47.   Jervis, *The Meaning of the Nuclear Revolution*, p. 80.

48.   Ibid., p. 85; see also Thomas C. Schelling, *Arms and Influence* (New Haven, Conn.: Yale University Press, 1966), pp. 89–99.

49.   Mueller, for example, contends that the horror of repeating World War II was sufficient to prevent U.S. and Soviet leaders from direct military conflict during the Cold War (*Retreat from Doomsday*, p. 116 and *passim*). Of course, the fear of global war that, according to Mueller, deterred any shooting war between Americans and Soviets from 1945 to 1990, is irrelevant for most potential proliferators after the Cold War. A credible threat to wage global conventional war now must be replaced by a credible threat to wage regional conventional war at an acceptable cost, as in Desert Storm.

50.   Alexander L. George, ed., *Avoiding War: Problems of Crisis Management* (Boulder, Colo.: Westview Press, 1991) includes an insightful selection of theoretical articles and empirical case studies on crisis management. See also Richard Ned Lebow, *Nuclear Crisis Management* (Ithaca, N.Y.: Cornell University Press, 1987); Alexander L. George, David K. Hall, and William L. Simons, *The Limits of Coercive Diplomacy: Laos, Cuba and Vietnam* (Boston, Mass.: Little, Brown, 1971), pp. 86–143; Scott D. Sagan, *Moving Targets: Nuclear Strategy and National Security* (Princeton,

N.J.: Princeton University Press, 1989), Chap. 4; Scott Sagan, "Nuclear Alerts and Crisis Management," *International Security* (Spring 1985), reprinted in Sean M. Lynn-Jones, Steven E. Miller, and Stephen Van Evera, eds., *Nuclear Diplomacy and Crisis Management* (Princeton, N.J.: Princeton University Press, 1990), pp. 160–99; Richard K. Betts, *Nuclear Blackmail and Nuclear Balance* (Washington, D.C.: Brookings Institution, 1987). See also Ole R. Holsti, "Crisis Decision Making," in *Behavior, Society and Nuclear War*, Vol. 1, eds. Philip E. Tetlock, et al. (New York: Oxford University Press, 1989), pp. 8–84; Blight and Welch, *On the Brink*. See also Scott D. Sagan, *The Limits of Safety: Organizations, Accidents and Nuclear Weapons* (Princeton, N.J.: Princeton University Press, 1993); Sagan, "The Perils of Proliferation," pp. 66–107.

51.   Bruce G. Blair, *Strategic Command and Control: Redefining the Nuclear Threat* (Washington, D.C.: Brookings Institution, 1985); Blair, *The Logic of Accidental Nuclear War*; Desmond Ball, *Can Nuclear War Be Controlled?* Adelphi Papers No. 169 (London: International Institute for Strategic Studies, 1981); Desmond Ball, *Soviet Strategic Planning and the Control of Nuclear War*, Reference Paper No. 109 (Canberra: Australian National University, Research School of Pacific Studies, 1983); Bracken, *The Command and Control of Nuclear Forces, passim*. On nuclear operations, see Ashton B. Carter, John D. Steinbruner, and Charles A. Zraket, eds., *Managing Nuclear Operations* (Washington, D.C.: Brookings Institution, 1987). John Steinbruner's work on command and control was also very seminal: see John Steinbruner, "Choices and Trade-offs," in *Managing Nuclear Operations*, eds. Ashton B. Carter, John D. Steinbruner, and Charles A. Zraket (Washington, D.C.: Brookings Institution, 1987), pp. 535–54; John Steinbruner, "Nuclear Decapitation," *Foreign Policy* (Winter 1981–82): 16–28.

52.   Feaver, *Guarding the Guardians*, pp. 12–25; Feaver, "Proliferation Optimism and Theories of Nuclear Operations," p. 166.

53.   On the significance of strategic culture for U.S. and Soviet Cold War forces, see Colin S. Gray, *Nuclear Strategy and National Style* (Lanham, Md.: Hamilton Press, 1986), pp. 33–96.

54.   As an illustration of what might be done, John Gaddis notes that World War I is generally thought to have broken out after six crises and World War II in Europe after five crises. He then tabulates some 37 major crises between 1945 and 1991, none of which led to a world war. His point is that this may say something about the significance of nuclear weapons for stability. See Gaddis, *The United States and the End of the Cold War*, p. 246, fn. 18 for the list of cases.

55.   For a sense of recent debates about deterrence, see the special issue of *World Politics*, January 1989, and the articles therein by Christopher Aachen and Duncan Snidal, Robert Jervis, Alexander L. George and Richard Smoke, Richard Ned Lebow and Janice Gross Stein, and George W. Downs. See also Ned Lebow and Janice Gross Stein, *When Does Deterrence Succeed and How Do We Know?* (Ottawa: Canadian Institute for International Peace and Security, 1990); Morgan, *Deterrence: A Conceptual Analysis*; Alexander L. George and Richard Smoke, *Deterrence in American Foreign Policy: Theory and Practice* (New York: Columbia University Press, 1974). See also the collection of articles in Steven E. Miller, ed., *Strategy and Nuclear Deterrence* (Princeton, N.J.: Princeton University Press, 1984).

56.   An exception is George and Smoke, *Deterrence in American Foreign Policy*, which draws important theoretical observations from detailed case studies. See also Michael Mandelbaum, *The Fate of Nations: The Search for National Security in the Nineteenth and Twentieth Centuries* (Cambridge: Cambridge University Press, 1988).

57.   Garthoff, *Deterrence and the Revolution in Soviet Military Doctrine*, Chap. 1. See also Raymond L. Garthoff, "Mutual Deterrence and Strategic Arms Limitation in Soviet Policy," in *Soviet Military Thinking*, ed. Derek Leebaert (London: Allen and

Unwin, 1981), pp. 92–124; David Holloway, *The Soviet Union and the Arms Race* (New Haven, Conn.: Yale University Press, 1983), esp. Chaps. 2 and 3; Raymond L. Garthoff, "Soviet Perceptions of Western Strategic Thought and Doctrine," in *Soviet Military Doctrine and Western Policy*, ed. Gregory Flynn (London: Routledge, 1989), pp. 197–328.

58.   Feaver, "Proliferation Optimism and Theories of Nuclear Operations," p. 162.

59.   See Gaddis' comments on the views of Waltz and Mearsheimer in Gaddis, *The United States and the End of the Cold War*, pp. 171–72.

60.   Mueller can be read to argue that nuclear weapons were irrelevant in both positive and negative senses: they neither supported nor undermined stability to a significant degree. However, I think a fairer reading is that they were unnecessary and gratuitously dangerous (otherwise, why devote a book to a discussion that they were unnecessary, if not also dangerous?).

61.   A.J.P. Taylor, *The Struggle for Mastery in Europe: 1848–1918* (Oxford: Clarendon Press, 1954), p. xix.

62.   John J. Mearsheimer, "Disorder Restored," in *Rethinking America's Security: Beyond Cold War to New World Order*, eds. John J. Mearsheimer, Graham Allison, and Gregory F. Treverton (New York: W. W. Norton, 1992), p. 229 contends that a totally denuclearized Europe would be the most dangerous option, compared with a Europe with the current number or an increased number of nuclear powers. For conventional deterrence failures, see John J. Mearsheimer, *Conventional Deterrence* (Ithaca, N.Y.: Cornell University Press, 1983), Introduction.

63.   Sagan, "The Perils of Proliferation," p. 71.

8

Military Persuasion and Peace Operations: Risks and Opportunities for U.S. Policy

Military persuasion is harder than military destruction. In this chapter, I define the concept of military persuasion, marking it off from other uses for armed forces.[1] I then consider some of the contentious issues surrounding U.S. military persuasion in the Cold War past and post–Cold War present. Those issues include whether the U.S. armed forces are suited for, or institutionally compatible with, various kinds of military persuasion missions, including peacekeeping. The costs of military persuasion in relation to other expected military roles and missions for the U.S. armed forces are also assessed.

MILITARY PERSUASION: THE CONCEPT

Military persuasion is the use of armed force for purposes other than destruction. A significant literature exists about the coercive political uses of military power. For example, Thomas C. Schelling's studies of bargaining games between states and Alexander George's investigations of "coercive diplomacy" demonstrated that armed forces can be used to influence the intentions of opposed states in crisis and other conflict situations.[2] Not all uses of military capability for political influence apart from destruction are coercive, though. There are a number of noncoercive but significant ways in which military power can be, and has been, used to persuade instead of destroy.[3]

Four examples of the use of armed forces for noncoercive persuasion are civic action and related political or military assistance, tripwire or "plate glass window" functions, military demonstrations and representations, and, of most immediate interest here, military diplomacy. In each category, there are borderline behaviors that, one might reasonably argue, partake of coercive and noncoercive influence. I suggest, nevertheless, that each of these four categories has a center of gravity that is closer to noncoercive than to coercive persuasion. In coercive persuasion, the threat to use force is manifest or apparent and often

involves the credible threat to escalate a crisis or war to a more dangerous or destructive level. Coercive persuasion is more like Schelling's
compellence than deterrence: it is a more active than passive form of
persuasion, and the threat of military action looms in the foreground,
not the background. President Kennedy's quarantine of Soviet military
shipments to Cuba in October 1962 was an act of compellence, with the
objective of forcing Khrushchev to remove the missiles, as well as
deterrence, precluding other missiles from being shipped to Cuba.[4]

Civic action includes a great variety of activities, centered on the
development of viable local institutions for health, education, security,
and other requisite state functions. Tripwire or plate glass window missions interpose one state's forces in the path of possible, although not
necessarily imminent, attack. The UN Emergency Force interposed
between Egypt and Israel from 1956 to 1967 performed this function, as
does the U.S. contingent of the United Nations force deployed in
Macedonia in 1993. Military demonstrations include, for example,
timely and well-placed navy activities to "show the flat" or overhead
reconnaissance that the observing state makes little effort to conceal.
Military maneuvers that are not actually concealed preparations for
surprise attack but that, nonetheless, signal a defender's readiness
to surprise can also be included among noncoercive military
demonstrations.

Military diplomacy ranges widely, too, from military to military
contacts for the purpose of confidence building to the undertaking of
explicitly diplomatic missions by uniformed personnel. Peacekeeping
and peace enforcement are forms of military diplomacy. Both peacekeeping and peace enforcement are nonwar operations by intent,
although peace enforcement requires the coercive use of military power
for ends other than the destruction of a state's military power. A
schematic representation of the forms of military persuasion appears in
Table 8.1.

PEACEKEEPING AND MILITARY MISSIONS

This study treats peacekeeping as a basically noncoercive form of
military diplomacy. Different agencies of the U.S. government employ
variable terms for peacekeeping, peacemaking, and the like. Other
states and UN terminology add more variety.

The U.S. Department of Defense makes a distinction between
traditional and "aggravated" peacekeeping missions as follows:

1. Traditional peacekeeping — deployment of a UN, regional
organization, or coalition presence in the field with the consent of all the
parties concerned, normally involving UN regional organization or
coalition military forces and/or police and civilians; noncombat military
operations (exclusive of self-defense) that are undertaken by outside

TABLE 8.1
Forms of Military Persuasion

Basically Coercive	Basically Noncoercive
Coercive bargaining or compellence (e.g., Kennedy's imposition of a blockade against Soviet shipments to Cuba in 1962)	Civic action (e.g., construction of roads, schools, and hospitals)
Ultimatums (e.g., Kennedy's insistence upon removal of the Soviet missiles by a certain deadline)	Plate glass window or tripwire (e.g., interpose noncombatant force between or near combatants to preclude initiation of war or war widening)
Maneuvers accompanied by threat (e.g., United States and Soviets during several Berlin crises)	Demonstrations not accompanied by explicit or strong latent threat of actual war (e.g., reconnaissance to which state being observed has resigned itself)
Fait accompli (e.g., incursion of forces into territory previously off-limits, as in Hitler's Rhineland invasion)	Military diplomacy (e.g., confidence-building measures to increase transparency against planning for surprise attack)

Source: Compiled by the author. See also Alexander L. George, "Strategies for Crisis Management," in Avoiding War: Problems of Crisis Management, ed. Alexander L. George (Boulder, Colo.: Westview Press, 1991), pp. 377–94.

forces with the consent of all major belligerent parties, designed to monitor and facilitate implementation of an existing truce agreement in support of diplomatic efforts to reach a political settlement to the dispute.

2. Aggravated peacekeeping — military operations undertaken with the nominal consent of all major belligerent parties but that are complicated by subsequent intransigence of one or more of the belligerents, poor command and control of belligerent forces, or conditions of outlawry, banditry, or anarchy. In such conditions, peacekeeping forces are normally authorized to use force in self-defense and in defense of the missions they are assigned, which may include monitoring and facilitating implementation of an existing truce agreement in support of diplomatic efforts to reach a political settlement or supporting or safeguarding humanitarian relief efforts.[5]

UN peacekeeping operations active as of April 1994 are listed in Table 8.2.

TABLE 8.2
Active Peacekeeping Operations of the United Nations, April 1994

Operation	Beginning	Approximate Cost (millions of dollars per year)	Strength as of February 1994	Fatalities
UN Truce Supervision Organization (UNTSO)	June 1948	30	221	28
UN Military Observer Group in India and Pakistan (UNMOGIP)	January 1949	8	39	6
UN Peacekeeping Force in Cyprus (UNFICYP)	March 1964	47	1,235	163
UN Disengagement Observer Force (UNDOF)	June 1974	32	1,048	35
UN Interim Force in Lebanon (UNIFIL)	March 1978	145	5,216	195
UN Iraq-Kuwait Observation Mission (UNIKOM)	April 1991	73	1,187	1
UN Angola Verification Mission II (UNA-VEM II)	June 1991	25	81	3
UN Observer Mission in El Salvador (ONUSAL)	July 1991	24	310	2
UN Mission for the Referendum in Western Sahara (MINURSO)	September 1991	40	336	3
UN Protection Force (UNPROFOR), former Yugoslavia	March 1992	1,245	30,500	77
UN Operation in Mozambique (ONUMOZ)	December 1992	329	6,754	10
UN Operation in Somalia II (UNO-SOM II)	May 1993	1,000	22,289	100
UN Observer Mission in Uganda/Rwanda (UNOMUR)	June 1993	Included in costs for UNAMIR	75	0
UN Observer Mission in Georgia (UNOMIG)	August 1993	7	20	0
UN Observer Mission in Liberia (UNOMIL)	September 1993	70	374	0
UN Assistance Mission for Rwanda (UNAMIR)	October 1993	98	2,131	0

Source: Congressional Budget Office, *Enhancing U.S. Security Through Foreign Aid* (Washington, D.C.: Congressional Budget Office, 1994), p. 33, based on data from the United Nations.

IS IT OUR JOB?

Former Chairman of the Joint Chiefs of Staff General Colin L. Powell expressed some of the misgivings of the U.S. officer corps about military involvement in operations other than war in a September 1993 press conference. Powell did not dismiss the possibility that policy makers might call upon armed forces for peacekeeping or other non-combat missions. He emphasized, however, that the main business of the U.S. armed forces must be war:

Because we are able to fight and win the nation's wars, because we are warriors, we are also uniquely able to do some of these other new missions that are coming along — peacekeeping, humanitarian relief, disaster relief — you name it, we can do it . . . but we never want to do it in such a way that we lose sight of the focus of why you have armed forces — to fight and win the nation's wars.[6]

In his testimony before Congress in September 1993, Colonel Harry G. Summers, Jr., also pointed to the concern among U.S. military professionals that an overemphasis on peacekeeping and other non-military operations would erode the military's sense of its core missions and responsibilities.[7] According to Summers, persons calling for massive involvement of U.S. armed forces in peacekeeping, nation building, and additional operations other than war are "unwittingly turning traditional American civil-military relations on its head."[8] Summers is concerned that taking on social or political tasks may displace a military ethos centered on war, to the detriment of both the U.S. armed forces and U.S. society:

Growing out of civilian academic conceits that one can change the world with the tools of social science, this wrongheaded notion that political, social and economic institutions can be built with the sword flies in the face of not only our Vietnam experience, but also the centuries-old American model of civil-military relations.[9]

Other experts are as optimistic as Summers is pessimistic about the potential uses of soldiers, including the U.S. military, for civic action and nation-building missions. Edward Bernard Glick, for example, points out the extensive involvement of the U.S. armed forces in activities thought of as "civilian" occupations throughout the nineteenth and twentieth centuries.[10] During the nineteenth century U.S. westward expansion, U.S. troops built roads, railways, and communications systems; engaged in frontier agriculture; protected civilian settlements; and were involved in numerous civic action projects. Commanders and enlisted personnel frequently objected to these assignments. Military contributions to science and technology were equally noteworthy in U.S.

history: West Point was created as the premier engineering school of the United States.

The U.S. Army Corps of Engineers in the twentieth century built or supervised building of the Pentagon, State Department, Washington Monument, and other important federal buildings, and the corps completed the Panama Canal after President Theodore Roosevelt gave up on civilian engineers for the job.[11] U.S. Navy and Coast Guard contributions to polar exploration and oceanography are too numerous to mention. Perhaps the most visible example prior to World War II were the Civilian Conservation Corps camps operated from 1933 to 1942. Although the Department of Labor chose men for the camps and the interior and agriculture departments administered the program, the war department built the camps and "clothed, cared for and disciplined the men."[12]

U.S. civil or military involvement outside the United States is more complicated, however, and problems of military mission pluralism often are compounded by the need to coordinate the activities of several national forces. Knowing this, U.S. and allied North Atlantic Treaty Organization (NATO) military leaders have been reluctant dragons when intervention in other states' civil strife has been proposed. This reluctance is typical even when the proposed intervention calls for strictly military skills and tasks.

FROM PEACEKEEPING TO COLLECTIVE SECURITY?

The civil war in Yugoslavia leading to the breakup of that country in 1992–93 provided a case study of the difficulty in obtaining commitments by the great powers to multilateral military intervention. Reports of widespread genocide and the potential for this conflict to escalate beyond the Balkans called for some kind of concerted European or UN action, either to separate the combatants or to impose a cease fire and return to the status quo ante. However, none of the European security organizations seemed able to take the lead. NATO had been designed for an entirely different mission. The Western European Union was enjoying a welcome rebirth, but it had not yet matured as a center of gravity for preventive diplomacy or for multilateral military intervention. The Conference on Security and Cooperation in Europe was the most inclusive body capable of taking a stand, but its very inclusiveness precluded harmonious action of a military sort.

NATO's air strikes against Bosnian Serbs besieging Sarajevo and other UN-declared safe havens in the spring of 1994 were intended as acts of coercive diplomacy. Their purpose was not to inflict military defeat on Bosnian Serb forces nor to undo the territorial gains previously made by Serbs fighting in Bosnia; instead, the purpose of NATO air strikes was to signal a sense of UN and Western alliance resolve in favor of some viable peace settlement. The problem was that military actions taken by the saving remnant of a Cold War anti-Soviet military alliance, NATO, were being used to backstop a UN peacekeeping mandate. The peacekeeping mission presumed political neutrality on the part of the United Nations as among the combatant parties, but NATO's strikes were clearly asymmetrical in their intended message and alarming to Russian diplomats, who complained about their not being forewarned of NATO's air strikes. Another controversial act of coercive diplomacy, the UN embargo against arms shipments to all sides fighting within former Yugoslavia, was also asymmetrical in its impact. Rump Yugoslavia (Serbia/Montenegro), already a productive manufacturer and prewar exporter of arms, suffered not at all, while Bosnian Muslims were denied weapons for self-defense.

Both collective security and peace enforcement pose the question of on whose side intervention should be undertaken. Collective security presupposes that one can identify an aggressor and a defender, a bad guy and a good guy.[13] In a multinational civil war of the Yugoslav type, the problem of identifying aggressors and defenders would be one that defied consensus or political objectivity.[14] If taking sides in collective security is plagued by the problem of objectivity in defining aggressors and defenders, the opposite problem obtains in peacekeeping operations. In peacekeeping operations, taking sides is contrary to the basic political purpose of the military operation.[15] Peacekeeping in civil wars, however, easily converts itself into "aggravated" peacekeeping, or into peace enforcement, if the restoration of order is resisted by one side, as in UN operations in Somalia in 1993.

Prominent U.S. politicians and media pundits called for military interventions of various kinds in 1992, and some made compelling cases that the chaos in former Yugoslavia could not be ignored. However strong the imperative, the "how" remained controversial. The necessity for multilateral intervention was easier to demonstrate that the feasibility of any military operation involving multinational ground forces under UN or other mandate. The case of U.S. intervention in Somalia in December 1992 for humanitarian relief, and with UN blessing, also showed the gap between the logic of necessity and the logic of the possible. It was deemed necessary to prevent widespread starvation: in order to do so, the U.S. and allied forces engaged in combat with Somali warlord gangs. The feasibility of intervention without taking on combat missions against Somali factions, and, therefore, assuming a different and nonhumanitarian mission was more complicated. U.S. forces were withdrawn after it became clear that the line between noncombatant and combatant roles could not be drawn with sufficient clarity to satisfy both the United Nations and the U.S. Congress.

In late November and early December 1994, the desperation of Bosnian Muslim defenders in Bihac (in northwest Bosnia-Herzegovina) against Bosnian and Croatian Serb pressure led to an embarrassing denouement for UN and NATO peacekeeping efforts in Bosnia. NATO could obtain no trans-Atlantic consensus on its next steps. British and French governments with peacekeepers on the ground in Bosnia were reluctant to approve broad air strikes against Serb artillery and other military targets. The Clinton administration was divided among one faction that preferred escalation in the form of airstrikes, one favoring continued emphases on diplomatic solutions, and one (finding echoes in a newly elected Republican majority on Capitol Hill) proposing prompt withdrawal of all peacekeepers and acknowledgment of Serb victory. NATO conceded that a contact group (United States, Britain, France, Germany, and Russia) peace plan giving 49 percent of Bosnia to Serbs and 51 percent to a Muslim-Croat alliance could not be imposed at an acceptable military and political cost. While NATO fiddled, Bihac literally burned.

The questions about operational feasibility of post–Cold War contingency operations for U.S. or for multinational military forces are the same. What is the political objective? What are the military objectives that follow from this political objective? Are these military objectives attainable with the forces that the United States or the United Nations are willing to commit? Similar questions, in the case of U.S. unilateral involvement or U.S. commitment of troops to multistate operations, must be answered with regard to U.S. domestic politics and its unavoidable connection with foreign policy.

REGULAR OR IRREGULAR WARS?

Future war is likely to be marked by a mixture of high technology equipment and low technology strategy. Reconnaissance-strike complexes using satellite or airborne detection, rapid data processing, and precision guided weapons will make possible deep strategic attack without nuclear weapons.[16] At the same time, terrorists and other nonstate actors will challenge states and their militaries for the monopoly of war related information. The electronics and communications revolutions of recent years empower small groups of clandestine warriors with access to global communications networks, with the potential for spoofing or otherwise interfering with military command, control, and communications networks.[17]

Future technology might enable both the big battalion armies and the flea warriors to reduce uncertainty and to minimize friction. In addition, even without high technology, some unconventional wars may fulfill Clausewitz's prescription about the relationship between policy and force better than conventional war does. Few who experienced Vietnam would now argue, even if they had prior to U.S. involvement in that conflict, that counterrevolutionary wars are more military than they are political.[18] As Sam C. Sarkesian notes, in revolutionary wars

The people of the indigenous area compose the true battleground. Clause-witzian notions and high-tech military capability are usually irrelevant in unconventional conflicts. Conventional military capability and the "largest" battalions rarely decide the outcome. The center of gravity is in the political-social milieu of the indigenous populace, rather than in the armed forces.[19]

The need to fight syncretic wars that are simultaneously conventional and unconventional in one sense drives U.S. military historians and planners back to the Revolutionary War roots of U.S. military practice. As Historian Russell Weigley has noted, General George Washington preferred to model the Continental Army along the lines of eighteenth-century European military forces.[20] Washington feared that irregular forces could not be counted on against British regular forces, and he also remained wary of the potential costs to the U.S. social fabric of guerrilla warfare. Even his postwar efforts to shape the peacetime U.S. armed forces favored a small regular army supported by a compulsory-service and federally regulated militia.[21]

On the other hand, the United States' revolutionary war against Britain also included successful U.S. unconventional campaigns against British regulars, such as the guerrilla attacks on Burgoyne's lines of communication and flanks, contributory to his defeat at Saratoga.[22] U.S. professional military heritage from the War of 1812 was also a mixed estate. On one side stood the Battle of New Orleans, suggesting that citizen-soldiers could fight with distinction against regular British forces. On the other wide stood the battles of Chippewa and Lundy's Lane, in which U.S. regulars acquitted themselves well against their British counterparts in open field battles without use of unconventional tactics.[23]

Two opposed views on the issue "what kind of war?" have been stated by Martin Van Creveld and Harry G. Summers, Jr. According to Van Creveld, large scale conventional war is mostly obsolete. The future of warfare lies in low intensity conflict, terrorism, and the like.[24] The reason for the obsolescence of large scale, conventional war, according to Van Creveld, is that large scale warfare does not pay political and military dividends relative to its costs. Van Creveld argues that this trend represents the dismantling of the Clausewitzian paradigm that dominated military strategy formation from the Peace of Westphalia until the end of World War II.

Van Creveld contends that the realist-statist model is no longer very realistic. The state can no longer assert its monopoly over the resort to violence. If he is correct in this argument, the implication are profound. Once the assumption that trinitarian war is the normative model for all armed struggle is relaxed, all intellectual hell breaks loose in military studies. We return to the pre-Westphalian environment in which tribes and tribunes resorted to war with the same assumption of political legitimacy as did governments. The contemporary conflicts within or among states of the former Soviet Union, as in Georgia and as between Armenia and Azerbaijan, may be normative for the future of warfare. So, too, may the upheavals in the Balkans, which have pitted ethnic and nationality groups against one another in a holy war of satanic proportions.

Harry Summers argues, in contrast to Van Creveld's view, that low intensity conflict cannot be normative for the U.S. armed forces.[25] Given U.S. political culture and military traditions, the Gulf War of 1991 is more representative of the kinds of wars that the American people and the U.S. Congress will support: high intensity warfare in which U.S. manpower is spared, technology is exploited to the fullest, and war termination is obtained in the shortest possible time.[26] Undoubtedly, the Gulf War was one of a kind, but Summers' argument holds more broadly that high technology conventional war is the kind of war that the United States has traditionally waged with great effectiveness. On the contrary, the U.S. track record for low intensity warfare is dismal. One scholar notes that the United States has even failed to learn very much about low intensity conflict from its own historical involvement in wars of this type, including nineteenth century wars on the U.S. continent itself.[27]

There is something to be said for both the Van Creveld and the Summers positions. One does not entirely exclude the other. For example, the war in Vietnam (Second Indochina War) was both a conventional and an unconventional war, adding to its complexity.[28] In each instance, we might ask, will future Congresses and publics support the manpower, muscle, and money to fight those kinds of war? Will popular support be conditional upon combat performance, as reported through the news media and interpreted by armchair military experts having obtained their information from television? The questions are not frivolous. Whether the U.S. armed forces will be able to wage high intensity warfare, low intensity conflict, both, or neither in the future is as much dependent on the U.S. public's understanding of the U.S. way of war as it is on the military-technical issues such as force size and weapons modernization. Public perceptions of international threats are notoriously fickle, and Cold War policy makers deliberately exaggerated the degree of threat in order to obtain defense commitments from the U.S. Congress. One defense scholar argues that the United States was virtually free from serious threat of invasion and conquest, slow strangulation through global blockade, or nuclear attack during the Cold War years.[29] Robert J. Art compared threats to U.S. security during three eras, summarized in Table 8.3.[30]

Many would argue that Art's definitions of possible dangers in the Cold War and post–Cold War eras are adequate to address worst-case scenarios. However, at levels of threat or potential conflict below those worst cases, Cold War experience and events since 1990 offer less

TABLE 8.3
Threats to U.S. Security in Three Eras

Type of Threat	Geopolitical Era (pre-1945)	Cold War Era (1945–90)	Post–Cold War Era (after 1990)
Invasion and conquest	Quite difficult after 1900	Practically zero probability	Practically zero probability
Slow strangulation by global blockade	Of indeterminate feasibility	Practically zero probability	Practically zero probability
Nuclear attack from Soviet Union		Not probable	Highly improbable
Nuclear attack from states other than Soviet Union or sub-national groups		Highly improbable	Not probable

Source: Robert J. Art, "A defensible Defense: America's Grand Strategy After the Cold War," *International Security* (Spring 1991): 11, Table 2. I have slightly revised Art's category labels with no effect on his meaning.

reassurance that other security objectives can be guaranteed at an acceptable cost. As John Lewis Gaddis has noted:

Victories in wars — hot or cold — tend to unfocus the mind. They encourage pride, complacency, and the abandonment of calculation; the result is likely to be disproportion in the balance that always has to exist in strategy, between what one sets out to do, and what one can feasibly expect to accomplish. It can be a dangerous thing to have achieved one's objectives, because then one has to decide what to do next.[31]

There are some cautions that we can derive from Cold War history. One caution is that forces that are optimized for high intensity conflict against industrial strength armies cannot simply be reduced in size and reassigned to low intensity warfare or to operations other than war. During the 1960s and prior to the Vietnam escalation, for example, it was assumed by planners that forces adequate for war between NATO and the Warsaw Pact countries would easily brush aside smaller and less heavily armed foes. It now is acknowledged that low intensity conflict or unconventional warfare, including counterinsurgency and counterterrorism, is qualitatively different from larger scale warfare.[32] Another caution derived from the Cold War is that low intensity conflicts involve ambiguous political missions for which U.S. popular support cannot be assumed and must be assiduously built. A third lesson is that the U.S. armed forces' sense of military professionalism may be compromised by missions outside the competency of military training and experience.[33] Assigning to military forces the mission of "nation building" invites possible confusion between a military mission and a broader political one, to the probable detriment of both military and political objectives.

PEACEKEEPING AFTER THE COLD WAR

As noted earlier, collective security implies a majority coalition of law-abiding states precommitted to wage war against any state that wages an aggressive war contrary to international law. Thus, most UN peacekeeping and peace enforcement operations during the Cold War were not true expressions of collective security theory.[34] The post–Cold War world has already found the U.S. military involved in a number of peacekeeping, peace enforcement, humanitarian assistance, and other nontraditional operations, as summarized in Table 8.4.

Peacekeeping operations may combine conventional and unconventional warfare with civic action and nation building. The cognitive complexity of peacekeeping or peace enforcement adds to the difficulty of obtaining good fit between policy objectives and political-military means. For example, the United States chose to intervene in Somalia in December 1992 in the face of the collapse of a militarily undersubscribed UN relief mission. President Bush declared that the objectives of the U.S. military commitment were to restore a sufficient degree of order for the shipment of food to where it was needed. It soon became clear in 1993 that the maintenance of order in Somalia required pacification of Mogadishu and other areas against the terrorist potential of various warlords, especially warlord Mohamed Farah Aideed. Ultimately, the United States became engaged in major combat operations against Aideed's forces, culminating in a firefight on October 3, 1993, which cost the lives of 18 U.S. soldiers. The same battle caused a domestic political flap in Washington and caused President Clinton to do two things: to send immediately 17,000 U.S. forces to the region and to announce that the United States would withdraw all but a few hundred of its forces from Somalia by the end of March 1994.

The disastrous engagements of October 3, 1993, between U.S. and warlord forces resulted in part from problems of UN and U.S. command and control interoperability. Another issue forcing congressional scrutiny of U.S. commitment to peacekeeping or peace enforcement operations was cost. Costs were both financial and in terms of the readiness of U.S. combat forces to meet national policy requirements. We consider first the problem of readiness, then cost.

The U.S. National Military Strategy requires that U.S. combat forces be capable of fighting in two major regional contingencies, for example, the gulf and Korea, almost simultaneously.[35] Members of the U.S. Congress, including Representative Ike Skelton (D–MO), have warned that the United States would have to draw forces away from their commitments to peacekeeping missions to fulfill the wartime requirements of national military strategy. According to Skelton, there are five Army contingency divisions that are supposed to be war ready at a moment's notice. Three of them — the Tenth, Twenty-fourth, and One Hundred First — were, as of October 1993, partially committed to peacekeeping operations from Somalia to the Sinai.[36]

According to a report by former Secretary of Defense Aspin in January 1994, peace enforcement or unilateral intervention operations may require forces equipped to accomplish one or more of the following objectives:

forced entry into defended ports, airfields, and other facilities and seizure and holding of these facilities;

controlling the movement of troops and supplies within a target country and across borders, including the enforcement of a blockade or quarantine against maritime commerce;

establishing and defending zones (e.g., Bosnian "safe havens" in which civilians are protected from external attacks;

securing protected zones from internal threats, including snipers, sabotage, and terrorism;

TABLE 8.4
Selected U.S. Military Post-Cold War Nontraditional Operations

Location	Date	Mission	Involvement
U.S. Borders: "JTF Six"	December 1990–	Drug interdiction	100 military plus civilian law enforcement
Kurdistan Operation "Provide Comfort"	April–June 1991	Refugee relief	12,000 U.S. forces with 11,000 partners
Bangladesh Operation "Sea Angel"	May–June 1991	Flood relief	8,000 U.S. Marines and Navy
Philippines Operation "Fiery Vigil"	July 1991	Mt. Inatubo volcano rescue	5,000 U.S. Navy and Marines
Western Sahara	September 1991–	Observer force	UN military with U.S. officers
Zaire	September 1991	Rescue foreign nationals	French, Belgian troops with U.S. airlift
Cuba	November 1991–May 1992	Haitian refugee relief	U.S. military
Russia, Operation "Provide Hope"	December 1991–February 1992	Food relief	Western and U.S. airlift
Former Yugoslavia, "UN Protection Force"	March 1992–	Peacekeeping	NATO and WEU naval deployments offshore, NATO AWACS monitor no-fly zone over Bosnia
Italy, Operation "Volcano Buster"	April 1992	Mt Etna volcano rescue	Small force of U.S. Navy, Marines
California, "Joint Task Force LA"	May 1992	Restore domestic order	8,000 U.S. Army and Marine Corps and 12,000 Guard

Florida, "JTF Hurricane Andrew"	August–September 1992	Disaster relief	21,000 U.S. Army, Air Force, and Marines and 6,000 Guard
Iraq, Operation "Southern Watch"	August 1992–	Surveillance	U.S. Air Force and Navy
Hawaii	September 1992	Hurricane Iniki disaster relief	National Guard and small number of U.S. Marines and Air Force
Somalia, Operaiton "Restore Hope"	December 1992–	U.S. "invasion" and pacification for famine relief, restore order	All arms of service, plus allied UN forces

Source: Adapted from John Allen Williams and Charles Moskos, "Civil-Military Relations after the Cold War," prepared for delivery at American Political Science Association, Annual Meeting, September 2–5, 1993, pp. 5a, 5b.

preparing to turn over responsibility for security to a reconstituted administrative authority and/or to peacekeeping units.[37]

According to the same document, the "prudent" level of forces that should be planned for a major intervention or peace enforcement operation is as listed in Table 8.5.

TABLE 8.5
Prudent Force Level for Peace Enforcement or Major Intervention

1 air assault or airborne division
1 light infantry division
1 mechanized infantry division
1 Marine brigade equivalent
1–2 carrier battle groups
1–2 composite wings of Air Force aircraft
Special Operations Forces, including PSYOP (psychological operations) and civil affairs units
Airlift and sealift forces
Approximately 50,000 total combat support and combat service support

Source: U.S. Department of Defense, January 1994.

Former Army Chief of Staff General Carl E. Vuono discussed the impact of U.S. commitments to peacekeeping operations during congressional hearings in October 1993. He noted that, in autumn 1992, available U.S. Army forces were committed in part to the following peacekeeping and peace enforcement or humanitarian operations:

Somalia: major elements of three Army divisions, one corps and theater Army logistical support;

Sinai: major elements of two brigades in two Army divisions and associated logistical support;

Macedonia: major elements of two brigades and two Army divisions and associated logistical support; and

Bosnia: forces held in readiness to meet possible NATO peacekeeping or peace enforcement requirements (about triple the force requirements for Somalia).

Overall, according to Vuono, Army forces in autumn 1993 prepared for commitment, committed to, or recovering from commitments to peacekeeping or humanitarian operations constituted a force equal to the major elements of about two corps, for a strength, including rotation base, of about 150,000 troops.[38]

The Clinton administration strategy of "engagement and enlargement" accommodated U.S. support for, and participation in, multinational peace operations. Experience in Somalia and elsewhere soon taught wariness about the selection of cases for intervention and about the degree of optimism for success. For example, the Clinton White House statement on national security strategy issued in July 1994 cautioned that U.S. audiences:

Must recognize that peace operations make demands on the UN that exceed the organization's current capabilities. The United States is working with the UN headquarters and other member states to ensure that the UN embarks only on peace operations that make political and military sense and that the UN is able to manage effectively those peace operations it does undertake.[39]

In its discussion of the criteria used to determine whether U.S. participation in UN and other peace operations was called for, the Clinton State Department outlined the following considerations:

Participation should advance U.S. national interests, and both the unique and general risks to U.S. personnel have been weighed and judged acceptable.

Personnel, funds, and other necessary resource for the operation are available.

The role of U.S. forces is tied to clear objectives, and an endpoint for U.S. participation can be identified.

U.S. participation is necessary for the success of the operation.

Domestic political and congressional support exists or can be obtained.

Command and control arrangements are acceptable to U.S. commanders and policy makers.[40]

Additional, more demanding criteria are added, according to Clinton documents on U.S. participation in peacekeeping, when U.S. participation in peace enforcement operations likely to involve combat is possible: there exists "a determination to commit sufficient forces to achieve clearly defined objectives"; a plan exists to achieve these objectives decisively; and a commitment is evident to reassess and to adjust, as necessary, the size, disposition, and composition of U.S. forces to achieve U.S. objectives.[41]

The U.S. Congress in 1993 was also interested in the financial as well as the readiness costs to U.S. forces of peacekeeping operations. In fiscal year (FY) 1993, the armed services reprogrammed about $953 million from other accounts, usually operations and maintenance, to support the unfunded costs of peacekeeping and humanitarian operations. During the same fiscal year, Congress increased the funds designated for peacekeeping by more than $1 billion. According to some congressional sources, however, this funding did not cover all of the services' additional expenses because of peacekeeping operations. For example, Representative Norman Dicks (D–WA) claimed in October 1993 that the Army currently faced a shortfall of more than $600 million in its operations and maintenance accounts because of its support for activities in Somalia, Southwest Asia (Iraq), and domestic crisis response.[42] A summary of peacekeeping and humanitarian missions costs and congressional appropriations by service for FY 1993 appears in Table 8.6.

TABLE 8.6
U.S. Service Costs for Peacekeeping and Humanitarian Operations, FY 1993
(in millions of dollars)

	Added Funds Sought	*Approved by Congress*
Army	201.1	201.1
Navy	222.4	197.5
Air Force	240.2	340.2
Other	288.9	311.9
Total	952.6	1,050.7

Source: John G. Roos, "The Perils of Peacekeeping," *Armed Forces Journal International* (December 1993): 17.

In addition to readiness and financial costs of U.S. involvement in peacekeeping operations, there are also the potentially dysfunctional strategic ones. Harry Summers' and others' skepticism about the suitability of nation building as a mission for armed forces and the well-documented U.S. allergy against protracted low intensity conflicts raise notes of caution for presidents and planners alike. The UN flag can legitimize an operation that might otherwise be doubtful of support in the U.S. Congress or in public opinion, but approval in the Security Council does not translate directly into military preparedness for, or public acceptance of, the strategic risks inherent in peacekeeping or peace enforcement. U.S. experience from Korea to Somalia seems to show that operations under one national command, although nominally under the aegis of multinational bodies, have a higher probability of success than military interventions commanded by multinational forces. The Gulf War experience was not really normative in this regard, because U.S. and allied NATO experience provided ready-made inter-operability and planning guidance for tactical operations.

CONCLUSION

Important constraints and risks for U.S. strategy and policy are apparent in present, and foreseeable future, commitments to multinational peacekeeping or other operations involving military persuasion. First, the ability of U.S. armed forces to meet the requirements of national military strategy for two nearly simultaneous major regional contingencies may be compromised.[43] Second, the lapse of command between multinational policy directives and individual state armed forces makes peacekeeping operations potentially more difficult than traditional combat. Third, financial costs of U.S. participation in peacekeeping may be temporarily swallowed in service operations and maintenance accounts, to the possible detriment of wartime readiness.

Nor is this all. There is more optimism in our house about the capacity of the U.S. armed forces to adapt to new missions, including missions other than war, than there is about the learning curves of Congress, the media, and the public. peacekeeping can evolve into pacification, and pacification has a hard edge. Operations to restore civil order may involve bitter struggles against bandits, including indigenous heroes. U.S. involvement in Somalia in 1993 and in Lebanon a decade earlier showed that it does not take a Vietnam, or even a war in the traditional sense, to put U.S. armed forces into mission malaise.

NOTES

1. This chapter elaborates some of my discussion in Stephen J. Cimbala, "Military Persuasion and the American Way of War," *Strategic Review* (Fall 1994): 33–43.

2. Thomas C. Schelling, *Arms and Influence* (New Haven, Conn.: Yale University Press, 1966); Alexander L. George, David K. Hall, and William L. Simons, *The Limits of Coercive Diplomacy: Laos, Cuba, Vietnam* (Boston, Mass.: Little, Brown, 1971).

3. Ned Lebow's discussions of the risks inherent in brinkmanship strategies and of the availability of reassurance as an alternative to deterrence are pertinent here. See Richard Ned Lebow, *Between Peace and War: The Nature of International Crisis* (Baltimore, Md.: Johns Hopkins University Press, 1981); Richard Ned Lebow, "The Deterrence Deadlock: Is There a Way Out?" in *Psychology and Deterrence*, eds. Robert Jervis, Richard Ned Lebow, and Janice Gross Stein (Baltimore, Md.: Johns Hopkins University Press, 1985), pp. 180–202.

4. Alexander L. George, "The Cuban Missile Crisis," in *Avoiding War: Problems of Crisis Management*, ed. Alexander L. George (Boulder, Colo.: Westview Press, 1991), pp. 222–68; Graham T. Allison, *Essence of Decision: Explaining the Cuban Missile Crisis* (Boston, Mass.: Little, Brown, 1971); Raymond L. Garthoff, *Reflections on the Cuban Missile Crisis* (Washington, D.C.: Brookings Institution, 1989); James G. Blight and David A. Welch, *On the Brink: Americans and Soviets Reexamine the Cuban Missile Crisis* (New York: Hill and Wang, 1989).

5. John G. Roos, "Perils of Peacekeeping: Tallying the Costs In Blood, Coin, Prestige, and Readiness," *Armed Forces Journal International* (December 1993): 14, for these Department of Defense definitions. Donald M. Snow's uses of "peacekeeping" and "peacemaking" are comparable to the above definitions of "traditional peacekeeping" and "aggravated peacekeeping," respectively. See Donald M. Snow, *Distant Thunder: Third World Conflict and the New International Order* (New York: St. Martin's Press, 1993), p. 131.

6. General Colin L. Powell, then chairman of the Joint Chiefs of Staff, press conference, September 1, 1993, cited in statement by Colonel Harry G. Summers, Jr., USA (Ret.), before the U.S. House of Representatives, Committee on Foreign Affairs,

Subcommittee on International Security, International Organizations and Human Rights, September 21, 1993, and reprinted in *Strategic Review* (Fall 1993): 70.

7.   Ibid., pp. 69–72.

8.   Ibid., p. 71.

9.   Ibid.

10.   Edward Bernard Glick, *Peaceful Conflict: The Non-Military Use of the Military* (Harrisburg, Pa.: Stackpole Books, 1967), esp. pp. 45–66.

11.   Ibid., pp. 47–51.

12.   Ibid., p. 58.

13.   Comparison of the theoretical principle of collective security with the actual practice of it appears in Inis L. Claude, Jr., "Collective Security After the Cold War," in *Collective Security in Europe and Asia*, ed. Gary L. Guertner (Carlisle, Pa.: U.S. Army War College, Strategic Studies Institute, 1992), pp. 7–28. Claude notes that excessive optimism about the probable success of collective security frequently follows in the aftermath of successful coalition wars (see esp. pp. 14–15).

14.   For an analysis of possible uses of ground forces and airpower in Bosnia and the degree to which force employment can or cannot satisfy U.S. or UN objectives, see Brett D. Barkey, "Bosnia: A Question of Intervention," *Strategic Review* (Fall 1993): 48–59.

15.   Paul F. Diehl, *International Peacekeeping* (Baltimore, Md.: Johns Hopkins University Press, 1993), pp. 4–13 and *passim*.

16.   The term "reconnaissance-strike complex" originated in Russian/Soviet military discourse to describe combinations of increasingly accurate conventional munitions, improved target identification and location, and enhanced control and communications systems for directing the employment of munitions against selected targets. See V. G. Reznichenko, I. N. Vorob'yev, and N. F. Miroshnichenko, *Taktika* (Tactics) (Moscow: Voyenizdat, 1987), p. 24. Deficiencies in U.S. performance in providing current target imagery for tactical air operations is noted in Les Aspin and William Dickinson, *Defense for a New Era: Lessons of the Persian Gulf War* (Washington, D.C.: U.S. Government Printing Office, 1992), esp. p. 36.

17.   Alvin Toffler and Heidi Toffler, *War and Anti-War: Survival at the Dawn of the 21st Century* (Boston, Mass.: Little, Brown, 1993).

18.   Harry G. Summers, Jr., *On Strategy: A Critical Analysis of the Vietnam War* (New York: Dell Publishers, 1984), argues that the United States should have followed a conventional military strategy in Vietnam, leaving counterinsurgency, civic action, and the like to the South Vietnamese. In his view, U.S. strategy failed in Vietnam because it strayed from military traditionalism into political-military amateurism, especially graduated escalation and counterinsurgency. Sam C. Sarkesian, *America's Forgotten Wars: The Counterrevolutionary Past and Lessons for the Future* (Westport, Conn.: Greenwood Press, 1984), pp. 194–218, provides a different assessment, contending that the military aspects of the war were especially complex and involved an unusual mixture of conventional and unconventional campaigns.

19.   Sam C. Sarkesian, "U.S. Strategy and Unconventional Conflicts: The Elusive Goal," in *The U.S. Army in a New Security Era*, eds. Sam C. Sarkesian and John Allen Williams (Boulder, Colo.: Lynne Rienner, 1990), p. 199. See also Leslie H. Gelb with Richard K. Betts, *The Irony of Vietnam: The System Worked* (Washington, D.C.: Brookings Institution, 1979), for an argument that bad foreign policy resulted from a U.S. domestic policy-making process that worked as it was designed to. For counterpoint to the Gelb-Betts arguments, see D. Michael Shafer, *Deadly Paradigms:*

The Failure of U.S. Counterinsurgency Policy (Princeton, N.J.: Princeton University Press, 1988), pp. 240–75, esp. 260–61.

20. Russell F. Weigley, "American Strategy from Its Beginnings through the First World War," in *Makers of Modern Strategy*, ed. Peter Paret (Princeton, N.J.: Princeton University Press, 1986), pp. 408–43, esp. 410–12; Russell F. Weigley, *The American Way of War: A History of United States Military Strategy and Policy* (New York: Macmillan, 1973), esp. pp. 12–13. See also Russell F. Weigley, *History of the United States Army* (New York: Macmillan, 1967), esp. pp. 16, 66–67, and Chaps. 2–3.

21. Weigley, "American Strategy," p. 412; Weigley, *History of the United States Army*, p. 66. Washington was never very enthusiastic for guerrilla or partisan warfare, but he did encourage the development within the Continental Army of light infantry. These forces specialized in rapid movement and sudden strikes and were carefully recruited from among the available manpower. Men for these companies "should be mostly of a middle size, Active, robust and Trusty, and the first Twenty (chosen for each light company) must be all old Soldiers the remainder will have a proportion of Levies" (cited in Weigley, *History of the United States Army*, p. 67). Confusion between the methods and tasking of light infantry and partisans and guerrillas is a recurring problem for scholars and analysts: an example is provided by the frequent misdescriptions of North Vietnamese infantry operations against U.S. forces from 1965 through 1968.

22. Weigley, "American Strategy," p. 410; Sarkesian, *America's Forgotten Wars*, p. 107.

23. Sarkesian, *America's Forgotten Wars*, p. 110.

24. Martin Van Creveld, *The Transformation of War* (New York: The Free Press, 1991).

25. Summers, *On Strategy: A Critical Analysis of the Vietnam War*.

26. Harry G. Summers, Jr., *On Strategy II: A Critical Analysis of the Gulf War* (New York: Dell Publishers, 1992).

27. Sarkesian, *America's Forgotten Wars*, esp. pp. 155–94.

28. Bruce Palmer, Jr., *The 25-Year War: America's Military Role in Vietnam* (Lexington: University Press of Kentucky, 1984), esp. 172–88.

29. Robert J. Art, "A Defensible Defense: America's Grand Strategy After the Cold War," *International Security* (Spring 1991): 5–53.

30. Ibid., p. 7. Art offers a deliberately narrow and specific definition of security: the ability of the United States to protect its homeland from attack, conquest, invasion, or destruction.

31. John Lewis Gaddis, *The United States and the End of the Cold War: Implications, Reconsiderations, Provocations* (New York: Oxford University Press, 1992), pp. 193–94.

32. Sam C. Sarkesian suggests that the term "unconventional conflict" is preferable to "low intensity conflict." Unconventional conflicts are nontraditional and not in conformity with the U.S. way of war. These kinds of conflicts emphasize social and political variables, especially the problem of revolution and counterrevolution, instead of the military dimensions of conflict. See Sarkesian, "U.S. Strategy and Unconventional Conflicts: The Elusive Goal," pp. 195–216.

33. Sam C. Sarkesian, *Beyond the Battlefield: The New Military Professionalism* (New York: Pergamon Press, 1981), Chaps. 4–6.

34. For perspective on the theory of collective security and its implications for present U.S. and UN options, see Claude, "Collective Security After the Cold War," pp. 7–28.

36. Secretary of Defense Les Aspin, *Annual Report to the President and the Congress, January 1994* (Washington, D.C.: U.S. Government Printing Office, 1994), p. 16, states that "it is prudent for the United States to field forces that in aggregate

are sufficient to fight and win two MRCs (major regional contingencies) that occur nearly simultaneously."

36.   Roos, "Perils of Peacekeeping," pp. 13–16.

37.   Aspin, *Annual Report 1994*, pp. 23–24.

38.   Testimony of General Vuono cited in Roos, "Perils of Peacekeeping," p. 17.

39.   The White House, Office of the Press Secretary, *A National Security Strategy of Engagement and Enlargement* (Washington, D.C.: The White House, 1994), p. 21.

40.   U.S. Department of State, *The Clinton Administration's Policy on Reforming Multilateral Peace Operations* (Washington, D.C.: U.S. State Department, 1994), p. 5.

41.   Ibid.

42.   Roos, "Perils of Peacekeeping," p. 16.

43.   The Aspin-projected U.S. force structure for FY 1999, according to the Pentagon's 1994 annual report to Congress, is "not intended to support simultaneous U.S. involvement in MRCs while also sustaining active force involvement in major peace enforcement operations." Aspin, *Annual Report 1994*, p. 27.

Conclusion

There are some who almost lament the end of the Cold War. Those who do so evaluated the Cold War as an exceptionally stable period in international politics. Others, seeing the Cold War as more dangerous or more turbulent than their more optimistic peers, welcomed its end. Regardless of optimism or pessimism about the facts of Cold War, both optimists and pessimists must have been surprised by some of its aftermath.[1]

Experts agreed well before 1990 that the military reach of the "superpower" Americans and Soviets would have to retract from its Cold War peaks. The oil embargos of the 1970s demonstrated that security issues could be displaced from policy makers' agendas by economic issues or, put another way, that economic and security issues were sometimes inseparable. The economic unification of Europe was still far from complete as the 1980s began, but the progress already taken down that road ensured that economic autarchy would have little or no appeal for the future elites of Europe. The economic collapse of the Soviet Union and its East European security glacis was more rapid than many dared hope, but it was foreseeable in the stagnated Soviet economy beginning in the latter 1970s and continuing for the next decade.

One thing that was not foreseeable and that defied normal rules of international history was that the Soviet Union, even prior to disintegration, gave up its military reach beyond its borders voluntarily. Although not without precedent, it was uncommon for hegemonic states to abandon their imperial rule against outside challengers or inside revolutions without a fight. Twentieth-century experience showed that decadent empires, as in the cases of pre–World War I Austria-Hungary and Russia, chose war as a possible alternative to serious reform of their internal politics. Imperial Japan and Hitler's Germany later waged world war in order to avoid limitations on their imperial reach and in order to avoid the domestic economic and social consequences of international shrinkage. Empires customarily do not go gently into the good night.

Gorbachev's reforms in the Soviet Union eventually led to a splintering of that empire into some 15 individual republics, including Russia.[2] The new Russia inherited most of the problems inherent in the old Soviet Union but without the Soviet authority structures of the Cold War. There were no longer the Communist Party, the Red Army, and the KGB (Committee for State Security) to enforce compliance with government dictates. Boris Yeltsin's Russia also inherited an economic quagmire along with Soviet political uncertainty. The effort to introduce capitalism into Russia was bound to confront entrenched interests and entrepreneurial growing pains. Russia's fate as a unitary political state was uncertain as of spring 1994.

Russia's disorder was symptomatic, not just of the end of the Cold War but also of the concluding movements of the symphony that began at the end of World War II. Liberation of formerly colonized territories from their European rulers enlarged the number of states in the international system from the end of World War II until, by 1994, more than 170-odd sovereign political entities were entitled to membership in the UN General Assembly. Of course, some of these were mini or micro states, sovereign in name only, but the plethora of international recognitions gave evidence of a deeper syndrome of political complexity, because it was not only in the outer reaches of international power politics that undemocratic governments with destabilizing international objectives came to rule. Challenges to international order within the very heartland of Eurasia, including former Yugoslavia and the former republics of the Soviet Union, posed threats to regional security that called for multinational responses.

These post–Cold War disorders were predictable in general, if not in all specifics, according to my preceding arguments. So, too, were the difficulties the leading powers would have in the aftermath of the Cold War in adjusting to the fine print of the "new world order." Cold War reflexes were no longer adequate, and new reflexes to fit the newer threats posed to global security were not yet learned. Individuals may learn behaviors at rapid rates, but governments learn only slowly, after many failures and repetitions. Governmental learning requires, in addition to many repetitions, initial bludgeoning of the mass mind, as Dean Acheson once said, by means of a dramatic event or institutional shock. So it was that Pearl Harbor was required to drive home the lesson that the United States had to have a central intelligence service, and it took George Kennan's "long telegram" from Moscow in 1946 to coalesce the U.S. foreign policy machine around a centralized perception of the Soviet threat and of its potential long-term vulnerabilities.

In an age of global electronic supermarkets and rapid communications, we expect learning curves to move more rapidly than they did in 1946, even for governments. The actuality is that governments today are, in all likelihood, going to learn more slowly than their predecessors. They will have more information, and they will process it faster. Great storehouses of electronic gobbledygook will accumulate, and networks will proliferate. Chronic indigestion will be the result of all this information. Bureaucracies will have to work harder to sift the significant from the trivial. Intelligence agencies will be the acquirers of scraps of information in unprecedented plenitude. Adding the pieces together to produce a coherent mosaic will be ever more difficult.

The normal tendencies of bureaucracies and the electronics and communications global supermarket will add to confusion about the new world order. Also adding to confusion will be the variety of wars and conflicts in which states and nonstate actors are engaged. War, from the origin of the modern European state system in the seventeenth century, has meant something very specific to Western audiences. It meant that uniformed troops, provisioned and authorized by state governments, carried out missions of destruction against other armies so designated.[3] The distinction between combatants and noncombatants was not always observed successfully, but the norm of avoiding gratuitous harm to innocents remained an admirable guidepost for governments until well into the twentieth century.

Twentieth-century warfare nibbled at the edges of the laws of war as understood in Western society (excluding noncombatants from unnecessary and avoidable harm) in at least two ways. First, the use of air power for strategic attacks against the opponent's homeland often involved, especially in World War II, deliberate attacks on civilians and their social livelihoods. Second, insurgency and counterinsurgency wars mixed civil and military strategies together in hopeless entanglement. The very purpose of insurgent warfare was to convert the majority of people against the government and for the revolutionary side, by political as well as military means. Chairman Mao's apt metaphor that guerrillas were fish and the larger population was the sea that sustained them pointed to the principal difficulty for states fighting against insurgents: how to wage war against revolutionaries without sliding into a campaign of annihilation against a people in its entirety.

War is in some senses returning to its nonstatist, or antistatist, past. Before states, at least in Europe, monopolized legitimate violence, wars were fought by tribes, knights, chieftains, entrepreneurs, mercenaries, and other adventurers who received authorization from a variety of sources or required no approval save their own.[4] Nowadays, for example, a former Soviet and now Russian army in Moldova serves loyally its commanding officer, Aleksandr Lebed. It is for all intents and purposes his army, not Russia's or Moldova's. It supports the cause for independent trans-Dniester and stands as a symbol of the breakdown of authority in the former Soviet armed forces. In Peru, Shining Path Maoist guerrillas have their own armies, working in cooperation with international narcotics traffickers and controlling parts of Peru that are

simply inaccessible to government forces.[5] In Russia, criminal gangs
practice the economy of violence that Machiavelli recommended to his
prince: they bribe whenever possible to get their way and resort to
violence, including political assassination, when less dramatic methods
will not work.

Antistatist breakdowns of political legitimacy and legality are not
entirely new in world politics. However, added to the return to pre-
statist wars is the spread of new weapons technology to states and to
nonstate actors. Weapons of mass destruction, including nuclear,
biological, and chemical weapons, as well as ballistic missile delivery
vehicles are now finding their way from the developed to the developing
worlds. Iraq's near miss in acquiring nuclear weapons and North
Korea's potential as an international nuclear shopping bazaar are only
two examples of the potential danger to the United States or to its
regional allies in the spread of technology across countries and cultures.
The potential breakup of Russia into autonomous regions, some with
the most modern weapons, is a nightmare most dreaded that may not
come to pass because of concerted efforts to prevent it, but, on a smaller
scale, there are potential trouble spots throughout the world in which
aspiring regional hegemonies or unstable political regimes, some
military dominated, could acquire nuclear weapons and ballistic missile
delivery vehicles of considerable range.[6]

The picture, thus far, sounds like unrelieved chaos. Yet, the difficulty
lies not so much in a world of unprecedented chaos as in our images of
that world and its predecessor. If we accept that there was more chaos
and small war in the Cold War years than most paid attention to, we
can see the growing pains of niche wars and unstable regimes emerging
from the past 40 years or so and continuing into the future.[7] One can
interpret that past as a glass half full or half empty, as we have seen.
The number of new states since 1945 that have survived, and the
number that have maintained democratic governments, is a remarkable
and historically unprecedented feat. On the other hand, more states and
more activity by nonstate actors, from terrorists to multinational
corporations, result in a set of international behavior patterns that defy
easy interpretation.

Based on the preceding observations, the following conclusions for
U.S. policy makers and military planners seem prudent.

1. The major security problem of the immediate past has been
states' fears of external aggression, of an attack from enemies outside
their frontiers. The major security problem of the immediate future will
be the failure of states to maintain internal public order and political
legitimacy.[8]

The failure of states will, in turn, lead to some replacement of
professional armed forces by private militias, warlords, and other
wielders of force not subordinated to any functioning state authority.

Notions of civil-military relations that developed states, especially those of North America and Western Europe, have taken for granted in the past will be problematical. In addition, as states disintegrate and armed forces are deprofessionalized and "de-state-ized," more lethal technology will spread from the developed to the developing world. This will make some states' legitimate armed forces more powerful than formerly, as in North Korea or in Iraq until 1991. However, it will also empower the insurgents, terrorists, narcotraffickers, and other illegals in states with military power not subject to government control.

2. Outsiders intervening in someone else's civil war are almost certain to undergo punishment and disappointment in excess of the presumed benefits. This is true for peacekeeping and for counterinsurgencies and counterterrorist and counternarcotics operations.[9] Many of these problems require competent and incorrupt domestic police forces for their solutions more than military operations. U.S. leaders should be especially wary of military interventions in other states' civil wars unless those conflicts involve obvious and easily explained U.S. security interests. Somalia is a textbook example of a necessary task for multinational forces other than U.S. ones and, preferably, for regional entities like the Organization of African Unity. Leaders should be especially sensitive to the need for an "exit strategy" prepared in advance for U.S. or for multinational peacekeeping operations.[10]

3. Because of the fears held by leaders of their obsolescence in the face of state disintegration and armed insurrection, the contractors and entrepreneurs will move in where traditional armed forces fear to tread. New technologies for the suppression of domestic revolt and opposition will become a growth industry. Special interest will focus on "nonlethal" technologies for crowd control and for noncombatant evacuation operations (hostage rescues).[11] As one Global Strategy Council discussion of "calmative agents" explained:

When we must incapacitate people as well as equipment, calmatives or sleep agents mixed with DMSO (which quickly delivers chemicals through the skin into the bloodstream) can curb violence and limit casualties wherever full (nuclear, biological, chemical) gear is not worn. In anti-terrorist actions, counterinsurgency, ethnic violence, riot control, or even in select hostage situations, calmative agents offer an underrated tactic whose effectiveness depends only on modern precision and area delivery systems.[12]

A key aspect of future peace enforcement may be behavior modification. Soft kill systems could expedite diplomatic resolution of a crisis by containing the military aspects of a conflict and minimizing loss of life. For example, biotechnical antimaterial agents, according to a National Research Council study, could "disable propulsion systems (attacking fuel and lubricants or clogging airways and critical passages); change the characteristics of soil or vegetation (to deny terrain to vehicles and troops); or degrade warfighting material (particularly those with organic components)."[13] Peace operations could also be assisted by advances in robotics and electronics. A "no man's land" patrolled by remote sensing devices and robot soldiers might be enforced by long range, precision guided standoff weapons.[14] The potential for advanced nonlethal technology to contribute to covert operations and commando missions of the future was envisioned by some special operations futurists thusly:

The commando crawls up to a nuclear research facility that the CIA believes is secretly producing an atomic bomb. His mission has been subliminally fed into his brain by tape recorders while he slept during the plane ride to the Third World country. Sensory enhancement pills enable him to see every detail of the facility in the dark and to hear the conversations of the scientists inside. From a wristwatch radio connected to a throat mike he can communicate with the Pentagon in Washington. To divert a sentry, the commando projects a three-dimensional hologram of himself at the main gate's guardhouse. A laser beam delivers a voice projection so the hologram speaks. The commando aims his shoulder-fired "Brilliant Pebbles" rocket launcher at the facility and fires.[15]

The information superhighway is a potential area of great vulnerability for governments and for antistate terrorists. Vulnerable cyberspace has already been exploited by hackers who have made unauthorized entry into U.S. government networks, including unclassified Department of Defense files. In some cases, hackers have succeeded in altering records in government files. The potential for cyberterrorism has been recognized for some time by the U.S. government and by users of the information highway. A computer Emergency Response Team based at Carnegie-Mellon University monitors instances of network misuse or tampering and investigates suspected cases.

New technologies for terror and counterterror raise a host of ethical and public policy issues. Governments could be tempted to use nonlethal technologies for suppression of political dissidence, even in cases of legitimate political protest. The rights of citizens may be more readily abridged when, for example, demonstrations can be broken up by dispersing temporarily paralyzing agents with no acknowledged or obvious lasting effects. Governments can manipulate the information highway in order to compile dossiers on citizens that would have been inconceivable to the framers of the U.S. Constitution. While third world governments are shooting their citizens' freedoms away, first world governments may be digitizing theirs.

4. Geography matters. In deciding whether the United States or the United Nations can intervene successfully in interstate or civil wars, it is important to note the potential for isolation of that conflict or contamination of the surroundings. Therefore, the Clinton administration

made the proper decision when it decided to station U.S. forces as part of a UN contingent in Macedonia in order to contain the spread of the former Yugoslav civil war. Containment and isolation of the conflict was the only realistic option open to U.S. leaders after 1992, however strong the arguments for more assertive intervention at an earlier stage. Geography also matters in deciding whether unilateral U.S. military intervention is worth the cost or risk. The feasibility of intervention to change regimes or to relieve human suffering is stronger for the United States in Haiti, for example, compared with Somalia.

5. Domestic politics matters, and it may be decisive. The U.S. president, before undertaking unilateral intervention for peacekeeping or peace enforcement or before authorizing U.S. forces to join a UN multinational mission, should be certain of congressional and public support. That support is not found in nature. The president must use the bully pulpit to build it, as George Bush did for the U.S. Desert Shield and Desert Storm operations against Iraq. There is no substitute for presidential leadership in building public and congressional support for the use of force. Once a president has done so, he or she is virtually unstoppable by foreign enemies or domestic political foes.

6. Some threats are overrated — threat deflation would be a useful cottage industry. The spread of weapons of mass destruction to countries not now in possession of them is not fated to occur. The present nuclear powers have strategies open to them to slow down or to halt the spread of nuclear weapons, especially to states most likely to threaten regional neighbors. One important weapon against proliferators is the Nuclear Nonproliferation Treaty, up for renewal in 1995. Even if nuclear weapons spread to countries currently lacking those weapons, the international community can and should make clear that consequences will obtain for irresponsible behavior. States first acquiring usable nuclear weapons in the 1990s or thereafter will never have arsenals even approximately as large and diverse as the acknowledged Cold War nuclear powers (the United States, Soviet Union, France, Britain, and China). For irresponsible behavior, the international community can make clear that the great powers have at least three options against malefactors armed with weapons of mass destruction: talk them out, squeeze them out, or, if necessary, shoot them out, possibly with conventional weapons.

7. The United States no longer has a single dominating scenario for military planning, as it did during the Cold War years.[16] However, this is not as different from the past as it appears. The dominant scenario of Soviet tanks rolling across the Central European plains was oversold and of low probability, although admittedly it involved the worst possible consequences for European democracy. The wars that did take place during the Cold War were more like the regional contingencies that are now normative for U.S. policy planners: Korea and the Gulf War of 1991. Vietnam, having begun as an unconventional war, was by

1965 mostly a conventional military contest between U.S. and North Vietnamese main force units (although the politics of the war, including the character of the South Vietnamese government and armed forces, added complexity).

8. Soft power is important in the post–Cold War world. Soft power is the power of U.S. representative institutions, democratic ideals, and public relations to obtain values without fighting or coercing others.[17] As the United States approaches the twenty-first century, it must acknowledge that not all problems related to global insecurity can be solved by military power. Some instabilities are the results of demographic and economic forces, including overpopulation and environmental deterioration, that are not amenable to solution by war or by deterrence.[18] The United States does set an example, which may be despised or emulated by others, because of its prodigious economy, openness to immigration, and international influence apart from military. The reputation of the United States as a country that stands for international norms favorable to human rights, including the humane treatment of citizens by governments, is an important asset and one that can be used to influence international outcomes short of war. Military power cannot, and should not, do everything — this Cold War reflex is one of which the United States is well rid.

CHOICES FOR THE FUTURE

If these conclusions are justified, what do they imply about choices of emphasis in U.S. military capabilities and doctrines for the early twenty-first century? Although this is not primarily a policy-prescriptive work or what Allan Millett refers to as "military-utilitarian" history, the problems of policy and strategy are as meaningful for academics as they are for policy makers.[19]

As the U.S. military enters the next century, it is faced with challenges primarily in three areas. First, the geopolitics of threat assessment and alliance cohesion have chanted as a result of the demise of the Soviet Union and its succession, for military purposes, by Russia. Second, advances in technology with military applications are providing new options for commanders and planners, but the same technologies also call for tougher decisions at the margin between competing research and development missions. Third, the management of U.S. involvement in "low intensity" or unconventional conflicts, including unilateral or multilateral peacekeeping that might include U.S. forces, continues from this century into the next.[20] Because the preceding chapters have already made some arguments pertinent to each of these headings, I will add here only some additional, and admittedly more speculative, points.

A NEW THREAT ENVIRONMENT

The post–Cold War shift in international geopolitics changes the security mission in Eurasia from one of collective defense to one of collective security, if earlier arguments are correct. It follows that the priority political task of the next several decades in Europe is to establish security community through economic and political integration. This necessarily involves some leaps of faith into supranationalism, including supranational military institutions. The North Atlantic Treaty Organization (NATO) has already shown that, faced with a sufficiently daunting threat, supranational military organization is possible. Removal of the immediate threat from Moscow leaves unresolved the question of whether military supranationalism can obtain in the absence of imminent threat, goaded only by the more vaguely expressed objective of stability or mutual security.

It will be objected by some that NATO is not a case of pure supranationalism in military institutions. Forces assigned to NATO during the Cold War were dual hatted: they remained under the command of their national state armed forces and were "chopped" to NATO command on demand. Dual hatted or not, NATO's Cold War forces were truly supranational in terms of their extensive peacetime cross-training, commitment of infrastructure by participating states, and advance contingency planning for war. One can hardly imagine the U.S. Congress settling for more integration than this under peacetime conditions; it took all the mugging of the leadership in the Truman and Eisenhower administrations to get this much commitment out of them to trans-Atlantic security.

Can NATO transform itself into a Eurasian security community "from the Bering sea to the Bering sea"? At some point, NATO may need to be integrated within a larger and looser security framework. One issue is NATO's receptivity to those Partners for Peace in East Central Europe and in the former Soviet Union who now wish to join NATO as members. Poles and Hungarians are beating on NATO's door; even Boris Yeltsin's Russia has indicated interest. NATO has, thus far, been a reluctant bridegroom even for membership by the "Visegrad" countries: Poland, Hungary, the Czech Republic, and (less certain) Slovakia. NATO's 16 nations are, to put it plainly, wary of additional members for the following reasons, among others: not all prospective members are stable democracies; NATO requires extensive commitments of infrastructure, which many aspiring members might not have the resources to provide; and the status of the market economy of some aspiring members, especially in the states of the former Soviet Union, is unpredictable. NATO tends to assume that market economies and democratic polities go together.

Enlargement of NATO beyond its present membership, even with a redefined and less explicitly military mission, raises difficult issues of military doctrine and threat assessment. An alliance is about the business of deterring or warding off an attack from someone. If there is no putative attacker who poses a common threat to most or all alliance members, what is the rationale for continued existence of the alliance? Russia is, thus, NATO's best friend and worst enemy at the same time. Russia cannot provide the unifying threat that will hold NATO together in the same way that the former Soviet Union did. At the same time, Russia's normalization following Soviet demise entitles it to a seat at the table of European security arrangements for the new world order. A worst-case Russia in the early twenty-first century for NATO is not a reborn Soviet Union but a Russia that flies apart.

If denuclearization is a security priority in Europe, it follows that conventional forces have to do part of the job of deterrence and crisis management that nuclears used to. A denuclearized Europe will have to be put together while NATO's search for a new identity is in progress. A European security identity within NATO has been encouraged by the Americans for some time — during the Cold War it was a polite speech taken to apply to some future and utopian time, like Marx's classless society. The sudden collapse of Cold War security structures makes the nature of a European security identity an immediate as well as a long range issue. A European identity within the Atlantic alliance is NATO's dream, assuming that a more assertive Europe does not cut its umbilical cord to the United States. However, a stronger Eurosecurity identity within NATO is, at the margin, a contradiction in terms. A Europe less tightly coupled with North America is policing itself against itself.

NATO, however it remains intact, will also have to confront the difference between military strategies that support collective defense and those that support collective security. Collective defense is, especially with nuclear weapons, a matter of persuading potential aggressors that there is no gradation between initial attack and potentially uncontrolled escalation. It matters hardly at all from this perspective who wins on the battlefield. Collective security, on the other hand, must provide for gradations or intermediate steps between the first rumblings of discontented actors and the last gasp of military exhaustion. Collective security does not pose the threat of total military or social annihilation but that of superior force sufficient to deny the aggressor his objectives. Collective security relies upon implementable and controllable military options, for many reasons including the most obvious one: its objective is a better peace at the lowest possible cost in violence and loss of value.

TECHNOLOGY AND MILITARY STRATEGY

The second prospective issue has to do with the evolution of technology related to military art and strategy. The end of the Cold War and the use of high technology conventional weapons in the Gulf War of

1991 have rekindled interest in nonnuclear weapons technology. Some Soviet military strategists anticipated in the early 1980s the revolution in military affairs brought about by high tech conventional weapons and put on display by the U.S. and allied forces in the Persian Gulf in 1991. The Gulf War was actually fought by the U.S. and coalition forces according to the paradigm of conventional deep strike originally devised for war in Europe. Whether this paradigm will carry forward into the next century or be modified in significant ways is a topic worthy of further discussion by military experts.

It would be almost impossible to overstate the danger that techno-fetishism holds for U.S. and other high technology military planners.[21] The Gulf War only encouraged a fallacy that high technology by itself wins wars. It follows that the United States has only to stay ahead of other states on the power curve of advanced technology research and development. Strategy, it is assumed by techno-fetishists, will catch up with technology. No one can deny that advanced technology will have more to do with winning weapons of the future, but military strategy and political science find nothing new in this. Someone's wonder weapon of the month is always immediately over the horizon. It bears recalling that the United States won the Gulf War of 1991 not only because of advanced technology, but also because of a highly sophisticated targeting and bombing campaign strategy designed to attack many of the opponent's command and control capabilities and a highly trained and motivated U.S. and allied ground force that rapidly and decisively closed with and neutralized the fighting power of the opponent.

Military related technologies in communications and electronics will create an even larger gap between the haves and have nots in the early twenty-first century than exists now. The ability to exploit space for military purposes also promises to be a very stratified international enterprise, with the affluent few states capable of using space continuously for reconnaissance and surveillance, for communications, and for detection and targeting of hostile weapons platforms. At the same time, the war of the flea among irregular force and terrorists will take on a partially high tech cast. New communications and electronics technologies will allow unconventional forces to strike deeper into enemy territory against more strategic targets, such as command centers and communications nodes. Special operations in support of conventional warfare and special operations as self-contained efforts will use advances in technology to diversify their missions and to take on some missions previously assigned to conventional forces now decommissioned or mothballed.

The "regional contingencies" strategy used by Bush was a way station from the monolithic Soviet menace to the uncertainty of threat pluralism after 1990. Pluralistic threats of undetermined origin play havoc with military planning. The operative question is always "planning for what?" Fortuitously, U.S. naval war plans and exercises between World Wars I and II were focused on Japan. The continuing clash of Japanese and U.S. ambitions in the Pacific made this focus an obvious choice. Most choices among pluralistic and indeterminate threats are less obvious. U.S. regional contingencies strategy runs the risk of allowing international malefactors and media pundits to set the agenda for U.S. military involvements. However, how to prioritize among possible, but no more or less plausible, threats?

There are further difficulties ahead for U.S. policy planners. During the Cold War, a certain laziness developed. Armed forces and military options were always at hand and, when expedient, taken down from the shelf and applied to the immediate situation. This military reflex made possible by expansive Cold War defense budgets must now be supplanted by a more selective matching of military options with applicable problems. Declining U.S. defense budgets and the social, economic, and cultural roots of many future security problems will make a large proportion of those problems unamenable to any solution by arms. A large agenda of security related problems not amenable to solution by military intervention might include environmental destruction and resource depletion, overpopulation, migration, ethnic and religious hatred, mass poverty and starvation, and the collapse of states into anarchy.

A NEW PARADIGM

This brings us to the third set of future issues: the Gulf War paradigm for large scale coalition war may be the exceptional case instead of the rule in the next century. Actually, in terms of the numbers of wars fought during the Cold War, unconventional conflicts were, by far, the majority, even if we have a restrictive definition of those conflicts (excluding, for example, banditry, crime, and terror not related to revolutionary overthrow or destabilization of a ruling clique). The social forces driving across state borders and the economic destitution of peoples at century's end all but ensure that the next century will be marked by violence, including unconventional wars, in which involvement by the major powers is unavoidable.

UNCONVENTIONAL WAR BECOMES THE NORM

A proliferation of wars in the Third World offers a menu for which the United States and other dominant nuclear and conventional military powers may be least prepared. The U.S. and allied NATO study of war has been skewed away from low intensity conflicts and toward major conventional wars of the century or to nuclear deterrence and crisis management. The lingering influence of World War II and the preoccupation with Soviet postwar challenges accounted for some of this bias in Cold War Western military studies. As Ian Beckett notes, it is not only the force of scholarly inertia and preconceived notions about what "real" war (conventional and large scale) is that distorted the focus of academic and policy studies:

Low-intensity conflict is no shortcut to the triumphant ride through Persepolis. In reality, it is distinctly unglamorous. results will not be obtained quickly and, in any case, success cannot often be measured in conventional military terms of decisive battles won. Careers may not be enhanced even by such success as can be demonstrated.[22]

In other words, there are institutional and societal inhibitions against the successful prosecution of low intensity and unconventional conflicts by modern, democratic, and industrial or postindustrial states. Professional disincentives for the U.S. armed forces to be engaged in low intensity conflicts are testified to by the surges and declines in the recognition given to Special Forces and special operations within the U.S. military establishment. The U.S. armed forces, despite numerous experiences in unconventional wars fighting in the American revolution, wars against native U.S. tribes, Philippine insurrection, Mexican expedition against Pancho Villa, and so forth, retained little of this experience in their professional memory bank.[23] Counterinsurgency wars in the third world do not make military careers in the first world, but the involvement in protracted and indecisive low intensity conflicts can wreck military careers, as French and U.S. experience in Algeria and in Vietnam showed.

If the developed states' militaries have difficulty with low intensity conflicts as poor professional risks, publics in democracies have equally strong doubts about the morality or effectiveness of the use of force in developing societies. As Donald M. Snow has noted: "Most Americans neither empathize with nor understand insurgency. In part, we may be too far from our own insurgent past to identify with what is going on in the Third World. Insurgencies occur in faraway places remote from the American consciousness, so they lack immediacy."[24] The first part of Snow's statement is uncontested, but the second part, about the remoteness of unconventional wars and their lack of immediacy, has been overtaken by the global reach of CNN and other international electronic media. U.S. policy makers may soon look with nostalgia upon the earlier periods when wars in the third world were remote from the immediate interest of the public and Congress. From George Bush's dispatch of Marines to Somalia in December 1992 through Bill Clinton's commitment of forces to Haiti in 1994, U.S. policy makers marched to an agenda largely dictated by media simulcast of fast breaking events. Clinton's decision to withdraw U.S. forces from Somalia after a firefight with warlords killed 18 U.S. Army Rangers in October 1993 was in part dictated by the visibility of broadcast information reaching U.S. public audiences and nervous members of Congress in nearly real time. CNN wars have put the public into airplane cockpits over the Gulf, on the ground with UN peacekeepers in Bosnia, and in front of Marines arriving in Somalia.

The increased visibility of remote wars makes the president's and the military's situation worse, not better. Public and congressional opponents of U.S. involvement in third world conflicts are frequently better informed, and faster informed, than officials working through approved diplomatic channels. New communications technologies and the worldwide networks made possible by them, including global information networks and electronic bulletin boards, have altered the ability of counterrevolutionary forces to isolate their battlefields from public scrutiny. Because the public now has a ringside seat on U.S. involvement in unconventional conflicts, the domestic political correlation of forces can shift rapidly for, or against, involvement.

Sam C. Sarkesian has argued that another problem with U.S. involvement in unconventional wars is the need for structural changes in the U.S. military establishment.[25] The special operations system, including an assistant secretary of defense for special operations and low intensity conflict and a joint command for military special operations, almost amounts to a "sixth service," but its components are mainly military. Sarkesian recommends that the civilian and military components of the U.S. special operations system be integrated within a central command structure that combines police, civil, and administrative structures, supported by military forces.[26] He also calls for a clearer distinction between special operations and Special Forces in U.S. military policy planning. Special operations emphasize short-term contingencies and the support of conventional operations by means of irregular warfare, including commando and partisan operations. Special Forces are more useful for long-term missions that involve a higher political than military component. Missions not directly pertinent to revolution and counterrevolution can erode the skills of Special Forces and turn them into specialized troops for the support of large scale, conventional military operations.[27]

Military officers, including those trained in U.S. academies, prefer clear political objectives, sufficient military means to accomplish those objectives in the shortest possible time, and an assurance of public and congressional support prior to the commitment of armed forces to war. Although these "Weinberger doctrine" criteria seem appropriate for large scale, conventional wars, it will be difficult to meet them in future unconventional conflicts that are more political than military.[28] Barring truly astonishing and unforeseen developments, there are few, if any, Pearl Harbors waiting out there to guarantee a unified public response to threatening events. The public rationale for U.S. Third World involvements will have to direct attention toward the nonmilitary side of the equation: humanitarian assistance, the spread of democratic values and institutions, and so forth.

The U.S. armed forces undoubtedly will have to turn to the history of so-called primitive wars and rebellions for lessons about the social, economic, and political backgrounds of ethnic, religious, and other conflicts based on primordial values.[29] There are two contrasting images of premodern cultures, in terms of the ways in which those cultures wage war, that have crept into Western anthropological and other social scientific work. The first, or benign, image is that war in premodern culture is much more restrained by ritual, myth, and symbol and, thus, is more eufunctional for cultural survival than is modern war. Premodern warriors, especially those preceding the arrival of large agricultural settlements, committed war and homicide within carefully prescribed limits and under self-imposed religious sanction. War was rarely, if ever, total in its effects.[30] The second, or relatively malign, image of warlike behavior in primitive cultures denies that it is more autolimited by cultural and religious traditions. In some anthropological accounts of primitive tribes surviving today, experts have argued that war was part of a process of natural selection and survival of the fittest. Anthropologist Napoleon Chagnon contended, for example, that Yanomamo men who slew others in war were rewarded with more wives and, therefore, had more children. Thus war was correlated with reproductive success.[31] Whether one's image of primitive war is that it was unrestrained or restrained, there are few isolated cultures remaining today and none posing any serious security risk for the first world. However, primitive war in the form of banditry or terrorism occurs from Spain to Peru, and much of it has explicit political overtones.

The implications for the size and character of the future U.S. armed forces are uncertain at this writing. Self-evidently, the post–Cold War armed forces of the United States will be smaller than their Cold War predecessors. The institutional boundaries between arms of service almost certainly will become less distinct as cross-trained special operations forces take over niche wars that conventional forces might previously have been tasked to fight. A smaller and more versatile active duty force will require reserves whose training makes them capable of rapid mobilization and deployment, compared with past standards. Smaller and more flexible forces will also require better educated soldiers, including enlisted personnel. Although even a downsized volunteer force is more expensive to maintain in peacetime than a conscript force, the wartime superiority of the volunteer force in motivation and in training spoke for itself in Desert Storm.

As great a danger as overcommitment for U.S. military forces in the twenty-first century is a return to isolationism of the kind that left the United States unprepared for its involvement in World Wars I and II. Already the trumpets sound for withdrawal of U.S. forward deployed forces in Europe and Korea; under favorable political conditions, this author has no objection. The absence of an obvious military threat to · U.S. security in the early twenty-first century, combined with pressures on the federal budget from tax-averse citizens and costly entitlement programs, argue for lesser willingness on the part of Americans to support foreign military involvements. As weapons of mass destruction spread and regional hegemonies gather unto themselves higher technology conventional forces, more obvious threats may materialize that turn U.S. government and public attention to problems of security. Consistent with earlier arguments, the more numerous decisions about future U.S. military involvements will be required for situations outside Europe and North America. A compromise position between world cop and global cop-out will be the task of presidents and military planners in the first decades of the next century.

It also seems evident that unilateralism will not be the way of the U.S. foreign policy future, especially with regard to military intervention. The end of the Cold War and the removal of any imminent global military threat to the United States and its NATO allies argues for a more equitable sharing of defense burdens compared with the lopsided U.S. military burden of the Cold War. The United Nations has already indicated a willingness to assume a more assertive peacekeeping role in the few years since the Soviet demise unlocked the Cold War stalemate from the Security Council. UN assertiveness is welcome, but conditional. The United Nations must match its growing ambitions to a more sustained development of capabilities for intervention.

For example, in Somalia, the United Nations learned, to its discomfort, that not all situations of intrastate anarchy have solutions that can be imposed or coerced by outside powers. Secretary-General Boutros Boutros-Ghali asked for U.S. military assistance in 1994 in order to complete the withdrawals of UN military personnel from Somalia. The secretary-general, noting that Somalia had no effective government or administration with which the United Nations could work, recommended that the UN military presence in that warlord-dominated state be terminated. In Bosnia in 1994, the United Nations found itself first helping Croats and Muslims preserve enclaves against attacking Serbs. Then, Croats and Muslims turned against one another. Finally, a Croat-Muslim alliance regained the initiative and placed into jeopardy areas previously taken by Serb militaries and assigned to Bosnian Serbs by tentative peace agreements.

Some have called for permanent assignment of national military contingents to the United Nations in advance of outbreaks of violence. The United Nations could then call upon "standing" forces according to the tastes of its commanders and policy makers, instead of cobbling together ad hoc forces for each contingency. It is unlikely that the Security Council would agree to do this for forces sufficient in size and capability for peace enforcement. International forces with substantial war fighting capabilities, of the kind required for peace enforcement, are politically controversial within and among the member states, including the permanent members of the Security Council. Having those kinds of forces precommitted in peacetime for missions as later determined by the secretary-general would raise fears, not least in the U.S. Senate, of international usurpation of national command prerogative over the combat arms.

What states might be more willing to do is to establish standing forces for humanitarian and disaster relief that could serve as a rapid deployment rescue force. Participating states could commit a battalion or so of troops specially trained for peacekeeping missions, including conflict resolution for low intensity conflicts. It would be understood that these forces, at the immediate beck and call of the secretary-general for fast breaking crises, were not to engage in combat except in emergency self-defense. If they were attacked, they would be extricated, perhaps by stronger, combatant forces authorized by Security Council fiat.

Another approach is to "deputize" one or more states to act as regional fire fighters for conflicts contiguous to their borders: the United States, say, for Central America and the Caribbean, or Russia for its "near abroad" of former Soviet republics. The advantages of deputizing as an approach are that unified command is maintained in the field and that the United Nations is acting through a state that has an obvious interest in maintaining regional order. The disadvantage of this approach is that the tail may wag the dog: a regional hegemony may use the United Nations for its own security objectives and not for stability as an end in itself. Some argue that the United States and Russia will act as regional stabilizers in this fashion, in any event; therefore, let the United Nations authorize their efforts and obtain residual credit. However, the United Nations needs to be wary of signing onto any state's unilateral peacekeeping or peace enforcement agenda. Pacification is often another term for subjugation or conquest.

The rising curve of social and economic chaos in the developing world and the unacceptability of large scale war in the developed world both argue for new concepts of security in the twenty-first century. The security of individuals will become as important as the security of states. Threats to the dignity and livelihood of persons on the part of their own or hostile governments, compounded by heartless social forces and mindless greed, will answer only to multilateral responses that are rooted in a clear concept of international human and civil rights. However arguable concepts of human rights are in the specifics, there is a genuine core of personal integrity and worth against which neither governments nor bandits should be permitted to encroach. Genocide on the "periphery" of the international system gradually erodes the values of spectators at the "center" of the same system.

NOTES

1.   John Lewis Gaddis, *The United States and the End of the Cold War* (New York: Oxford University Press, 1992), pp. 133–54 and 155–67, surveys his own faulty predictions.

2.   For analysis of the Gorbachev era and its mistakes, see Marshall I. Goldman, *What Went Wrong with Perestroika?* (New York: W. W. Norton, 1991).

3.   Martin Van Creveld, *The Transformation of War* (New York: Macmillan, 1991), pp. 33–62.

4.   Van Creveld, *The Transformation of War*; Martin Van Creveld, *Nuclear Proliferation and the Future of Conflict* (New York: The Free Press, 1993), pp. 1–31.

5.   Donald M. Snow, *Distant Thunder: Third World Conflict and the New International Order* (New York: St. Martin's Press, 1993), pp. 169–81.

6.   For example, North Korea's Nodong-1 ballistic missile has an estimated range of at least 600 miles with a conventional (nonnuclear) payload. Its nuclear range would be even longer. Launched from Iran, it could hit targets throughout the Middle East and South Asia, including Israel.

7.   For the term "niche wars," see Alvin Toffler and Heidi Toffler, *War and Anti-War: Survival at the Dawn of the 21st Century* (Boston, Mass.: Little, Brown, 1993), pp. 89–97.

8.   Gareth Evans notes four major reasons for the decline of interstate war: the ideology of bellicism has virtually disappeared from the advanced industrial countries; armed force is a decreasingly effective tool for resolving international and domestic issues; economic power has become more effective as a means of obtaining states' objectives in international relations; and complex, interdependent societies require voluntary cooperation from citizens. Therefore, conquered territories may be destroyed but not usefully pacified, compared with the past. Gareth Evans, "Cooperative Security and Intrastate Conflict," *Foreign Policy* (Fall 1994), Electronic Newstand e-mail.

9.   On counternarcotics, counterterrorism, and peacekeeping, see Snow, *Distant Thunder*, pp. 112–35.

10.   Gabriel Marcella, *Haiti Strategy: Control, Legitimacy, Sovereignty, Rule of Law, Handoffs, and Exit* (Carlisle Barracks, Pa.: U.S. Army War College, Strategic Studies Institute, 1994), provides an example for U.S. intervention in Haiti.

11.   Steven Metz and James Kievit, *The Revolution in Military Affairs and Conflict Short of War* (Carlisle, Pa.: U.S. Army War College, 1994).

12.   Quoted in Toffler and Toffler, *War and Anti-War*, p. 131.

13.   National Research Council, STAR 21, Technology Forecast Assessments (Washington, D.C.: National Academy Press, 1993), p. 346, cited in Metz and Kievit, *The Revolution in Military Affairs and Conflict Short of War*, p. 10.

14.   Ibid.

15.   Douglas C. Waller, *The Commandos: The Inside Story of America's Secret Soldiers* (New York: Simon and Schuster, 1994), p. 355.

16.   This has obvious, and not so obvious, implications. See Paul K. Davis, "Planning Under Uncertainty Then and Now: Paradigms Lost and Paradigms Emerging," in *New Challenges for Defense Planning: How Much Is Enough?* ed. Paul K. Davis (Santa Monica, Calif.: RAND, 1994), pp. 15–58.

17.   The term was coined by Harvard professor Joseph S. Nye, Jr., in *Bound To Lead: The Changing Nature of American Power* (New York: Basic Books, 1990), 188–201 where he referred to U.S. culture as a soft power resource. According to Nye, power is becoming less fungible (transferable across issues), less coercive, and less tangible.

18.   Paul Kennedy, *Preparing for the Twenty-first Century* (New York: Random House, 1993).

19. On military-utilitarian and other forms of military history, see Allan R. Millett, "American Military History: Clio and Mars as 'Pards'," in *Military History and the Military Profession*, eds. David A. Charters, Marc Milner, and J. Brent Wilson (New York: Praeger, 1992), pp. 3–22.

20. Leslie H. Gelb, "Quelling the Teacup Wars: The New World's Constant Challenge," *Foreign Affairs* (December 1994), Electronic Newstand e-mail.

21. For insight on this problem, see Colin S. Gray, *Weapons Don't Make War: Policy, Strategy and Military Technology* (Lawrence: University Press of Kansas, 1993).

22. Ian Beckett, "Low-Intensity Conflict: Its Place in the Study of War," in *Military History and the Military Profession*, eds. David A. Charters, Marc Milner, and J. Brent Wilson (New York: Praeger, 1992), p. 124.

23. Sam C. Sarkesian, *America's Forgotten Wars: The Counterrevolutionary Past and Lessons for the Future* (Westport, Conn.: Greenwood Press, 1984), argues this point at length.

24. Snow, *Distant Thunder*, p. 82.

25. Sam C. Sarkesian, *Unconventional Conflicts in a New Security Era: Lessons from Malaya and Vietnam* (Westport, Conn.: Greenwood, 1993), pp. 195–96.

26. Ibid., p. 196.

27. Ibid.

28. The Weinberger doctrine refers to a set of guidelines for U.S. military intervention outlined by then Secretary of Defense Caspar Weinberger in a speech before the National Press Club in November 1984. See Howard Means, *Colin Powell: Soldier/Statesman, Statesman/Soldier* (New York: Donald I. Fine, 1992), pp. 271–76.

29. E. J. Hobsbawm, *Primitive Rebels: Studies in Archaic Forms of Social Movement in the 19th and 20th Centuries* (New York: W. W. Norton, 1959).

30. John Keegan, *A History of Warfare* (New York: Alfred A. Knopf, 1993), pp. 1–60. See also the discussion of debates among anthropologists about the warlike behaviors of the Yanomami, the largest indigenous people in the Amazon basis, in *Chronicle of Higher Education*, October 26, 1994, pp. A10, A18–A19.

31. *Chronicle of Higher Education*, p. A18.

Selected Bibliography

Allard, C. Kenneth. *Command, Control and the Common Defense*. New Haven, Conn.: Yale University Press, 1990.

Allison, Graham T., Ashton B. Carter, Steven E. Miller, and Philip Zelikow, eds. *Cooperative Denuclearization: From Pledges to Deeds*. Cambridge, Mass.: Harvard University, Center for Science and International Affairs, 1993.

Art, Robert J. *Strategy and Management in the Post–Cold War Pentagon*. Carlisle Barracks, Pa.: U.S. Army War College, Strategic Studies Institute, 1992.

Art, Robert J., Vincent Davis, and Samuel P. Huntington, eds. *Reorganizing America's Defenses: Leadership in War and Peace*. New York: Pergamon Brassey's, 1985.

Aspin, Les and William Dickenson, U.S. Congress, House Committee on Armed Services. *Defense for a New Era: Lessons of the Persian Gulf War*. Washington, D.C.: U.S. Government Printing Office, 1992.

Atkinson, Rick. *Crusade: The Untold Story of the Persian Gulf War*. Boston, Mass.: Houghton Mifflin, 1993.

Ball, Desmond and Jeffrey Richelson, eds. *Strategic Nuclear Targeting*. Ithaca, N.Y.: Cornell University Press, 1986.

Bayliss, John, Ken Booth, John Garrett, and Phil Williams. *Contemporary Strategy, I: Theories and Concepts*, London: Holmes and Meier, 1987.

Beckett, Ian. "Low-Intensity Conflict: Its Place in the Study of War." In *Military History and the Military Profession*, edited by David A. Charters, Marc Milner, and J. Brent Wilson, pp. 121–30. Westport, Conn.: Praeger, 1992.

Betts, Richard K. *Nuclear Blackmail and Nuclear Balance*. Washington, D.C.: Brookings Institution, 1987.

____. *Soldiers, Statesmen and Cold War Crises*. Cambridge, Mass.: Harvard University Press, 1977.

Binkin, Martin. *Who Will Fight the Next War?: The Changing Face of the American Military*. Washington, D.C.: Brookings Institution, 1994.

Blackwill, Robert D. and Albert Carnesale, eds. *New Nuclear Nations: Consequences for U.S. Policy*. New York: Council on Foreign Relations, 1993.

Blair, Bruce G. *The Logic of Accidental Nuclear War*. Washington, D.C.: Brookings Institution, 1993.

Blank, Stephen J. and Jacob W. Kipp, eds. *The Soviet Military and the Future*. Westport, Conn.: Greenwood, 1992.

Blight, James G. and David A. Welch. *On the Brink: Americans and Soviets Reexamine the Cuban Missile Crisis*. New York: Hill and Wang, 1989.

Boutros-Ghali, Boutros. *An Agenda for Peace: Preventive Diplomacy, Peacemaking and Peace-keeping*. New York: United Nations, 1992.

Builder, Carl H. *The Masks of War: American Military Styles in Strategy and Analysis*. Baltimore, Md.: Johns Hopkins University Press, 1989.

Bundy, McGeorge, William J. Crowe, Jr., and Sidney Drell. *Reducing Nuclear Danger: The Road Away from the Brink*. New York: Council on Foreign Relations, 1993.

Carter, Ashton B., John D. Steinbruner, and Charles A. Zraket, eds. *Managing Nuclear Operations*. Washington, D.C.: Brookings Institution, 1987.

Cohen, Eliot and John Gooch. *Military Misfortunes: The Anatomy of Failure in War*. New York: Free Press, 1990.

Corbin, Ted, Arsen Hajian, and Kosta Tsipis. *Nuclear Arsenals for the 21st Century*. Cambridge, Mass.: MIT, Program in Science and Technology for International Security, 1991.

Davis, Paul K., ed. *New Challenges for Defense Planning: Rethinking How Much Is Enough*. Santa Monica, Calif.: RAND, 1994.

Diehl, Paul F. *International Peacekeeping*. Baltimore, Md.: Johns Hopkins University Press, 1993.

Dunn, Lewis A. *Controlling the Bomb: Nuclear Proliferation in the 1980s*. New Haven, Conn.: Yale University Press, 1982.

Dupuy, T. N. *Numbers, Predictions and War: Using History to Evaluate Combat Factors and Predict the Outcome of Battles*. Indianapolis, Ind.: Bobbs-Merrill, 1979.

Enthoven, Alain C. and K. Wayne Smith. *How Much Is Enough? Shaping the Defense Program, 1961–1969*. New York: Harper & Row, 1971.

Feaver, Peter Douglas. *Guarding the Guardians: Civilian Control of Nuclear Weapons in the United States*. Ithaca, N.Y.: Cornell University Press, 1992.

Freedman, Lawrence. *The Evolution of Nuclear Strategy*. New York: St. Martin's Press, 1981.

Gaddis, John Lewis. *The Long Peace: Inquiries into the History of the Cold War*. New York: Oxford University Press, 1987.

____. *The United States and the Origins of the Cold War, 1941–1947*. New York: Columbia University Press, 1972.

Garthoff, Raymond L. *Reflections on the Cuban Missile Crisis*. Rev. ed. Washington, D.C.: Brookings Institution, 1989.

George, Alexander L., David K. Hall, and William L. Simons. *The Limits of Coercive Diplomacy: Laos, Cuba, Vietnam*. Boston, Mass.: Little, Brown, 1971.

Glantz, David M. *Soviet Military Strategy after CFE: Historical Models and Future Prospects*. Ft. Leavenworth, Kans.: Soviet Army Studies Office, 1990.

Glick, Edward Bernard. *Peaceful Conflict: The Non-Military Use of the Military*. Harrisburg, Pa.: Stackpole Books, 1967.

Goodpaster, Andrew J. *Tighter Limits on Nuclear Arms: Issues and Opportunities for a New Era*. Washington, D.C.: Atlantic Council of the United States, 1992.

Gray, Colin S. *Strategic Studies: A Critical Reassessment*. Westport, Conn.: Greenwood, 1982.

Guertner, Gary L., ed. *Collective Security in Europe and Asia*. Carlisle Barracks, Pa.: U.S. Army War College, 1992.

Hemsley, John F., ed. *The Lost Empire: Perceptions of Policy Shifts in the 1990s*. New York: Brassey's, 1991.

Howard, Michael. *The Lessons of History*. New Haven, Conn.: Yale University Press, 1991.

Huntington, Samuel P. *The Soldier and the State: The Theory and Politics of Civil-Military Relations*. Cambridge, Mass.: Belknap Press/Harvard University Press, 1957.

Jaffe, Lorna S. *The Development of the Base Force, 1989–1992.* Washington, D.C.: Office of the Chairman, Joint Chiefs of Staff, Joint History Office, 1993.

Jervis, Robert. *The Meaning of the Nuclear Revolution.* Ithaca, N.Y.: Cornell University Press, 1989.

_____. "Cooperation under the Security Dilemma." In *International Politics: Anarchy, Force, Political Economy and Decision Making,* edited by Robert J. Art and Robert Jervis, pp. 86–101. New York: HarperCollins, 1985.

Jervis, Robert, Richard Ned Lebow, and Janice Gross Stein. *Psychology and Deterrence.* Baltimore, Md.: Johns Hopkins University Press, 1985.

Jones, David R. "The Napoleonic Paradigm: The Myth of the Offensive in Soviet and Western Military Thought." In *Military History and the Military Profession,* edited by David A. Charters, Marc Milner, and J. Brent Wilson. Westport, Conn.: Praeger, 1992.

Kecskemeti, Paul. *Strategic Surrender: The Politics of Victory and Defeat.* Stanford, Calif.: Stanford University Press, 1958.

Kennedy, Paul. *Preparing for the Twenty-first Century.* New York: Random House, 1993.

Kennedy, Paul, ed. *Grand Strategies in War and Peace.* New Haven, Conn.: Yale University Press, 1991.

Korb, Lawrence J. *The Fall and Rise of the Pentagon: American Defense Policies in the 1970s.* Westport, Conn.: Greenwood, 1979.

Krauthammer, Charles. "The Unipolar Moment." In *Rethinking America's Security,* edited by Graham Allison and Gregory F. Treverton. New York: W. W. Norton, 1992.

Lafeber, Walter. *America, Russia and the Cold War, 1945–1975.* New York: John Wiley and Sons, 1976.

Lewis, Kevin N. *Historical U.S. Force Structure Trends: A Primer.* Santa Monica, Calif.: RAND, 1989

Lynn-Jones, Sean M., Steven E. Miller, and Stephen Van Evera, eds. *Nuclear Diplomacy and Crisis Management.* Princeton, N.J.: Princeton University Press, 1990.

Martel, William C. and William T. Pendley. *Nuclear Coexistence: Rethinking U.S. Policy to Promote Stability in an Era of Proliferation.* Montgomery, Ala.: U.S. Air War College, 1994.

Mastny, Vojtech. *Russia's Road to the Cold War: Diplomacy, Warfare and the Politics of Communism.* New York: Columbia University Press, 1979.

May, Ernest R., ed. *Knowing One's Enemies: Intelligence Assessment before the Two World Wars.* Princeton, N.J.: Princeton University Press, 1984.

May, Michael M., George F. Bing, and John D. Steinbruner. *Strategic Arms Reductions.* Washington, D.C.: Brookings Institution, 1988.

Mazarr, Michael, Don M. Snider, and James A. Blackwell, Jr. *Desert Storm: The Gulf War and What We Learned.* Boulder, Colo.: Westview, 1993.

Mearsheimer, John J. *Conventional Deterrence.* Ithaca, N.Y.: Cornell University Press, 1983.

Miller, Stephen E., ed. *Strategy and Nuclear Deterrence.* Princeton, N.J.: Princeton University Press, 1984.

Millett, Allan R. and Williamson Murray, eds. *Military Effectiveness, Vol. I: The First World War.* Boston, Mass.: Unwin Hyman, 1988.

Mosher, David and Michael O'Hanlon. *The START Treaty and Beyond.* Washington, D.C.: Congressional Budget Office, 1991.

Mueller, John. *Retreat from Doomsday: The Obsolescence of Major War.* New York: Basic Books, 1989.

Palmer, Bruce, Jr. *The 25-Year War: America's Military Role in Vietnam.* Lexington: University Press of Kentucky, 1984.

Prados, John. *The Keepers of the Keys: A History of the National Security Council from Truman to Bush.* New York: William Morrow, 1991.

___. *Presidents' Secret Wars: CIA and Pentagon Covert Operations Since World War II.* New York: William Morrow, 1986.

Quester, George H. *Deterrence before Hiroshima: The Airpower Background of Modern Strategy.* New Brunswick, N.J.: Transaction Books, 1986.

Ritter, Gerhard. *The Schlieffen Plan: Critique of a Myth.* London: Oswald Wolff, 1958.

Sagan, Scott D. *The Limits of Safety: Organizations, Accidents and Nuclear Weapons.* Princeton, N.J.: Princeton University Press, 1993.

Sarkesian, Sam C. *Unconventional Conflicts in a New Security Era: Lessons from Malaya and Vietnam.* Westport, Conn.: Greenwood, 1993.

___. *America's Forgotten Wars: The Counterrevolutionary Past and Lessons for the Future.* Westport, Conn.: Greenwood, 1984.

Sarkesian, Sam C. and John Allen Williams, eds. *The U.S. Army in a New Security Era.* Boulder, Colo.: Lynne Rienner, 1990.

Schelling, Thomas C. *Arms and Influence.* New Haven, Conn.: Yale University Press, 1966.

Shafer, D. Michael. *Deadly Paradigms: The Failure of U.S. Counterinsurgency Policy.* Princeton, N.J.: Princeton University Press, 1988.

Snider, Don M. *Strategy, Forces and Budgets: Dominant Influences in Executive Decision Making, Post–Cold War, 1989–91.* Carlisle Barracks, Pa.: U.S. Army War College, Strategic Studies Institute, 1993.

Snow, Donald M. *Distant Thunder: Third World Conflict and the New International Order.* New York: St. Martin's Press, 1993.

Spector, Leonard S. and Virginia Foran. *Preventing Weapons Proliferation: Should the Regimes Be Combined?* Warrenton, Va.: Stanley Foundation, 1992.

Summers, Harry T. *On Strategy: A Critical Analysis of the Vietnam War.* New York: Dell Publishers, 1982.

Svechin, Aleksandr A. *Strategy.* Translated and edited by Kent D. Lee. Minneapolis, Minn.: East View Publications, 1991.

Tarr, David W. *Nuclear Deterrence and International Security: Alternative Nuclear Regimes.* London: Longmans, 1991.

Taylor, A.J.P. *The Struggle for Mastery in Europe, 1848–1918.* Oxford: Clarendon, 1954.

Trachtenberg, Marc. *History and Strategy.* Princeton, N.J.: Princeton University Press, 1991.

Tritten, James John. *Our New National Security Strategy: America Promises to Come Back.* Westport, Conn.: Praeger, 1992.

U.S. Air Force, *Gulf War Air Power Survey (GWAPS),* Abbreviated Summary. 7 Vols. Washington, D.C.: U.S. Government Printing Office, 1993.

U.S. Department of State. *The Clinton Administration's Policy on Reforming Multilateral Peace Operations.* Washington, D.C.: U.S. State Department, 1994.

Van Creveld, Martin. *Nuclear Proliferation and the Future of International Conflict.* New York: Free Press, 1993.

___. *The Transformation of War.* New York: Free Press, 1991.

Von Clausewitz, Carl. *On War.* Edited and translated by Michael Howard and Peter Paret. Princeton, N.J.: Princeton University Press, 1976.

___. *On War.* Translated by J. J. Graham. London: Routledge and Kegan Paul, 1966.

Waltz, Kenneth N. *The Spread of Nuclear Weapons: More May Be Better.* Adelphi paper No. 171. London: International Institute for Strategic Studies, 1981.

Weigley, Russell F. *The American Way of War: A History of United States Military Strategy and Policy.* New York: Macmillan, 1973.
____. *History of the United States Army.* New York: Macmillan, 1967.
Weisner, Jerome, Philip Morison, and Kosta Tsipis. *Beyond the Looking Glass: The United States Military in 2000 and Later.* Cambridge, Mass.: MIT, Program in Science and Technology for International Security, 1993.
Woodward, Bob. *The Commanders.* New York: Simon and Schuster, 1991.

Index

ABOUT THE AUTHOR

STEPHEN J. CIMBALA, Professor of Political Science, Pennsylvania State University, Delaware County Campus, is well known for his many books on military strategy, arms control, and conflict deterrence and termination. His books from Greenwood Press and Praeger Books include *Conflict Termination in Europe* (1990), *First Strike Stability* (1990), *Strategy after Deterrence* (1992), *Controlling and Ending Conflict* (1992), and *Force and Diplomacy in the Future* (1992), among others.

ISBN 0-313-29656-1

90000>

EAN

9 780313 296567

HARDCOVER BAR CODE